Reading Alcoholisms

Reading Alcoholisms

Theorizing Character and Narrative in
Selected Novels of Thomas Hardy,
James Joyce, and Virginia Woolf

Jane Lilienfeld

St. Martin's Press
New York

ISBN 0-312-21709-9

Library of Congress Cataloging-in-Publication Data

Lilienfeld, Jane, 1945–
    Reading alcoholisms : theorizing character and narrative in selected novels of Thomas Hardy, James Joyce, and Virigina Woolf / by Jane Lilienfeld.
        p. cm.
    Includes bibliographical references and index.
    ISBN 0-312-21709-9 (cloth)
    1. English fiction—20th century—History and criticism.
2. Alcoholism in literature. 3. Joyce, James, 1882–1941. Portrait of the artist as a young man. 4. Hardy, Thomas, 1840–1928. Mayor of Casterbridge. 5. Woolf, Virginia, 1882–1941. To the lighthouse.
6. Drinking of alcoholic beverages in literature. 7. Characters and characteristics in literature. 8. Alcoholics in literature.
9. Narration (Rhetoric) I. Title.
PR888.A4L55   1999
823'.809355—dc21   99–21180
                                                                    CIP

Design by Letra Libre, Inc.

First edition: July, 1999
10 9 8 7 6 5 4 3 2 1

This book is dedicated
to
my mother, Edna R. Lilienfeld, 1907–1990
and
Cynthia Maude-Gembler, visionary and colleague

CONTENTS

ACKNOWLEDGMENTS

I WOULD LIKE TO THANK MY FAMILY for the generous financial assistance that sustained the research and writing of this book: my mother, Edna R. Lilienfeld; my uncle, Joseph Meyerhoff; my cousin Harvey Meyerhoff; all of Baltimore, Maryland.

Elizabeth Wilson, University Librarian, and Ivy Hui, Tesuk Im, and Connie May, Librarians of Lincoln University Library, were tireless in their help in locating and obtaining interlibrary loan materials. The following research librarians at the University of Missouri/Columbia libraries were generous in their assistance: Cindy Cottner, Assistant to the Director; Michael Cook, Executive Staff Assistant; Diane Johnson, Research Librarian, Health Sciences Library; Nancy Meyers, Sociology Research Librarian. I thank Martha Shirkey, former Research Librarian in Literature at the University of Missouri, Columbia, for her cheerful and indefatigable help. I am also grateful to the following librarians and library staff associates at Harvard University Libraries for their generous help: Carol Alexander, Director of Periodicals at Widener Library; Michael Currier, Head of Widener Library Privileges; Marcia Deihl, Staff Assistant, of Tozzer Library; and Maureen Mahoney, Library Assistant, of Tozzer Library. Thanks also to Deborah Grier, Head of Circulation, at the Fine Arts Library. I deeply appreciate the extensive help and electronic expertise provided by Greg Finnegan, Associate Librarian for Public Service and Head of Reference of Tozzer Library. Additionally, I am grateful to Barbara Haber, Curator, Schlesinger Library of Radcliffe College; and Robert Prescod, Acting Department Head for Circulation Privileges, Countway Library, Harvard Medical School; and Lyn Dietrich, Acting Director, McLean Library Services, McLean Hospital, for access to library materials. Without Carol Gilligan's creative and generous support of my library research, I could not have completed this book.

For taking the time to share their work about Alcoholism with me I thank Ben Adams, M. Ed; Elaine Black, CAC, LICCS; Tommie Bower, MA; Celia Dulfano, MSW; Sally Duncan, MSW; Priscilla Johnson, MA; the late Mark Keller; Sally O'Leary, RN, MA; Amy Stromsten, MFA; and Susan Waldstein, CAC, MSW. For many theoretical discussions about codependence and its relation to violence against women, I thank Kate Cloud, Director, RESPOND; and Susan Hoye, Counselor, RESPOND, Somerville, MA.

My appreciation goes to the many scholars that have graciously given my work time and attention, often putting aside their own work to help me with this book in its various stages. My deepest gratitude to Louise DeSalvo, who has generously and indefatigably provided inspiration and guidance as well as critical responses to my text. Eileen Barrett, Michael Beard, David Eberly, Cynthia Maude-Gembler, and Steve Wall-Smith kindly took the time to read and respond to various drafts of the entire manuscript. Elaine Black; Sally Duncan; Helen Losckky; Steve Infantino; Jeffrey Robinson; Dennis Taylor; and Marilyn Zuckerman generously critiqued earlier drafts of the Thomas Hardy chapter. Marilyn Brownstein; Diane Filby Gillespie; Michael Gillespie; Richard Pearce; and Marilyn Zuckerman tirelessly responded to various drafts of the James Joyce chapter. Krystyna Colburn; Patricia Cramer; Toni McNaron; and Vara Neverow provided extensive critical responses to the Virginia Woolf chapter. John Bicknell generously shared his incomparable knowledge of Virginia Woolf's family with me, and allowed me to read some of his unpublished work on Leslie and Julia Stephen. Panthea Reid discussed her research on Maria Jackson's drug use with me. Thomas J. Staley cordially and quickly responded to my many questions about Stanislaus Joyce and John Stanislaus Joyce. To all these scholars I give my heartfelt thanks. Jean Herbert and my other colleagues in the Alliance of Independent Scholars supported this project in its earliest stages. My warm thanks, as well, to Flavia Alaya; Beth Daugherty; Carol Gilligan; Evelyn Haller; Mark Hussey; Susan Lanser; and Lucio Ruotolo for taking the time to discuss the ideas in this book with me. Those who have helped me are not responsible for my choices of emphasis and interpretation.

I would especially like to thank Dr. Rosemary Hearn, Vice President for Academic Affairs of Lincoln University, for her unwavering commitment to my scholarly endeavors, and for providing me with the financial support of a Summer Mentorship of my student Brenda Brandt, whose work on my manuscript I appreciate. I am grateful to Professors Ken Luebbering and Susan Mattingly, the Chairpersons of the Department of English, Foreign Language and Philosophy, Lincoln University, for their support of my scholarship. I thank my colleagues at Lincoln University, Professor Tom Gage and Professor Ann Harris, for their support of my work.

For their help I thank Mildred Adler; Ronald and Sandra Avola; Donald and Nancy Bateman; Bev Brooks; Margot Chamberlain; Daisy and the late Al Droge; Alison Friedman; Helen and Albert Hurwitz; Edmund and Mandy Kudarauskas; Charles and Valia B. Langsam; Karen Lindsey; Jean Macrae; New Words Bookstore; Sheron and John Thompson; Fred Smith; Cynthia Solomon; and Berni Zisserson.

I appreciate the editorial support and guidance of Maura Burnett and Kristi Long, my editors at St. Martin's Press. For their generous editorial and manuscript preparation assistance, my thanks to Alan Bradshaw, Donna Cherry, Susan James, Amy Reading, Karen J. Shepard, and Jennifer Simington.

My partner and dear friend Steven MacNiven Jerrett has been an invaluable resource; I appreciate our discussions, and his challenging questions, insight, and wit. I greatly appreciate the support and interest of my aunts, Dora Lee Chayt and Mimi Gray. The late Edna Lilienfeld, my mother, and Dr. Louis Kaplan, Rabbi and scholar, have for many years sustained and encouraged all my scholarly endeavors, thus helping me to undertake and to complete this project. My deepest thanks go to all of them.

I gratefully acknowledge permission to reprint excerpts from the novels on which this study is based:

I thank Harcourt Brace & Company for permission to use excerpts from *To the Lighthouse* by Virginia Woolf, © 1927 and

INTRODUCTION

I BEGAN TEACHING THE MATERIAL that became *Reading Alcoholisms: Theorizing Character and Narrative in Selected Novels of Thomas Hardy, James Joyce, and Virginia Woolf* in the mid-1980s while working at several Northeastern liberal arts colleges. After two students at one college died within two weeks of each other in alcohol-induced accidents, I became determined to use classroom discussion about novels to demythologize alcohol use.

In doing so I discovered that such discussions sometimes performed an indirect intervention as students confronted their own or others' problematic drinking. I faced ethical questions I had not anticipated, for I am neither a therapist nor am I trained to use the classroom as a therapeutic tool.

As a result of this experience, I developed a team-taught course on literature and addiction with an alcohol counselor who worked in the nationally known Cambridge and Somerville Program for Alcohol Rehabilitation (CASPAR) program at Cambridge City Hospital in Cambridge, Massachusetts (Vaillant, *Revisited* 189–94). We taught our course on addiction and literature at Cambridge Center for Adult Education in Cambridge, Massachusetts in 1987.

I discovered that alcoholism discourse was an area of fiercely contested questions and approaches where one's choice of differing models of addiction and treatment modalities directly affected the lives of those suffering from alcoholism and those close to them. My colleague's approach arose from the medical model, providing an excellent resource for those of our students who sought help. But I found that the medical model had pedagogical limitations. I needed a model of addiction that situated literary studies in historical, social, gendered cultural context without denying the physiological facts of addiction. Hence I was led to apply the biopsychosocial model of alcoholism to my study of novels and thence to write this book, which focuses on alcoholism and addiction in Thomas Hardy's *The Mayor of Casterbridge,* James Joyce's *A Portrait of the Artist as a Young Man,* and Virginia Woolf's *To the Lighthouse.*

ADDICTION DISCOURSE

Alcoholism theory is as contested a site as literary theory. My book destabilizes hegemonic medical and scientific discourses of alcoholism by making visible the struggles between various positions. The resulting conversation among competing interpretations yields overlapping definitions, emphasizing the complexity of alcoholism.

My book is based on the biopsychosocial model of alcoholism, which recognizes the irrefutable physiological facts of addiction without obscuring the social and gendered constructions of addiction as experienced by men and women within the context of family, society, and culture.

One of the greatest strengths of the biopsychosocial model is that it represents the competing models of alcoholism as equally important[1] rather than hierarchically ordered. Its dialogic specifies the physiological, problematizes the thinking distortions produced (or preceding) alcoholism, acknowledges subjective suffering, and critically examines, yet includes, laboratory research and clinical findings. It thus moves alcoholism discourse forward because it invites rather than discourages multiple voices and views. As a literary critic I seek ways to read, not ways to cure. I have adopted the biopsychosocial approach while shaping it to my needs as a reading tool, not a therapeutic strategy.

The reader will notice a certain rhythm running through my dual discourse of theory. I interweave alcoholism and literary theory, discussing characters and narratives from that vantage, turning again to the interwoven theories, and then again to characters and narrative throughout this work. Each discourse interrogates the other, deepening the reader's understanding of the authors' methods of character creation and choices about narrative strategy by examining these in context of theoretical debates within alcoholism theory.

Many North American scholarly discussions of addiction and literature rely on the Alcoholics Anonymous model, which is a simplified form of what is called the medical model (Zinberg and Bean, "Introduction" 10–14). The medical model posits physiology as the cause of addiction, discouraging speculation about those psychological, social, and cultural factors that may encourage and support addiction (Vaillant, *Revisited* 115–19; Miller and Chappel 198–99, 201–203).

AA and the medical model define alcoholism as a progressive disease and advise abstinence to gain remission. In discussing why the mayor of Casterbridge returns to drinking after 21 years, I investigate these contested assertions.

The deconstructionist discourse on addiction and literature minimizes the physiological aspects of addiction, conceptualizing addiction as a trope or metaphor. Such work is exemplified by Barry Milligan's *Pains and Pleasures: Opium and Orient in Nineteenth-Century British Culture.* Sociological discourses of addiction, like the deconstructionist model, focus on the social uses of addictive substances, making meaning of addiction that clarifies cultural context at the expense of a focus on the physiology and emotions of the addict. Joseph Lanza's *The Cocktail: The Influence of Spirits on the American Psyche,* Joseph Gusfield's *Contested Meanings: The Construction of Alcohol Problems,* or Robin Room and Susanna Barrows' theoretical statements in the introduction to their coedited anthology, *Drinking: Behavior and Belief in Modern History* demonstrate that approach. I discuss the ramifications of using an anthropological model when I problematize placing Simon Dedalus's drinking in *A Portrait of the Artist as a Young Man* in cultural context.[2]

North American popular culture promulgates a model of alcoholism in a conflicted discourse found, for example, in films, TV shows, routines of comics, and the confessional pages of Ann Landers (a strong supporter of Alcoholics Anonymous).

Much debate in the American media suggests that AA enables drunks to avoid censure by claiming the label of "victimization" (Gordon, "More" 25). Such a view distorts issues of victimization, responsibility, and accountability that must be considered when discussing human behavior.[3] To others, AA's moral philosophy of strict accountability as embodied in AA's twelve steps is repugnant, indicating as it does AA's origin in the spiritual principles of the Judeo-Christian tradition (Blau; Karlen 32–35; Hirshey 24–25). To these critics, AA is too much like right-wing religious precepts that deprive the member of his or her will and individuality.

Contemptuous views of abstinence, which AA advocates, have historical precedents in conflicted views about the Temperance Movement, dating back to Colonial and Puritan history (Miller and Chappel 197–98). Within the last ten years, popular media hostility to its distorted model of AA has expanded to include attacks on the so-called Recovery Movement by literary critics and feminist therapists who write in the elite print media, attacks I discuss below in chapter 3.

My book is not based on Alcoholics Anonymous, neither as defined by itself nor as distorted by the popular media, but on the more inclusive biopsychosocial model. In the course of writing this book, I have met and talked with a number of treatment professionals and members of AA. I am convinced that the methods of treatment AA advances are effective for many people. But AA is not the subject of my book, nor does its model of alcoholism serve as the basis for my literary analyses.

My argument is that alcoholism is a biopsychosocial illness. That view of alcoholism acknowledges that it is a multicausational disease, has a physiological component, may be genetic, but occurs within an individual embedded in a family system that is located in a particular social class, historical time, and socioeconomic actualities. In its specificity, close attachment to historical, psychological, and cultural analyses, the biopsychosocial view has similarities to the approaches used in cultural studies of literature.

SCRUTINIZING THE SCIENTIFIC MODEL

The biopsychosocial view of alcoholism is based on a series of ideas that claim scientific validity, a claim that is contradicted by some current feminist theories and some modes of literary critical practice.

Sandra Harding and other feminist epistemologists have suggested methods of scrutinizing scientific material, some of which I have adopted. Harding synthesizes extensive work on the histories of science, noting many researchers' conclusions that scientific methods and arguments are inseparable from social situations and unexamined cultural biases (143–49).[4] Harding posits critical scrutiny (149) and "strong objectivity" as a solution to the problems resulting from the bias inherent in socially situated knowledge (138–52). Harding suggests that using gender and race to defamiliarize researchers' unexamined assumptions about methods and observed results produces more balanced information (149–50), problematizing "the 'winner's stories' . . . which men's interpretations of men's lives tend to produce" (150).

Because alcoholics have been silenced, acknowledging their experiences destabilizes "the winner's stories." Hence Harding's methodological stance is directly relevant to my scholarly method. The authors whose works on alcoholism have influenced my textual analyses in this book are not all medical professionals, and their views on science and medicine are sometimes at variance. But most of them rely on some form of scientific investigation to buttress their arguments.

What my most frequently cited sources on alcoholism have in common, however, is "strong objectivity." At some point in their analyses each writer will offer an empathic reading of the subjective experience of alcoholism. In using the biopsychosocial model of alcoholism, my sources respect the alcoholic's subjective experiences of suffering while also exploring from varied viewpoints aspects of the alcoholic's experiences unavailable to him or her.

Currently, scientific models may be challenged because medicine is seen by some to have developed historically as a form of power-based manipulation of people and resources (Berridge and Edwards; Peterson). The possibility of scientific objectivity is challenged by Sandra Harding, among others, because of the biases inflecting the practitioners' methodologies and unexamined basic assumptions. Feminists and feminist therapists decry the male model of health that underlines the tone of the *DSM-III* and *DSM-IV* (discussed later) in descriptive analysis of women who are "diagnosed" as unhealthy when they fail to meet men's needs or challenge male prerogatives and power. Grassroots groups, such as Al Anon Adult Children of Alcoholics and Al Anon, that claim to assuage suffering related to alcoholism are scoffed at by some feminists who find twelve-step groups inimical to white middle-class American feminist beliefs and practices. Thus my sources are often conflictual in their basic assumptions and methodologies.

I make no claim to resolve these contradictions. However, I recognize that while the development of medicine has included gendered, racial, and economic motivations, not all male-identified science is malevolent, that not all medical practitioners want to victimize women and the weak, and that some people involved in twelve-step movements might have succeeded in helping alleviate some aspects of human suffering that politically based groups might not consider to be worthy of being called "suffering." My intention is to present such conflicting views as in dialogue with one another so that divergent views will be represented.

In popular North American media discourse, alcoholics and drug addicts function as derided Others onto whom are projected that which is deemed culturally unacceptable. Currently, alcohologists (to use Jerome Levin's term) who are sensitive to gender concerns note that the stigma attaching to the female alcoholic is greater than that attaching to the male alcoholic (Vaillant, *Revisited* 123–24). Most of the studies that have been conducted by North American alcohologists focus on male alcoholism. Partly this is a result of "decades of neglect and denial of alcoholism in women" (Vaillant, *Revisited* 122). That bias is part of the reason that I focus on the male alcoholic. Because I wanted to locate my account within the biopsychosocial debates of alcoholism, I have been limited by how much and what kind of accumulated, interrogated knowledge base has been established. Research on female alcoholism is still being compiled and has not yet been synthesized into current debates about male alcoholism. I briefly note this skewed view of male and female alcoholism in discussing how Hardy fictionalizes the populace of Casterbridge's responses to the dramatic irony of the female alcoholic furmity woman's serving as the instrument by which Michael Henchard acknowledges his past alcoholic crimes. Biased medical assumptions about women have contributed to the protracted media and clinical debate over the acceptability of the concept of codependence. I address those disputes in chapter 3.

A racialized hierarchy is implicit in the North American popular culture discourse on addiction. In popular discourses, alcoholics are culturally constructed as white males, while drug addicts are constructed as black men or black, crack-addicted welfare mothers. By this means, alcoholism, which kills many more people yearly than drug addiction, is constructed as more benign than drug addiction, which is constructed as an affliction deliberately sought by the racialized Other. As a recent statistical report noted, the yearly alcohol-related death rate in America is almost twice as high as the drug-related death rate (Institute for Health Policy, *Substance* 36–37). Further, in its chemical properties, alcohol functions as a drug (Miller and Chappel 197). Shifting the focus away from the realities of alcoholism, popular media distort both drug addiction and alcoholism.

I will respond indirectly to this media stereotyping by focusing on the addiction of white working-class men and upper middle-class white British men and women. This focus reflects my refusal to participate in the unethical racist stereotyping so frequent in media discussions of alcoholism and addiction. Alcoholism and addiction are not concentrated in one gender or in one group but affect members of all ethnic groups and social classes.

Familial Addiction

In the *DSM-IV Sourcebook,* Mark Schuckit presents a reasoned analysis of why the subcommittee of psychiatrists who arrive at the diagnostic criteria utilized in the *Diagnostic and Statistical Manual* have rejected the term *familial alcoholism* (Widinger 159–67). Their objections, however, are but one aspect of a protracted debate. As I note in the body of my book, many others who advocate diverse treatment modalities have long studied alcoholism as a family illness, recognizing that alcoholism in a parent can have deleterious effects on his or her children.

That alcoholism can be inherited is an aspect of the disease I mention briefly in considering whether the father of Michael Henchard, the mayor of Casterbridge, might have been affected by "the gin epidemic" in eighteenth-century England. I analyze Elizabeth-Jane, Michael Henchard's step-daughter, as a daughter of an alcoholic, although such a discussion is peripheral to my major focus on Henchard's alcoholism. My discussion of Stephen Dedalus in *Portrait* focuses on his position as the eldest son of an alcoholic. My analyses incorporate aspects of the protracted current debates about the offspring of alcoholics, including the points of view of those researchers' work that finds no scientific value in the concept of "children of alcoholics." I historicize this controversy, legitimating the use of the accumulated evidence of the impact on children of parental alcoholism as a tool of literary analysis.

Before examining what I call "the opium narrative in *To the Lighthouse,*" I consider the biographical and fictionalized narratives of Virginia Woolf's maternal grandmother Maria Jackson's use of chloral and morphia. The biopsychosocial approach to alcoholism and addiction authorizes my consideration of Victorian medical debates about legal drug use, which were inflected by gender, social class, and racialized stereotypes buttressed by tropes of British imperialism.

LITERARY THEORY

During the years that I researched and wrote most of this book, poststructuralist and postmodernist discourses (arising from the work of Jacques Derrida, Michel Foucault, Roland Barthes, and Paul de Man, among others) interrogated the fact that authors write texts, that their lives are complexly refracted and denied and examined by those texts, and that the selves represented in novels and the selves of the readers are more than fragmented positionalities formulated in language.

Current literary criticism is now as much cultural as textual. Newer approaches reattach texts and their readers and writers in a more nuanced way to social, economic, and historic life, without losing the gains in the analysis of narrative and textual meanings produced by the postmodernist literary revolution.

I discuss these methodological issues throughout this book, particularly in my study of the impact of parental drinking on the fictional character Stephen Dedalus, and in the representations of narratives of denial in *Portrait* and in *To the Lighthouse*.

Postmodernist theory revolutionized feminist understandings of social, cultural, and historical circumstances. Most feminist scholars now acknowledge that the term *woman* represents diversities of class, race, and sexualities (Flax, *Thinking* 220; Martin 16–17). Like many other feminists, I continue to use gender as a category of analysis because, as Biddy Martin so cogently argued, "if we fail now to assert the category woman from our own shifting and open-ended points of view, our oppression may easily be lost among the pluralities of new theories of ideology and power" (Martin 17).

In the aftermath of postmodern theory, by what scholarly methods can a feminist conceptualize a "self" and its affective experience? I believe that a self can occupy multiple sites, but I do not disbelieve in "deep subjectivity," that privileged consciousness which is cognizant of aspects of itself. In a balanced assessment of the usefulness of postmodernism for feminist theory, Jane Flax examined the history of Western philosophy. Flax historicizes the "postmodern deconstructions of self" in the context of "a long line of philosophical strategies motivated by a need to evade, deny or repress the importance of early childhood experience, especially mother-child relationships in the constitution of the self and the culture" (*Thinking* 232). However, Flax recuperates some aspect of the postmodern view of the dispersed self by suggesting that interiority be conceptualized as "fluid rather than solid, contextual rather than universal, and process oriented rather than topographical" (*Disputed* 93). This multiply-situated self is constituted by a complex inner world of imagined and actual relations as well as diverse "affective relations with others and our feelings and fantasies about them" (*Thinking* 232).

I will use such philosophical and feminist critiques as Flax's to authorize my reliance on concepts of the self that underpin alcoholism theory. For to discuss alcoholic subjectivities as these are differently constructed by various models depends on the ability to utilize (and to question) long-standing modes of psychological discourse. That discourse includes but is not limited to constellations of definitions around such words as "self," "ego structures," "defenses," "personalities," and "denial." Although alcoholism theorists on whom I rely do not all use these words the same way, nor always refer to classic psychoanalytic concepts by such words, they do utilize an extensive vocabulary of psychological terms in order to discuss why people become alcoholics in certain societies under certain conditions, and what it feels like to experience that process.

Ironically, the process of becoming an alcoholic is a process by which the self becomes less integrated. I do not think this process is what postmodernists have in mind by the concept of fragmented positionalities, but, in fact, the onset of and living with alcoholism express the miseries of such a fragmented positionality. No alcohol theorists that I have read would consider such disintegration to be a philosophical good (Bean-Bayog, "Psycopathology"; and Bean, "Denial"; Levin, *Treatment* and *Introduction*).

In formulating the alcoholic subjectivity illuminated by my dual discourse of theory, my book draws on such work as that of Janet Liebman Jacobs's feminist discussion of the effects of incest on survivors, and feminist family theorists such as Monica McGoldrick and Deborah Luepnitz whose interpretations of the position of women in family, society, and culture depend on grassroots community feminisms. The works of Linda Gordon, the Dobashes, Judith Lewis Herman, and Louise DeSalvo have informed my insistence on the realities of incest and abuse in my discussions of the narrativity of alcoholism in literature.

Alcoholism is a multidimensional disorder that transforms the personality of the alcoholic in such a way that certain feelings, perceptions, denial strategies, and thinking distortions characterize the illness in many if not all of the afflicted. Chapters 1 and 2 of this book examine this contested assertion about the characterological manifestations of alcoholism, based on overlapping results from twentieth-century North American empirical research and therapeutic assessments. I argue that Michael Henchard's binge drinking is not a symptom of an underlying problem, but is a manifestation of well-established alcoholism, an illness that underpins his rages, his inarticulate and manipulative quest to bend others to his will, his obsessional and distorted thinking; it exacerbates his suicidal depressions and exhibits itself, too, in his wildly impulsive and often destructive behavior.

Alcoholism affects those involved with the alcoholic, who frequently manifest similar characterological deformations such as mood disorders, thinking distortions, and severe difficulties in intersubjective and intrasubjective relations. As Simon Dedalus suffers his economic reversals in *A Portrait of the Artist as a Young Man*, his alcoholism negatively affects his beloved son almost as much as it disrupts his own life, as I will argue in chapter 2. Using the simplified AA view as a tool of literary investigation can flatten rather than expand understanding of characterization, whereas the subtle, flexible biopsychosocial model of alcoholism can produce a more subtle examination of character, narrativity, and the varied alcoholic subjectivities under discussion.

LITERATURE AND ADDICTION

My book is part of the emerging field of alcohol and literature studies.

The pioneering work in the field in America was done by an Americanist, Roger Forseth, whose careful and provocative studies of such writers as William Faulkner, F. Scott Fitzgerald, and Ernest Hemingway use close textual analysis of novels in context of the medical model of addiction. His analyses interweave the writers' alcoholism with that of the characters in their novels.

This pattern Forseth established is emulated by other major analytic works such as those by Tom Dardis, Thomas B. Gilmore, Donald Goodwin, MD, and Donald Newlove. These works focus on much the same group of North American male alcoholic writers, adhere to the medical model, and interweave textual and biographical analyses.

John Crowley's *The White Logic*, although it explores cultural contexts, is nevertheless deeply indebted to the medical model, relying on such concepts as "the rummy's rummy," the loneliness of the male alcoholic, and the inevitable alcoholic progression downward toward helplessness and death. Crowley's work is the closest to my own in discussions of the cultural constructions of masculinity as inseparable from hard drinking, although Crowley focuses on male alcoholism as this was constructed and inflected by the fashionable angst of male modernism in North American writers. Relying on postmodernist interpretive strategies, Crowley's focus is more language-centered than mimetic.

My book creates a dialogue with the pioneering works of my predecessors. Like my predecessors, I do not accede to characters', narratives', or readers' denials of alcoholism. Like my predecessors, I respond to the textual representation of the alcoholic's subjectivity. Biographical investigation informs my approach also, although I interrogate one-to-one correspondences between art and life. My book participates in an ongoing critical conversation in an emerging field of literary analysis.

Within each of the three British novels that I analyze is embedded a literary discourse on addiction to alcohol (and in the case of To the Lighthouse, to opium). Recognizing the complex narrative resonances that are variously defined as dialogic, or "the free indirect discourse hypothesis" (Rimmon-Kenan 131). I argue that each of these narratives constructs characters whose fragmentation of self is situated within a narrative of the effects of alcoholism on personhood. Additionally, not only do the multiselved characters in these narratives exhibit the psychological behaviors frequently associated with alcoholism in the self or the parent, but the narrative strategies in each of these novels at times mimic the behaviors often arising from alcoholism.[5]

CHAPTER ONE

"AN ALTAR TO DISEASE IN YEARS GONE BY"

Alcoholism in
The Mayor of Casterbridge

Michael Henchard, the one-term mayor of Casterbridge, is well aware that he has a problem with alcohol. Early in their relationship, he declines his new friend Donald Farfrae's invitation for a drink because "'[w]hen I was a young man I went in for that sort of thing too strong—far too strong—and was well-neigh ruined by it . . . '" (M 38). He continues, explaining that he abstains from liquor because, while drunk, "'I did a deed on account of which I shall be ashamed to my dying day'" (M 38). He is thus aware that had he not been drinking, he would not have sold his wife. Almost two decades later, when he once again meets the woman he had sold, the first thing he tells her is that he does not drink (M 56). Even so, Michael Henchard enacts the effects of his drinking through his struggle to achieve economic power, his denied homoerotic dependencies, and his familial relationships. Further, certain emotional aspects indicative of his troubled relation to alcohol appear as narrative strategies, manifested partly in Henchard's fatalism, and in the lives of Christopher Coney and Solomon Longways, those work-folk whose lives appear to shadow or double Henchard's life.

Henchard's abstinence is underpinned by a time-bound oath. Once he drinks again, he loses control of his drinking and his destiny, eventually dying in self-imposed exile from the human community like a King Lear of the Heath. Michael Henchard is an alcoholic, and the story built around his life, *The Mayor of Casterbridge*, is a tragedy of an alcoholic.

Several years before writing *The Mayor of Casterbridge* in 1883–84, Thomas Hardy returned to his native Dorset where he had been born the first of four children to his temperamentally mismatched parents, Thomas and Jemima Hardy. Unlike James Joyce's father (aspects of whose downward financial course are fictionalized as the overt plot of the autobiographical *A Portrait of the Artist as a Young Man*), Thomas Hardy's father gained increasing financial and social security during his lifetime (Gittings, *Young* 7). The writer's paternal forebears had been master-masons for four generations when Thomas Hardy, Sr. (along with his brother) inherited their father's business in 1847. Although financial difficulties were sometimes severe, by the time of the elder Hardy's death in 1892, his property was valued at £850 (Gittings, *Young* 7).

In the society of Thomas Hardy's youth, minute class differentiations were of life-shaping importance (Millgate, *Hardy, Biography* 4–5, 26; Gittings, *Young* 12–13). The extended Hardy family was composed of numerous relatives who suffered the range of financial distresses common to many skilled artisans in the Dorset region of nineteenth-century England (Millgate, *Hardy, Biography* 31–32). According to Robert Gittings, Hardy "omits" the financial and social backgrounds of "about thirty first cousins" (*Young* 3) in *The Early Life of Thomas Hardy*, which is now widely assumed to be his autobiography (published originally as the work of his second wife). A self-educated man who began life as the eldest son of a skilled artisan who had not yet achieved the financial success of his later life, Hardy had good reason to disguise his class origins from Victorian and Edwardian readers reared, as he had been, when class barriers were almost impregnable, and were, in fact, regarded by many as divinely ordained (Millgate, *Hardy, Biography* 55).

In his autobiography, Hardy also elides the impact of alcoholism on his own family and the culture of his youth (Gittings, *Young* 3–5). If this were a conscious choice, there was good reason for it. Although Hardy has long been chastised by literary critics because his omniscient narrators are regarded as enjoying their characters' difficulties, in fact, Hardy's narratives are designed to encourage readers to take enlightened and compassionate views of human beings (Marks). His "work-folk," as he called them, though clearly of a class below that of the narrators, are never mocked. As Denis Thomas and Frank Giordano have pointed out, no one with an alcohol problem in any Hardy novel is the object of derision. Although the narrator does tease Joseph Poorgrass about the "multiplying eye" caused by grog in *Far From the Madding Crowd,* and Bathsheba Everdene does caution her new husband Sergeant Troy against giving too much liquor to the "work-folk," the narrator does not equate British agricultural workers with drunkards (Gittings, *Young* 177). However, the attitudes of many middle-class and upper-class people in Victorian and Edwardian England toward alcohol abuse were neither compassionate nor enlightened, as it was generally assumed that workmen were drunkards (Berridge and Edwards 97–107; Sournia 21).

Thomas Hardy was born within two and a half miles of Puddletown, the town fictionalized in *Far From the Madding Crowd* as Weatherbury (Millgate, *Hardy, Biography* 5). The scene of much poverty, the town witnessed political retaliation against injustice and privation as machines replaced skilled workers (Millgate, *Hardy, Biography* 32–33). Its inhabitants were reputed to be hard drinkers (Gittings, *Young* 14). In Puddletown lived many of those who Gittings suggests are Hardy's hidden paternal and maternal relatives, some of them with serious alcohol problems (Gittings, *Young* 13–16).

Drinking was a way of life for Hardy's maternal relatives, the Hand brothers, and for some of the men the Hand sisters married; but the perpetual financial troubles of James Sparks, Maria Hand's husband, may not necessarily be attributable to alcohol (Millgate, *Hardy, Biography* 15). Gittings suggests that the absence of alcohol problems in Hardy's father's family had allowed them to rise higher in that society of minute class differentiations than had his mother's family (*Young* 14). However, drink was involved in every aspect of working men's lives in the preindustrial and industrial British Isles (Stivers 31). The pressure on working men to drink was reinforced by the involvement of drink as part of payment for goods and service, status, social expectation, fines, and reprisals from other workers (Stivers 30–33). "Drinking was associated with literally every significant . . . social occasion . . ." (Stivers 32); marriages and religious ceremonies in the British Isles had included customary hard drinking for centuries (B. Harrison 43–44).

Gittings and Millgate report the impact of alcohol on Hardy's extended family. Millgate states that Jemima Hardy was the daughter of Elizabeth Swetman and George Hand, a "violent, drunken, unregenerate father" (12).[1] "His meagre wages were largely consumed in drinking, a propensity for which his sons were also to be notorious" (Millgate, *Hardy, Biography* 12). Left penniless and with seven children at her husband's death, Betsy Swetman Hand was forced to accept parish relief, a sign to the upper and middle classes of moral degradation.[2]

Hardy's mother Jemima had worked as a domestic servant to the Earl of Ilchester before her marriage (arranged because she was pregnant with Thomas). Jemima's brother "Christopher's drinking and knocking his wife about when she was with child distressed his own mother" (Gittings, *Young* 14). Her sister Mary had married the shoemaker John Antell, "a wild and interesting character" (Gittings, *Young* 15).

A bright, self-taught man, Antell was prevented from attending a university by the chasm of social class. Antell's bitter rage had increased over the years as he drank more, and as his skilled trade, the shoe-making business, was undermined by machine-made goods (Millgate, *Hardy, Biography* 107–8; Gittings, *Young* 15; Antell 28). So serious was Antell's alcoholism that "[h]e left behind a family of alcohol abstainers and many times the cottage at Bockhampton echoed to his daughter, Polly, singing 'Lay down the bottle and never pick it up again'" (Antell 29).

Hence, as Gittings observes, "Puddletown provided Hardy not only with a glimpse of the larger world, but, through his own relatives there, contact with broad and coarse social realities" (*Young* 16). Within his own family, Thomas Hardy observed the realities of the lives of the impoverished, the struggling, the occasionally solvent, and those, like his own parents, who were at first precariously perched on the edge of apparent success but who finally, through luck and hard work, were able to attain financial security.

Even so, the unremitting poverty and consequent social derision that Jemima Hardy had endured as a child goaded her all her life. She made certain that the elder two of her four children were pushed, through education and her work ethic, out of their social class of origin and into the professional classes (Millgate, *Hardy, Biography* 103). This is understandable and is by no means a behavior limited to Jemima Hardy. Many late Victorian autobiographies of successful people who rose above their class origins attest to parental prodding (Houghton 191).

No matter how ambitious for him she was, however, Jemima Hardy could not shield her son from the daily realities of life in so poor a district and extended family. The boy accompanied his father on numerous musical outings and saw the kinds of scenes he later recorded in euphemisms as the drunken and sexual behavior of the work-folk at the Harvest dance in *Tess of the D'Urbervilles* (Gittings, *Young* 24–25). As a boy, Hardy had heard talk of a young shepherd boy who had literally starved to death (Millgate, *Hardy, Biography* 33). Like many raised in the country, Hardy could remember winters so harsh that the very birds starved to death (Gittings, *Young* 19). Further, one of the reasons Jemima could not shield her son from the misery of the lives of those around him below them in the social scale was that her deeply pessimistic view of life shaped his own.

Hardy's relatives were master storytellers; Hardy not only was brought up on the oral tradition in song, story, and local legend, he himself was its "last and greatest" representative (Millgate, *Hardy, Biography* 37). Many of the stories he heard were savage, stark, of murders, hangings, thievery, smuggling, illicit love and illegitimate children, infanticides, suicides, supernatural events, and ghost stories. As Gittings points out, these tales of life in harsher times were to others merely interesting stories, but to a boy of

Hardy's "morbidly sensitive temperament," they had an impact of which his relatives were perhaps unaware (*Young* 18). Gittings suggests that the boy was "perhaps over-quick to read horror into any situation" (*Young* 18).

Both Millgate's and Gittings's biographical accounts of Jemima's attitudes suggest that she took delight in the miseries of others and in expecting the worst. Some contemporary readers may speculate that Jemima's attitudes were shaped perhaps both by the severe alcoholism of her father and by the effects of gender and social class on her prospects in life. Additionally, Jemima Hardy is known by her relatives to have been affected by a "dangerous miscarriage" in the period between 1843 and 1846 (Millgate, *Hardy, Biography* 20). She seems to have developed abrupt mood swings, and her nature, which had earlier been given to warmth and humor, changed (Millgate, *Hardy, Biography* 20–21). After the illness she emerged "harder, sterner, altogether more assertive in her relationship with her husband and children . . . even at times, 'tyrannical'" (Millgate, *Hardy, Biography* 20–21).

Millgate and Gittings do not suggest a connection between Jemima's depression and illness resulting from the loss of the baby with prolonged exposure as a child to the effects of a "violent, drunken, unregenerate [alcoholic] father." But it is perhaps significant that the characteristics Jemima exhibited—unbidden mood swings, embittered negativity, and the need to control everyone and every event—are said by some contemporary North American clinicians to result frequently from chronic trauma situations like those of Jemima's childhood, a consequence of alcoholism that I will investigate in cultural context in chapter 2, pp. 111–115.

Nor were her attitudes aberrational. Formed as she was in a violent, alcoholic home, raised in poverty, and growing up in a culture that condemned both the poor and the drinker, it would have been odd had Jemima thought otherwise than she did. Nor did she relinquish her attitudes with her husband's increasing prosperity, for she well knew that in Victorian England, financial resources and property were necessary as shields against disaster.

It is thus understandable that Jemima Hardy "had inherited in full measure the ancient pessimism of the rural poor, their perpetual imagination of disaster" (Millgate, *Hardy, Biography* 21). The turns of narratives of the stories Hardy had heard as a boy from his mother and other relatives stressed not just the unpleasant, but also the strange and the unpredictable, "hap," in fact, as Hardy later called it, the fact that circumstance is beyond human control.[3] The powerlessness of almost all Hardy's characters in the face of ordinary circumstances is a central fact of his narratives. This view certainly arose out of his training in the oral tradition, and was deepened by his mother's attitudes toward life. Nor were her attitudes aberrational or merely those characteristic of some contemporary North American adult children of alcoholics, as I will discuss later.

The obsessional imagination of disaster can be a spiritual ill, one inherent in the negative outlook produced by alcoholism, an attitude frequently cited by some contemporary clinicians who specialize in the treatment of alcoholism (see "Henchard's Return to Drinking," pp. 62–75).

Mayor is unusual in Hardy's novels. Events do not just happen to Michael Henchard; almost all occurrences grow out of choices he makes (Gittings, *Later* 40; disputed by Howe 90–92). Underpinning the narrator's sometimes sardonic voice and the implacability of coincidental circumstance to ruin human hopes is the characteristic depression and self-destruction of the main character. Hardy's unerring eye for the characteristics of "the clinical [male] alcoholic personality" (Levin, *Introduction* 124) enabled him to make the alcoholic temperament of his main character and the sometimes bitter commentary supplied by the subsidiary working-class characters bear the burden of what critics routinely call Hardy's pessimism.

Both Gittings and Millgate suggest that Michael Henchard, the mayor of Casterbridge, was partially created out of an amalgam of aspects of the writer and certain real-life characters in Hardy's past: John Antell, Hardy's maternal uncle, and Horace Moule, the upperclass mentor for whom Hardy felt an ambivalent love and resentment. But the narrative method that creates and sustains Henchard takes into itself also the characteristic attitudes toward life of Hardy's mother and his maternal relatives.

Robert Gittings has so convincingly argued that the suicide of Horace Moule on August 19, 1873 reshaped *Far from the Madding*

Crowd, the book Hardy was in the midst of writing, and forever altered Hardy's vision, his characterizations of the male protagonists in his fiction, and his plotting that even now, more than 20 years later, critics do not dispute this insight (Gittings, *Young* 178–86). Although Robert Gittings thoroughly documented Horace Moule's alcoholism, and discussed the hard drinking of Hardy's male forebears, Gittings did not focus on the implications of family alcoholism in shaping Hardy's mother and Hardy's attitude to life.

Horace Moule was the fourth of seven sons of Reverend Henry Moule, the Vicar of Fordington, a poor area of Puddletown and the site of what became, in *Mayor,* Mixen Lane. At first resented by many of his parishioners for his strict religious views (Gittings, *Young* 36), Reverend Henry Moule earned his parishioners' respect for his brave service to the afflicted during the cholera outbreak of 1854 (Millgate, *Hardy, Biography* 65).

The Moule family seems to have been unhealthily enmeshed by some contemporary North American family-treatment standards, lovingly close by Victorian standards. All of the sons except Horace enjoyed successful academic and clerical careers (Millgate, *Hardy, Biography* 65). Millgate speculates that "[h]is desperate search for approval from his austere father was at the heart of his difficulties" (70). The fact that Reverend Moule strongly opposed drinking (Brooks 56) can hardly have improved his relationship with Horace.

Because there was a coroner's inquest after his suicide in 1873, and perhaps because the family wanted Horace buried in consecrated ground, the family had to testify on record to the facts of his alcoholism and opium use (Millgate, *Hardy, Biography* 68).[4]

Horace's problems were apparent in his undergraduate years. He had been sent first to Oxford in 1851, and then in 1854 had transferred to Cambridge University. Although he won the Huslean prize in 1858 at Cambridge for a thesis on ancient history, he did not gain his Bachelor's degree until 1867. During the 1850s and 60s, he worked as a private tutor and wrote reviews for prestigious journals such as *Fraser's,* in which position he reviewed several of Hardy's novels (Millgate, *Hardy, Biography* 142; Gittings, *Young* 154–55, 158, 166–7). But depression and the alcohol Robert Gittings argues he drank to medicate it led to suicidal despair, imperil-

ing his chances to hold positions, and causing him and his family remorse and misery (*Young* 178).

His alcoholism was apparent as early as 1860. By then his illness was so advanced that Wynne Albert Bankes, one of the two
pupils whom he was tutoring, refused to continue with his work unless Moule agreed not to have alcohol in the house and not to go out
of the house unaccompanied (Millgate, *Hardy, Biography* 69). Even
after assenting to these conditions, Moule's alcoholism prevented his
honoring them. After many days of hard studying, the tutor and his
students separated. The next day he did not meet his students at the
proposed time, but instead ended up in France on a weeklong drinking binge. So seriously did the family take his drinking, that
Horace's "brothers Henry and Charles came to France to help" and
Bankes "made daily visits to the Paris morgue" during Moule's absence (Millgate, *Hardy, Biography* 69). Finally his brothers and
Bankes were informed by telegram that Horace had turned up in
England after having been missing for seven days.

Moule's experience in 1860 seems to have so shaken him that
he determined to stop drinking and "restore stability to his life"
(Millgate, *Hardy, Biography* 70). "In February 1861 he lectured on
temperance at East Fordington, urging total abstinence upon those
who lacked the self-discipline to drink in moderation" (Millgate,
Hardy, Biography 70). But in spite of this attempt to abstain, Moule
continued to relapse into periodic binges during which he "stayed
drunk for days at a time" (Millgate, *Hardy, Biography* 154; see also
Gittings, *Young* 123–24). Thus before his suicide "[h]e had been for
many years an alcoholic, perhaps an opium addict, certainly a potential suicide" (Millgate, *Hardy, Biography* 154).

Moule's family did not abandon him. But his more successful
brothers' constant intervention to rescue him may have been deeply
wounding to him. Shortly before his suicide, economic necessity had
forced Horace Moule to take a steady job in addition to his tutoring
and reviewing. As part of his duties, Moule visited workhouses
"among whose unhappy occupants he must often have seen examples of what he himself dreaded to become" (Millgate, *Hardy, Biography* 154). His job placed him in near proximity to his now grown
and highly successful younger brother Charles, who had obtained a

college fellowship at Corpus Christi College. Charles and Dr. James Hough were supposed to guard him should his depression worsen. Within 30 miles, also, was his brother Frederick, who frequently had "rescued him when stranded on his drinking bouts" (Gittings, *Young* 160). But the safeguards his family had hoped to supply could not prevent his suicide. On September 21, 1873, after a difficult weekend during which Dr. Hough had called a nurse and alerted Charles Moule, who had come the night before and had participated in "a distressing and all-too-familiar talk with him," Moule retired to his bedroom and slit his own throat (Gittings, *Young* 179). Thomas Hardy found out three days later.

Moule's influence on Thomas Hardy was formative and not altogether positive. They had met in 1857 when Moule was twenty-five years old and Hardy was seventeen, after Moule had left the university without a degree and was living at Fordington vicarage, tutoring and writing reviews.

Horace Moule is credited with encouraging Hardy in the study of Latin, Greek, and British classics, in guiding much of his reading during Hardy's youth and his five unhappy years as a young architect in London, and in shaping Hardy's taste in the other arts. The relationship always retained its character of university tutor and student (Gittings, *Young* 70). At first, as Hardy's biographers suggest, Moule must have served as the ideal of that which accidents of birth would prevent Hardy from ever becoming (Millgate, *Hardy, Biography* 67–69). Apparently, Moule was not convinced that Hardy had the abilities of another of his pupils, H. Tolbert, whose father's trade as an ironmonger afforded the son time to study for the Oxford Middle Class Examination. While tutoring Tolbert, Moule also tutored Hardy, but suggested that Hardy remain in his architectural apprenticeship and not work so hard on mastering the Greek classics (Millgate, *Hardy, Biography* 71). For one of Hardy's temperament, such a suggestion by a man of Moule's social class and learning might indeed have presented an insuperable mental obstacle to further aspirations to attend the university.

But with Hardyean irony, as Moule's professional life worsened, Hardy's improved. Moule lived long enough to see Hardy publish three novels, and receive a contract to write a fourth from the prestigious and influential *Cornhill Review,* edited by Leslie Stephen (eventually to become the father of Virginia Woolf).

Although sexual rivalry for Hardy's cousin Tryphena Sparks is said to have separated the two men, this is speculation on biographers' part. Moule's sexuality was ambiguous, as his biographers have suggested, and may have included something that Hardy construed as a homosexual advance. Further, some have suggested that Moule fathered an illegitimate child by a working-class woman (Millgate, *Hardy, Biography* 154–56). What is known, for certain, however, is the fact of the intertwined and progressively fatal impact of drink and depression on Moule's career. Hardy bore witness to a downward spiral and the consequent suicide that he was powerless to stop, as was Moule's family.

Thomas Hardy remained friends with Horace Moule and depended on his judgments even though three years after they had become friends in 1857, Hardy was made aware of Moule's alcoholism. Hardy's mother, with her determination to triumph over all circumstances combined with her fatalism and highly developed negativity, bore some temperamental resemblance to Moule, who suffered from depression and alcoholism. But Hardy was not just drawn to Moule by the perhaps unconscious comfort provided by the familiarity of Moule's temperament. Moule was the most highly placed and the most successful upper-class male intellectual and creative man Hardy's rural world and social class had provided him. Hardy envied Moule's education and sophistication, and he wanted to emulate the man (Millgate, *Hardy, Biography* 68). Nor is it likely that active alcoholism would scare or disgust him, as he was familiar enough with alcoholism in his family and in his neighborhood.

Elements of Moule's tragic life story are similar to aspects of the character and life story of Michael Henchard. Henchard's sexuality is ambiguous; although he has had a love affair with Lucetta while visiting the island of Jersey, which he has kept hidden for many years and whose consequences cause him remorse and fear, for most of the text Henchard is obsessed by Donald Farfrae. Henchard is a binge drinker whose bouts wreak havoc with his life. Perhaps as a result of his drinking he is subject to crippling depression. Henchard believes that temperance, that is, abstaining from liquor, is the solution to his problem—one he tries not once but twice. Like Moule, he commits suicide.

The character of Michael Henchard is formed partially from a complex composite of Hardy's experiences, friends, and relatives. Henchard combines traces of the gifted, tortured Horace Moule with aspects of Hardy's own temperament and the ambiguity of his feelings toward Moule. The trajectory of Henchard's life seems to offer proof of Jemima's aggressive negativity. Henchard's characterization clearly reflects John Antell's sufferings as well as Hardy's knowledge of the effects of alcoholism on the drinker and those around him. Millgate suggests that Henchard's qualities were those "Hardy knew to be most lacking in himself—though he had a 'source' for at least some of them in his maternal grandfather George Hand" (*Hardy* 253). Hardy's paternal grandfather, John Hardy, had come into town with only his tools, as did Michael Henchard to Casterbridge (Gittings, *Young* 7). All of these figures and experiences form part of the mix of elements fictionalized in Michael Henchard, the mayor of Casterbridge.

ALCOHOL AND THE SALE OF HENCHARD'S WIFE

In 1949 Albert J. Guerard summarized his assessment of what motivated Michael Henchard's behavior: "There is little justification for the critic who sums up Henchard's tragic flaws as temper and addiction to drink; these were symptoms of the self-destructive impulse rather than its cause" (148). Albert J. Guerard was writing at a time when there was little comprehension of alcoholism by educated, middle-class North Americans. The fact that much more is now generally known about alcoholism is reflected in the compassionate, careful scrutiny of Denis W. Thomas in his fine essay, "Drunkenness in Hardy's Novels." Here Denis W. Thomas states that "[Henchard's] alcoholism is thus not only an intrinsic part of Henchard's character but also a manifestation of some deterministic impulse which will ensure his fate" (204). But the language of Thomas's assertion separates "alcoholism" from "character," suggesting that alcoholism is one component rather than the structuring principle of Henchard's character. In his essay Thomas does not distinguish between "problem drinking," "heavy drinking," or "alcoholism," but uses these terms interchangeably, whereas in alcoholism discourse, the terms indicate differing degrees of alcohol problems. Thomas's inquiry is further complicated by a problematic aspect of Henchard's drinking that Thomas does not remark on: Henchard is not at first a daily drinker, but an episodic one who seemingly can stop at will. The questions that Thomas both raises and implies are at the center of my examination of *The Mayor of Casterbridge.*

Is Michael Henchard—at first a binge drinker—an alcoholic? Is what some critics refer to as his tragic flaw his alcoholism? Do his personality and character arise from his alcoholism, rather than his alcoholism arising because of his personality problems? Applying the biopsychosocial model of alcoholism as an illness best understood in cultural context, I will argue that Michael Henchard is an alcoholic and that his personality, motivation, and suffering are inseparable from his alcoholism.

Sociologists of addiction find medical models of addiction problematic because such models seem ahistorical: Even if biology were universal, the social construction of biology is not (Barrows and Room, "Introduction" 5–7; see also chapter 2 p. 95, and chapter 3 p. 168). As part of my examination of Michael Henchard, I will be using theories about alcoholism developed by twentieth-century North American psychologists, psychiatrists, and researchers. I do not think my method will result in anachronism.

The historical existence of the British and North American temperance movements proves that many in the nineteenth-century British Isles and North America saw clearly that there was such a thing as excessive drinking, that it followed certain physical patterns, that it seemed to be connected to male violence (Sournia 29–33, 120–26), and to what some might today term the construction of masculinity (Stivers 34). Further, the temperance movement enabled women to reject male violence and men's legal rights to women's and children's bodies; indeed, twentieth-century North American radical and middle-class white feminisms were greatly influenced by the nineteenth-century temperance movement (Flexner 185–91).

Because this is the case I do not believe that it is anachronistic to discuss the physiological consequences of nineteenth-century male alcoholism in terms established by twentieth-century North American medical literature. I assert this because the British and North American temperance movements developed a sophisticated understanding of alcoholism and an analysis of the interconnection of social class, male drinking, male violence, and women's lives. Hence I do not think it inaccurate to use twentieth-century feminist analyses of familial alcohol systems to analyze a nineteenth-century male/female working-class relationship. The oath that Henchard swears in order to stop drinking resembles some forms of nineteenth-century temperance oaths, suggesting that Thomas Hardy was incorporating temperance information in this text, information that some of his readers might have recognized. Indeed, "impressed by Henchard's vow of abstinence," *The Church of England Temperance Chronicle* thanked *The Graphic* (in which the serial version of *The Mayor of Casterbridge* appeared) for "giving our movement this friendly lift" (Millgate, *Hardy, Biography* 269). Further, Horace Moule, one of those whose alcoholism may be fictionalized in the figure of Michael Henchard, had for a time lectured on total abstinence and temperance.

Influenced by postmodernist assumptions, some scholars have recently suggested that Thomas Hardy's modes of characterization deliberately undermine the coherence of the human figure, producing fragmented, multiple, often unintegrated characters (G. Levine 141–43; Sumner). But Thomas Hardy was not a postmodernist. While working in a genre not entirely dependent on the tropes of Victorian realism, he created characters who, although they may not convince all readers of their verisimilitude, are intended to represent human beings. The full title of the novel is *The Life and Death of the Mayor of Casterbridge: A Story of a Man of Character*. It is perhaps anachronistic to impose a current expectation of the dispersed self on a novel written to explore the mystery of the dissolution of a man of character. Alcoholism is an illness that dissolves stable selfhood, if such a thing exists. Henchard's sufferings seem to me to reveal his alcoholism much more than Hardy's "protopostmodern" assumptions (G. Levine 142).

Unlike critics such as Albert Guerard who would see drinking as but one aspect of Henchard's problematic personality, the characters in the novel have no trouble realizing that the originating cause of what is to become the tragedy of the mayor of Casterbridge, Michael Henchard's selling his wife, arises from the amount of alcohol he consumes and what happens to him after he consumes it.

At the fair, Henchard goes not to the "Beer, Ale and Cyder" tent (M 5) but to the furmity (a nourishing wheat pudding) tent at his wife's urging. In the nineteenth-century British Isles such hiring fairs were places where drinking was an inescapable part of sale, barter, and masculinity rituals (Stivers 18). Susan's request suggests that Henchard's drinking and its probable violent consequences are "habitual" enough so that his wife, passive as she may be presented to be, is nevertheless worried enough about the effects of alcohol on him to want to modify his drinking. However, this is a novel by Thomas Hardy, and the ironic result of Susan's choosing the furmity tent is that Michael Henchard is therein able to drink as much if not more than had he gone into the "Beer, Ale and Cyder" tent.

How much does he drink? Hardy makes this quite clear. Henchard immediately notes that Mrs. Goodenough, the furmity saleswoman is lacing the furmity with rum. Henchard has one bowl. After Susan protests, he convinces her to have her furmity laced also. This is his second bowl (M 6). If the reader can extrapolate from Susan's behavior, her giving in may indicate that this may be a relationship wherein alcohol has become a problem. Some North American clinicians note that one strategy the nondrinking partner uses to take charge of the drinking partner's drinking is to join in (Davis 116). Susan does so (M 6). After having one bowl of furmity and rum, Henchard desires more. "At the end of the first basin the man had risen to serenity; at the second he was jovial; at the third, argumentative; at the fourth ... he was overbearing—even brilliantly quarrelsome" (M 6–7). Henchard's problem with alcohol is revealed: the more he drinks, the more he wants. As he drinks, he exhibits anger, self-pity, grandiosity, and aggression. The chemical effects of alcohol on his body lessen what self-control he had shown before he began drinking.

After the four "strongly laced" bowls of wheat and rum, Michael complains that his wife and child interfere with his economic potential (M 7). Susan "seemed accustomed to such remarks" and "acted as if she did not hear them" (M 7). The novel is set in Britain in the early days of the nineteenth century, a time when the wife as well as her child was legally the property of her husband. If she leaves Henchard, Susan has no social or economic recourse other than the workhouse and almost certain loss of her child, or the starvation wages of piecework or migrant farming, both of which alternatives were known to drive women with children to prostitution (Walkowitz 13–14). As the first chapter of the novel makes clear, she and Michael have discussed separating (M 10); presumably Susan is aware of just how difficult this would be for a woman of her social class in Regency England. Unless she is presented with a viable financial alternative to Michael Henchard, it is in Susan's economic if not emotional best interests to accede to the demands of her husband.

As Henchard drinks even more, Susan tries to ignore him to focus on their daughter. Some twentieth-century North American clinicians note that the denial that alcohol is a problem is frequently shared by those closest to the alcoholic, for whom denial of alcohol's effect is as much a survival tactic as for the drinker (S. Brown, *Treating the Alcoholic* 236–41; Dulfano 24–25). Meanwhile, the cattle auction proceeds outside. Suddenly Henchard realizes that he can sell Susan as the auctioneer is selling the livestock. (In the original draft, Henchard justifies his behavior by citing wife sales he had witnessed [Langbaum 128].) He decides to do so, but Susan protests (M 7–8). It seems likely that this is not her first experience of such hard drinking and his public blaming of his wife and child for his failure to rise in the world (M 7). In making this claim he denies the obvious social and economic realities of pre-Victorian England. Very few hay trussers could have risen from laborer to capitalist. Further, many twentieth-century North Americans who have problems with drinking cannot admit that their problem is alcohol. They lay the blame on circumstances external to the self (S. Brown, *Treating the Alcoholic* 236–41; Bean, "Denial" 70–77). Such denial is integral to the distorted thinking patterns that are characteristic of the problem drinker's inability to face the fact that alcohol dependence is a cause, not the solution, for difficulties (Morse and Flavin 1013).

Thus within four pages of the novel's opening, Hardy has located Michael and Susan Henchard in a troubled relationship (M 4). He has shown that Michael's drinking is habitual enough for his wife to try to control it. Showing that, he implies the question of whether the marriage is a failure because Henchard has legitimate grievances or whether the marriage is serving as a convenient screen onto which to project problems with alcohol. Finally he has shown that one drink of alcohol elicits Henchard's desire for more. There can be no doubt, even before the wife sale is actually concluded, that Michael Henchard, if not an alcoholic, is a problem drinker (Steinglass, et al. 31).

Henchard does not stop drinking. "But a quarter of an hour later the man, who had gone on lacing his furmity more and more heavily, . . . was either so strong minded or such an intrepid toper that he still appeared fairly sober . . ." (M 8). Here Henchard has had an additional two bowls of rum-laced furmity, possibly more, but even so, Henchard still has control of his bodily functions. Clinicians suggest that a drinker who can drink as much as Henchard has done and still maintain such external controls has the characteristic of tolerance for this amount of alcohol in the system, an indication of a serious problem with alcohol, if not chronic physical addiction (Levin, *Introduction* 118–19; Vaillant, *Revisited* 72–73).

Susan Henchard becomes so angry that she stands up, ready to be auctioned. The woman drinker in the tent urges her not to, blaming Michael's behavior on rum (M 9). This being a Hardy novel, a sailor enters at this exact moment and offers to buy Susan. The deal is concluded when Susan, after justifying her decision, joins the sailor—later identified as Newson—who pays five guineas for her (M 10–11).

Perhaps Newson's timely arrival signals Hardy's characteristic assessment of human powerlessness over circumstance; however, it is equally possible that the buyer arrives then because crafting an event-filled, suspenseful plot appropriate for magazine serialization demands that he appear, a problem of constructing a serial narrative that Hardy himself admitted (Page 25–26).

Why does Henchard sell his wife? What some alcoholism experts label the "disinhibiting effect" of alcohol has noticeably increased Henchard's belligerence and lessened his ability to appear to lose face and back down (Tarter, et al. 73; Barry 117). Hardy has previously indicated that Henchard is "perverse" (M 6), and throughout the narrative, the mere presentation of one alternative in such a way as to be perceived as a threat or a dare leads Henchard to take the opposite alternative. Psychologist John Wallace finds such behavior to be characteristic of the defense structures of many of his twentieth-century North American alcoholic clients (27–32).

As part of this constellation of characteristics, Henchard seems unable to conceptualize the fact that behaviors have consequences. Even though Hardy's 1895 introduction to the novel states that wife sales occurred in the Wessex of the 1820s, Hardy cut Henchard's self-justifying memory of such evidence from the final draft (Langbaum 128). This deliberate excision emphasizes Henchard's impulsive aggressivity, underlining the importance of Henchard's response to alcohol as a factor in the wife sale.

In concluding the wife sale, Henchard agrees that Susan can take the child, indicating this concluded bargain was part of an earlier quarrel in which they had discussed parting (M 10). Susan tells Michael that she is leaving him partly due to his "temper" (M 11) and partly to gain safety for herself and the child. How much did drinking have to do with "temper"? Did "temper" include physical violence? These questions are never answered. If not the prime cause of these events, alcohol is a major component of the problems in Henchard's handling of himself, his life, and his relationships. Thus, without further discussion of alcohol in the novel, a close analysis of the events of the wife sale casts considerable doubt on Albert Guerard's dismissal of alcohol as a secondary rather than causal factor in the structuring of character and action in the novel.

At this point Henchard is quite drunk. He asks the others in the tent whether Susan is indeed gone and gets up to seek her. "He rose and walked to the entrance with the careful tread of one conscious of his alcoholic load" (M 11). When he cannot see his wife, he blames Susan for having gone with the sailor and refuses to pursue her: "'If she's up to such vagaries she must suffer for 'em'"

(M 12). The spectators understandably soon leave, and Henchard passes out.

Perhaps it is Victorian propriety that keeps Hardy from mentioning some physical effects of so much liquor on Henchard. There is no indication of vomiting or losing control of his urine or bowels. The fact that Henchard has almost no hangover in the morning is interesting. His capacity to hold his liquor has been shown to be great, and the fact that he can drink that much without extreme physical reaction may indicate—besides readers' Victorian proprieties that even Hardy dared not yet challenge—that such behavior was usual if not habitual (Levin, *Introduction* 118–19).

On awakening, he wonders whether the wife sale were a dream, but the presence of his wife's ring and the five guineas reveals that the events happened. "'[A]m I sober enough to walk, I wonder?'" (M 13), one of his first remarks on waking, may indicate in yet another way that such hard drinking to the point of passing out is a not infrequent occurrence.

Henchard's characteristic inability to accept responsibility for his own behavior when he is drinking is immediately revealed. "'I must get out of this as soon as I can,'" (M 12) he thinks. He blames his wife that she "had taken him so literally," and not himself that he had sold her (M 13). "'[W]hy didn't she know better than bring me into this disgrace!'" (M 14) It takes him a great while before he can admit, "'[i]t was of his own making and he ought to bear it" (M 14). Drunk or sober, in this way, Henchard never changes. It is an almost impossible struggle for him to accept responsibility for his own being and his behavior. As I will discuss later, he either literally forgets almost immediately that he has behaved in certain ways or claims that other people caused his behavior and "forced" him to act as he did. Such rejection of his own part in his situation is another aspect of the denial that many twentieth-century North American clinicians note is a component of alcoholism. As Margaret Bean has explained so compassionately, the facing of the behavior consequent to alcoholic drinking requires facing the fact that one cannot drink in a socially acceptable way. Maintaining a coherent sense of oneself may become impossible if a failure at being able to drink without negative consequences is accepted ("Denial" 74–77).

But Michael Henchard is a determined man. Within one paragraph of his decision to accept responsibility for the wife sale, he takes an oath that he will stop drinking. Importantly, Hardy does not present the record of any of Michael's thinking. Hardy never shows Henchard thinking things through or reasoning logically, but instead externalizes Henchard's motives by other narrative means (Holloway, "Fiction" 345). To create a character who merely acts at the rudimentary level rather than reasons about feelings, actions, and motivations, ensures that the reader has no way except through the omniscient author's reports to gain access to the character's consciousness. In this way Henchard is at once made larger than life because he is almost all action, but he is also diminished, for the silencing of Henchard has the effect of making all his actions seem like sudden impulses. Whereas this makes Henchard quite convincing as the type of problem drinker who has but to get an impulse that he enacts it, it does not do justice to that part of Henchard that enables him to realize his economic ambitions.

Thus, without internal comment, Henchard leaves the Furmity tent, walks to the nearest town, finds a church and enters it. The reader seems as unprepared for this behavior as Henchard is. What did he think about as he walked to the church? Did he see the church as he was walking and then enter it on a whim? We will never know. Because Henchard is not a regular churchgoer, "he seemed to feel a sense of strangeness for a moment" (M 14). He kneels down and puts his head on the Bible on the Communion-table. He swears: "'I, Michael Henchard, on this morning of the sixteenth of September, do take an oath before God here in this solemn place that I will avoid all strong liquors for the space of twenty-one years to come, being a year for every year that I have lived. And this I swear upon the book before me; and may I be struck dumb, blind, and helpless, if I break this my oath!'" (M 14).

Henchard's oath has biographical and historical precedents. As I have noted, Horace Moule tried for a time to control his drinking by total abstinence from alcohol (Millgate, *Hardy, Biography* 70). Further, temperance was a current topic for Hardy's readers. During the early 1880s, when the novel was serialized and then published in book form, the Gospel temperance faction of the movement was enjoying a "phenomenal" national resurgence (Shiman 112).

The oath that Henchard swears has similarities to temperance oaths current in the nineteenth-century British Isles, for Hardy appears to have amalgamated aspects of several temperance pledges.[5] For example, members of the British and Foreign Temperance Society "pledged themselves to abstain from all spirits [distilled liquors such as whiskey and gin] 'except for medicinal purposes' and to 'discountenance the causes and practices of intemperance'" (B. Harrison 107). Because the BFTS members were evangelical Christians, they considered their oaths as religious vows. However, many working men who became total abstainers were atheists (B. Harrison 184–85).

The Mayor of Casterbridge begins "before the nineteenth century had reached one-third of its span" (2). The first temperance movements in Britain, Scotland, and Ireland were formed officially in 1829 (B. Harrison 103). Hardy knew that the action of a working man's swearing a solemn oath to abstain from "all strong liquors" for a set period of time would have been current in Henchard's time. For example, "[t]he story of the teetotaller who started life at the very bottom of the ladder as an itinerant handloom weaver, usually unemployed, and rose to be mayor of Chester and its first teetotal sheriff, was one duplicated by other temperance colleagues" (Shiman 30). Hardy had taken notes on a similar tale from the *Dorset County Chronicle* about "Sobriety and its beneficial consequences": A working man who pledged to abstain for seven years achieved financial stability, then drank again, renewed his pledge— and his economic success (Millgate, *Hardy, Novelist* 239–40).

Although Michael Henchard is not part of any society of abstainers, his pledge is respected by the work-folk, as were many such abstinence pledges of working men by their fellows (Shiman 19–20). Michael Henchard's pledge, thus, is historically accurate enough to sustain fictional verisimilitude and points also to Horace Moule as one of the biographical origins of the fictional character.

Several critics have suggested that this oath is a self-punishing way to deny himself pleasure (Howe 386; Giordano 83; Nelson 137). If drinking so much rum that he sells his wife and then passes out is a pleasure, this must come as a surprise to many readers. Henchard's oath is not an action of self-deprivation, but an action of self-acceptance and self-love. Henchard admits by this action that he knows that if he had not been drinking, he would not have shamed himself and his family. He indicates that he knows that he cannot control what happens to him when he drinks, and that he is willing to seek help beyond his own rational being that will control his use of alcohol. This admission and this oath are not the actions of a weak man inflicting pain on himself, but of a man great enough in mind and spirit to try, the only way he knows how, to take control of his own life. Such oaths were socially accepted, as Solomon Longways' respectfully calling Henchard "a banded teetotaller" makes clear (M 28). Further, although he himself is not a Christian, Henchard lives in a culture permeated with Christianity. Many of those who were not practicing Christians believed that socially sanctioned, church-based mechanisms could help control behavior.

The fact that liquor caused many of his problems is made clear in the revelation that he can only become the mayor of Casterbridge because he stops drinking. Only then does he rise from being a day laborer to farmer and merchant. From that position he can become mayor of those prosperous burghers with whom he has, through hard work and ambition, become aligned. As the events of the novel make clear, it was not his wife, but his drinking, that most likely used up his wages, exacerbated his self-hatred, and perpetuated a defeated cycle of marital misery. Safe from alcohol, he is able to exert himself to the full extent of his forceful, if primitive abilities. Hardy makes clear that Henchard's class rise and class fall are thus tied to his use of alcohol. (Increased prosperity due to abstaining was one of the themes of temperance oratory [B. Harrison 128–32].)

Shortly after swearing an oath against drinking, Henchard sets out for Casterbridge (M 15). Eighteen years pass in between chapters 2 and 3, as the conventions of the Victorian novel allow (O'Toole 19–20). Chapter 3 opens with a couple walking on the same road as in chapter 1: Susan Henchard and her daughter Elizabeth-Jane, who are seeking information about Michael Henchard from the furmity dealer (M 17).

The furmity dealer, no longer the prosperous owner of a thriving business, but a consumer of her own wares, has become an alcoholic (M 17). She reports that about a year after the wife sale, Henchard had returned and requested her to tell the bartered woman that he had gone to Casterbridge, were she ever to inquire for him. According to the narrator, Susan Henchard had believed that the wife sale formed a legal, matrimonial tie to Newson. However, upon being disabused of the idea that she was legally married, Susan could no longer comfortably sustain their connection. Newson obligingly "lost" himself at sea (M 223–24). Now "widowed," Susan needed Michael Henchard for financial support, but she also wanted to provide Elizabeth-Jane with a respectable life from which the young girl could make a good marriage.

Like her husband when he takes his oath not to drink for twenty-one years, Susan Henchard has no difficulty assessing the relation of alcohol to her public sale to Newson. In thinking over the likelihood that Henchard would prove an economic resource for herself and her daughter, she acknowledged to herself: "To . . . search for the first husband seemed . . . the best . . . step. *He had possibly drunk himself into his tomb*. But he might, on the other hand, have had too much sense to do so; for in her time with him he had been given to bouts only, and was not a habitual drunkard" (M 21; emphasis added). Stivers notes that "[w]hat we term alcoholism today was often referred to as 'habitual drunkenness' in the past. If habitual drunkenness was not addictive, it more often than not led to chronic alcoholism over a long period of time" (Stivers 5). Because it was episodic, Susan did not view Henchard's drinking as that which twentieth-century North American clinicians might term alcoholism. Hardy depicts Henchard's episodic drinking as a form of alcoholism, as I will argue later (see pp. 39–46, 242 n8).

Susan Henchard's observation raises a question and reveals several things. "[H]ad too much sense to do so," indicates her idea that Henchard had rational control over his drinking. Even though a medical contemporary of Susan Henchard, Thomas Trotter, at the turn of the century had argued that "[d]runkenness is an illness," Susan believed that Henchard could still control his drinking at the time of their marriage (Sournia 23). In retrospect, his "bouts" thus seemed to her to have been not only under rational control, but to have been separated by enough time to indicate that he was not a daily drinker, "a habitual drunkard."

It is significant that she did not mention his drinking as an explanation of why she was leaving him for the sailor as she walked out of the Furmity tent. Perhaps she was unable to condemn him as a drunkard in public, even after the shame of the wife sale. On the other hand, suppose Henchard's drinking had been worse than Susan admitted to herself 18 years after the event? Some twentieth-century North American clinicians suggest that the denial mechanisms of those who have problems with alcohol are similar to the denial mechanisms of their families (S. Brown, *Adult* 169–70; Steinglass, et al. 44–48[6]). Susan's not remembering the severity of Henchard's problem with alcohol may not indicate that his drinking was not severe so much as it may indicate Susan's denial and her need for hope that he would be in a position to provide economically for her and her child.

On their entrance into town, the two women overhear a conversation in which Henchard's name is mentioned. Susan will not allow Elizabeth-Jane to inquire of the speakers the whereabouts of Henchard: "He may be in the workhouse, or in the stocks, for all we know" (M 22). Drunkards were treated as common criminals in early Victorian England, and were frequently punished, as was the furmity-woman, who, when found wandering drunk and urinating in public (M 153), was sent to Casterbridge Court to be tried for drinking as a criminal offense. Rather than make direct inquiries, Susan goes to The King's Arms. Perhaps Susan inquires there because at an inn that served alcohol, the man she knew as her husband might most likely have been known (M 25).

But Henchard is not drinking. Elizabeth-Jane and Susan observe Michael through a window of the hotel (M 25).[7] He is wealthy and powerful, as attested to by his posture, expression, laughter, and "jeweled studs" (M 26). Susan seems overwhelmed more by the fact that he is sober than by his wealth and stature: "Three glasses stood at his right hand; but, to his wife's surprise, the two for wine were empty, while the third, a tumbler, was half full of water" (M 26).

He abstains while everyone around him is drinking to excess (M 27). Responding to her question, an old man next to Elizabeth-Jane confirms that Henchard is indeed "the celebrated abstaining worthy" before them: "He scorns all tempting liquors . . . I have heard tell that he sware a gospel oath in by-gone times, and has bode by it ever since" (M 27).

Those seated with the mayor drink a great deal (M 30–31). Thus the narrative makes scenic what is later stated clearly: Casterbridge is a hard drinking town, with three pubs for the three social classes, the burgher class, the working class, and the outcasts. It would be inaccurate to say that the whole respectable merchant class of Casterbridge drank too much. For instance, not all those burghers who later befriend Farfrae are tipplers. Even so, Henchard has long been sober within a hard-drinking community, a feat that would have aroused envy and admiration and given him the advantage of a clear head.

As the novel progresses, the cultural division between Henchard, who returns to "habitual drunkenness," and Farfrae, a sober man, takes on economic significance. Henchard stands for a rural way of life predating the Elizabethans; Farfrae stands for "modern" industrial methods (Paterson 357; D. Brown, "Harsher" 323). "The old patterns of occupational drinking proved incongruent with the increasing rationalization of economic life. Modern industrial techniques demanded a well-disciplined and regular work force" (Stivers 48; see also B. Harrison 95–96). Hence the fact that Henchard's economic rise coincides with his sobriety is an historically accurate representation of the changing cultural meaning of "occupational drinking," one of the themes that this novel depicts.

An abstainer in this town of drinkers, Henchard has not as yet forgotten about his problems with alcohol. After Farfrae has helped him by explaining how the ruined wheat (corn in British usage indicates grain or wheat) may be partially restored so that it is salable, Farfrae asks the mayor to join him for a drink. Henchard responds honestly about his problem and also his occasional desire for a drink, a desire that his self-knowledge and increased social status and the passage of many years have not dimmed: "'No, no; I fain would, but I can't,' said Henchard gravely. . . ." He explains to Farfrae, as I have noted, that when drunk, he committed "a deed," the shame of which he must endure the rest of his life:

> It made such an impression on me that I swore, then and there, that I'd drink nothing stronger than tea for as many years as I was old that day. I have kept my oath; and though, Farfrae, I am sometimes that dry in the dog days that I could drink a quarter-barrel to the pitching, I think o' my oath, and touch no strong drink at all. (M 38)

When a man says he can imagine himself draining—and sometimes still wants to drain—dry an eight-bushel barrel to its bottom, he is hardly cured of a problem with alcohol.

Whether or not abstinence must be the goal of treatment for every problem drinker or alcoholic is one of the most controversial of the many controversial questions in current Western alcohol studies. What this novel shows is that this particular drinker, once he returns to drinking increasingly deteriorates. Not only does Henchard behave in ways that are as socially stigmatizing as wife-selling, he moves from periodic to daily drinking. His temper, appearance, self-image, social status, living quarters, and job status worsen until he is reduced to occupying one room in a bitter enemy's house in the poorest slum in town, ending his days in a King Lear–1like hovel on a deserted heath (Paterson 356).

Further proof that the mayor of Casterbridge and his wife Susan are fully aware of his alcohol problem and its consequences, is the interchange between them when they meet again face to face for the first time since the wife sale. The first thing the mayor tells Susan is: "'I don't drink,' . . . 'You hear, Susan?—I don't drink now—I haven't since that night.' . . . He felt her bow her head in acknowledgment that she understood" (M 56).

As he could not bring himself to apologize directly, she could not bring herself to appear to forgive him (M 56). He offers her more money, promises to marry her again, agrees with her that they must keep Elizabeth-Jane from any knowledge of their legal tie. He urges her to "[j]udge me by my future works" (M 58). Indeed, during their brief courtship and during their marriage he is as good to her as he can be. She wants for nothing materially. And, most important, he abides by his oath and his promise to her. While she lives, he never drinks again.

As these scenes from the novel show, the narrative establishes the fact that Henchard's drinking was the immediate cause of his selling his wife, the action that sets the tragedy in motion. Although some critics have chosen to ignore the beginning of the narrative's insistence on alcohol as the cause of the wife sale, the major participants in the transaction, husband and wife, never do. Henchard accepts his problem with alcohol and uses a socially sanctioned religious oath, one modeled on a variant of a nineteenth-century Total Abstinence Pledge (B. Harrison 107), as a method to stop drinking. He tells Farfrae and Susan that he has stopped drinking and he tells Farfrae why. In fact, it is because she learns of his shame about what alcohol caused him to do that Susan gains the courage to contact him (M 38). There can be no mistake that Henchard's first words on seeing Susan again after an eighteen-year separation acknowledge that he is aware of his problem and has changed himself. There can be no doubt, then, that Henchard's problem with alcohol is a central fact of the events in the novel, that the writer saw it as such and shaped a narrative that would encourage readers to share this view.

THE MAYOR OF CASTERBRIDGE
AS AN ALCOHOLIC

In spite of the fact that definitions of alcoholism are the site of competing interpretations, several definitions illuminate aspects of Michael Henchard. Many current models of alcoholism agree that this is a multicausational illness, has a physiological component, may be genetic, but occurs within an individual embedded in a family system that is located in a particular social class, historical time, and socioeconomic reality.[8] For if there ever was a portrait of a certain kind of alcoholic male, Hardy has delineated it in the figure of Michael Henchard.

How can this assertion be made when many theorists of alcohol have concluded, after years of investigation, that there is no such thing as "the" alcoholic personality? (Syme; Ludwig 77) In fact, many clinicians now refer to "alcoholisms" (Cox 147–48), arguing that "alcoholism is anything but a unidimensional disorder" (Vaillant, *Revisited* 156).

A clinical portrait of one subgroup of male alcoholics can be found in varied sources. Publications by psychologists, psychiatrists, and alcohol counselors form a composite portrait of the male alcoholic client, drinking or sober. Facets of this composite picture are substantiated by the results of numerous empirical tests which have been administered to male alcoholics for decades.[9] Evidence drawn from longitudinal studies such as those by Vaillant substantiates the composite picture emerging from psychological and psychiatric clinical studies, one supported by some empirical test results.

The varied diagnostic criteria used to assess alcoholism, the divergence of patients' class, race, gender, age, and potential problems of countertransference (Vaillant, *Revisited* 368, 372; Wallace 32–35) need to be considered when synthesizing clinical and research findings. Even so, the resulting overlapping descriptions of a specific kind of drinker are remarkably consistent.

Many North American clinicians have noted consistent patterns of behavior, attitudes, and defenses of specific groups of male alcoholics (Levin, *Introduction* 129–33; Ludwig 19, 78; Kinney and Leaton 159–70; Wallace 26–32; Bean-Bayog, "Psychopathology" 343). For example, Ludwig states "the lack of a typical alcoholic personality does not mean that there is not a constellation of inchoate attributes common to alcoholics, or most individuals for that matter, which can become exaggerated . . . in response to a growing dependence upon alcohol" (78). After an extensive review of the medical literature through 1979 about "the alcoholic personality," Gordon Barnes concluded that a clinical alcoholic personality could be postulated (622–23). Recently Jerome Levin agreed that "the few facts that have been determined do hold up across studies and populations . . . [these] describe the clinical alcoholic personality . . ." (*Treatment* 124; see also Bean-Bayog, "Psychopathology" 343).

In the original search for the prototypic alcoholic personality, researchers hoped to establish which predisposing psychological problems might lead to alcoholism. As more became known about the disease, controversy continued, and has not been resolved about whether certain consistent characteristics of alcoholism may lead to or result from the illness (Miller and Chappel 202; Miller and Gold 285; Bell and Khantzian 273–75).

For my purposes, the question is not whether certain physiologies, genetic markers,[10] character traits, and defense structures predispose the alcoholic to the illness, but rather whether once the illness is established, certain traits and defenses—ways of construing life and others—occur as an inextricable part of alcoholism. Clinicians and empirical test results present extensive evidence that certain subsets of male alcoholics have poor self-esteem, grandiose and primitive defenses, sudden and severe rages as part of poor impulse control that leads them to act out rather than reason through choices about behavior, and little ability to conceptualize the long-range consequences of their actions (Wallace 26–32; Ludwig 18–24; S. Brown, *Treating the Alcoholic* 97; Khantzian, "Self Regulation" 30–31).

Several clinicians who believe alcoholism leads to characteristic behavioral and perceptual patterns view the loss of control of drinking as central to the definition of alcoholism. As loss of control increases, they note, alcohol becomes the organizing principle of the drinker's life. Distortions in thinking develop, which the alcoholic needs to maintain a central focus on alcohol while denying such a focus. Because alcohol, not themselves or others, becomes the primary concern, alcoholics lessen their physical and emotional self-care; their interpersonal relations suffer. Consequently alcoholism causes decreased work capacity, shame, guilt, self-preoccupation, and increasingly lowered self-esteem (S. Brown, *Treating the Alcoholic* 3–26, Bean-Bayog, "Psychopathology" 339–45; Wallace 28–32; Vaillant *Revisited,* 33–34, 48, 79–80, 82–85, 107, 118–19, 136–37, 142, 270, 274–75, 365, 371–73).

Still other clinicians such as Jerome Levin and E. J. Khantzian, for example, focus on what some term the "weak ego structures" of the alcoholic, although Levin postulates such ego-permeability as the result of alcoholism and Khantzian as a probable precondition. Among the painful characteristics caused by alcoholism, Levin cites low tolerance for frustration, low self-esteem, feelings of shame, and an inability to assess long-range consequences of actions or to control impulsive behavior (*Treatment* 129–33). Psychiatrist E. J. Khantzian concludes from his clinical work with addicts and alcoholics that specific behaviors of addiction are an attempt to palliate pre-existing severe psychic distress. Such "[d]isturbances in psychic structures" cause problems with "affect life, self-esteem, relationships and self care" (Bell and Khantzian 275). Khantzian argues that "substance abusers' self-protective, survival deficiencies are the consequences of deficits in a capacity for self-care" ("Self Regulation" 30). Michael Henchard demonstrates many of the characteristics associated with this postulated weak ego structure in his self-devaluation, lack of impulse control, belligerence, and aggressivity.

The narrative insists on the loneliness and suffering of this man who longs for human connection and can neither make healthy connections nor sustain those he has made. However he came by these characteristics, either as the result of his drinking or as part of the cause, Michael Henchard has those specific difficulties that arise because his core self is poorly developed, he perceives other people as objects, and he experiences his own feelings as intolerable attacks. Repeatedly he seems unable to think through the consequences of behavior, as I have argued earlier when analyzing the wife sale.

When called upon to explain or to defend himself appropriately, he cannot or will not. For instance, he remains silent when confronted by Elizabeth-Jane at her wedding (Giordano 93–94). As another indication of low self-esteem and lack of impulse control resulting from the impaired self-care of alcoholism, Henchard refuses to lie and discredit her when confronted by the furmity-woman, instead, agreeing with her denunciation of him as a wife-seller (M 154–5). His self-devaluation renders him incapable of defending himself even when the most important things in his life depend on it.

Discussions of the mayor's weak ego illuminate Henchard's inability to interact with others as an adult human being. He lost his position in Casterbridge for many reasons, but drunk or sober, his rages consistently cost him allies. When he learns that Farfrae's business is established, for instance, his tantrum could be heard "as far as the town pump" (M 86). This episode illustrates his lack of self-care skills, as observed in the intolerable and thus uncontrollable nature of his rage, and his inability to recognize and accept the long-term consequences of his ill-advised behavior. All are characteristics of alcoholism (Wallace 26–32; Ludwig 18–22; S. Brown, *Treating the Alcoholic* 97; Khantzian, "Self-Regulation" 30–31).

If alcoholism is a biopsychosocial disease, then cultural and sociological variables will affect its development and course. Cross-cultural studies that investigate interpersonal dependency as a factor in alcoholism are pertinent to any discussion of Michael Henchard as an alcoholic (Heath 393–94). Feminist theory, further, has long argued that the construction of masculinity is the partial result of the rejection of traits culturally marked as "feminine" (Chodorow 180–90). These assertions are pertinent to Blane's speculations about what would now be termed the construction of masculinity within white middle-class American norms of dependency (Blane 13–14, 37, 85). Blane suggested that alcoholics can be categorized into three types: openly dependent alcoholics who expect others to meet their primary needs, counterdependent alcoholics who cannot admit dependency except under the influence of alcohol, and dependent-independent alcoholics who swing from one extreme to the other.[11]

Although it is problematic to advance his ideas as a scientific analysis, Blane's reading of the white male in North American middle-class culture is an excellent metaphor for Henchard's behaviors in the novel. Michael Henchard sells his wife and child because they do not exist for him as subjects; he experiences them as nuisances who impede his rise. Once having shed his dependence on his wife, he lives superficially with other men and concentrates on work. His one sexual relationship[12] before his wife reappears takes place when he visits the island of Jersey on business. There he becomes physically ill and then falls into a severe depression that has weakened his resolve not to rely on others.

Once Henchard becomes interested in Farfrae, he is overcome by his need for the young man, a need that he goes to extreme lengths to satisfy. When Farfrae refuses to remain in his stranglehold, the mayor veers away from his dependence to a haughty independence that cloaks a fantasy of fused dependency on Farfrae, so that the majority of his actions relate either symbolically or directly to the young man. Michael Henchard thus embodies Blane's theories about dependent counterdependent male alcoholics (26–32). In all of these relations, Henchard demonstrates what John Wallace has described as the extreme self-referentiality and consequent flattening of other human beings to objects, characteristic of certain of his male alcoholic clients who "tend to . . . perceive the happenings around them largely as they impinge upon self," and "screen out" and "distort" other "information" (30). Later I will analyze in some detail Michael Henchard's struggle with dependency, both on alcohol and on Donald Farfrae.

An alcoholic's dependency on others, whether acknowledged or denied, may be related to what researchers speculate is an "external locus of control." This term refers to people's perceptions of "the source of control in their lives," (Cox 159) a contested measure of alcoholism on empirical tests. Although not all clinicians and alcohol theorists would agree with this finding, Levin asserts that "[a]lmost all studies of alcoholics show them to have an external locus of control" (Levin, *Introduction* 132).

Like Howard Blane's ideas, which I treat as metaphorical, I think this finding is nevertheless suggestive for an understanding of Michael Henchard. Even though Henchard is an independent laborer at twenty-one, he is nevertheless a member of a social class with very little control over their lives and social circumstances. Members of this social class at the beginning of the nineteenth century in England were at the mercy of forces to which those with more money were not subject.

A significant feature of many of Hardy's working poor is their insistence on fate rather than individual efforts and will. Michael Henchard's conviction of victimization by fate is exacerbated by his alcoholic inability to accept responsibility for his own behavior. Whether he is an unemployed hay trusser or the mayor of a prosperous town, Henchard cannot take responsibility for his actions. As I have noted, he blames his wife for the fact that he sold her. When he discovers that Elizabeth-Jane is not his own child, he is convinced that a "sinister intelligence" has decreed that he suffer (M

97). Instead of being able to recognize his own role in the fall of his corn empire, he strikes out at Jopp onto whom he projects all his problems (M 145).

Henchard's first reaction to events that do not go his way, drunk or sober, is to look to others' failures or behaviors as the cause. It is an almost impossible struggle for him to maintain contact with the fact that he is at the center of his life, not fate or another, thus demonstrating the perceptual style termed "external locus of control."

Depression has a high correlation with alcoholism, as numerous sources attest. However, the complexity and dimensions of this correlation continue to be contested (Hamm, et al. 580; Weissman and Meyers 372–73).

Alcohol is physiologically a depressive drug (Levin, *Treatment* 17). But does prior depression predispose some to become alcoholic? Is alcohol a "self-medication," then, to treat a preexisting condition? George Vaillant, advocating a medical model, argues that depression results from drinking (*Revisited* 82). Her clinical work with alcoholics leads Margaret Bean to suggest that depression results from shame over the loss of control in alcoholic drinking, and from the necessity for denial of the severe toll uncontrolled drinking takes on self-esteem, relationships, and adult functioning capacity ("Denial" and Bean-Bayog, "Psychopathology"). Acknowledging the devastation alcoholism brings, Edward J. Khantzian has consistently argued that intolerable feeling states, including depression, may lead to addiction as an alternative to such suffering (Bell and Khantzian 274, 279).

In 1952, Frederick Lemere, a Seattle psychiatrist, surveyed the life histories of 500 deceased alcoholic patients, discovering that 11 percent had killed themselves (Lemere 695). Earlier, Karl Menninger "conceptualized alcohol addiction as a chronic progressive suicide" (qtd. in Hamm, et al. 580); an interpretation that Frank R. Giordano's study of Henchard substantiates.[13]

Michael Henchard is depressed to the point of suicide several times in the novel, and his return to drinking has been interpreted as a suicidal gesture of rage turned against himself (Giordano 79, 96). In the first rapture of their friendship, the mayor tells Farfrae that his depressions were rather common and that he expected them in his life (M 60). One of his methods of handling depression is to become immobilized, as when he retreats to Jopp's lodgings and isolates himself from everyone for a time (M 169). He consciously contemplates suicide at least three times (M 97–98; 171; 226–27; 253–54); finally having decided to drown himself, he is only deterred by seeing his effigy in the weir-hole of Blackwater (M 227).

Henchard also handles his depressions by formulating external situations as the problem and becoming enraged about them, as for instance, when he maneuvers Farfrae into quitting. He does not want Farfrae to leave, but he lacks the impulse control necessary to tolerate his feelings and wait for an appropriate time to work things out with Farfrae in private.

After his return to drinking, Henchard moves from bouts of depression and inability to tolerate sadness to increasingly self-destructive behaviors. The note that he leaves on his deathbed (M 254) makes clear that his death is motivated by what Lemere might have interpreted as the suicidal despair of the drinking alcoholic.

So specific were Hardy's observation and understanding of the alcoholics around him that his fictional character presents a convincing portrait of an alcoholic. The creation of Michael Henchard indicates that Hardy closely observed the characteristic behaviors and sufferings of the many alcoholics he knew and used his compassionate observations to create the unforgettable figure of the mayor of Casterbridge.

LOVE AND THE MAYOR OF CASTERBRIDGE

The biopsychosocial view of alcoholism argues that as a physiological addiction with emotional and mental components, alcoholism is intimately tied to dependency. Deprived of alcohol, the alcoholic and the problem drinker do best if they can substitute another activity or passion (some would not hesitate to say obsession) for drinking (Vaillant, *Revisited* 246–54; see also Vaillant, *Natural* 190–95). This Henchard did when he turned from the loss of his wife and child to the dedicated hard work that enabled him to achieve his business ambitions. But it is most clearly in his relationship to Donald Farfrae, both as an interconnection with a real human being and as a search for the perfect object of a totalizing fantasy of fusion, that *Mayor* may be interpreted as a story of alcoholic dependency.

The circumspection and self-control he developed through many years of sobriety and financial success carry the mayor through his first interview with Donald Farfrae. In the midst of this conversation the facade of his new self—which the narrator later refers to as "the rind" (M 86)—Henchard had built up begins to crack. For Henchard sees in Farfrae something of his brother and at that moment his longing for fusion with Donald Farfrae begins. It becomes the obsessive force motivating Henchard's movements for some time:

> Your forehead, Farfrae, is something like my poor brother's—now dead and gone; and the nose, too, isn't unlike his. You must be what—five foot nine, I reckon? I am six foot one and a half out of my shoes. . . . In my business, 'tis true that strength and bustle build up a firm. But judgment and knowledge are what keep it established. Unluckily I am bad at science, Farfrae. . . . You are just the reverse . . . *I have been looking for such as you these two year, and yet you are not for me.* . . . Can't ye stay just the same? (M 37–38; emphasis added)

This passage combines narrative exposition with psychological motivation, dramatizing the contrasts between the two men. But as the words emphasized make clear, it is also much more.

This is one of the few details ever presented about Michael Henchard's past or his family life. The narrative never reveals the site of Henchard's birth, the size or birth order of Henchard's family, nor parental child-rearing practices. But his reactions to Farfrae in this scene allow the reader room to speculate.[14]

The fact that Farfrae's resemblance to Henchard's brother elicits Henchard's trust is both an effective narrative device and an indication of Henchard's infinite need for human love. Henchard neither knows how to control such yearning nor to express it so that his needs can be met (J. H. Miller, *Distance* 147). His passionate longing for a reciprocal love from Farfrae exacerbates Henchard's increasingly immature behavior and leads to the losses that precipitate his return to drinking.

Obsessed as Henchard becomes with Lucetta briefly and with Elizabeth-Jane for longer periods, neither they nor his wife Susan ever inspire the overriding passion in Henchard that Donald Farfrae does. It is Henchard's relation to Farfrae that causes much of the external action, and brings about the circumstances that make possible the eruption of Henchard's past into his present so that he is ruined. The women are but stand-ins. Michael Henchard's most passionate feelings revolve around another man.

Little explanation other than Farfrae's reminding him of his lost brother is given for the beginning of Henchard's obsessional attachment to the younger man. He speculates that perhaps his loneliness is the cause (M 44), but why had his loneliness not bothered him before? Apparently work had taken the place of people for Henchard during his two decades as a successful Casterbridge businessman (Showalter, "Unmanning" 106). His business does not begin to slip, nor do his troubles overwhelm him, until he involves himself with Farfrae.

Just as "the female world of love and ritual" (Rosenberg) sanctioned passionate friendships between women, so too did the Victorian ideal of manly love encourage strong friendships between men which were not then viewed as homosexual attachments. Because of the enormous constraints on heterosexual interaction within the middle class, same-sex relationships served for many as their primary attachments in Victorian England (Davidoff and Hall 416, 419–21, 429, 445–49).

Henchard's complex homoerotic attachment to Farfrae is demonstrated in the way Henchard seeks Farfrae as a potential employee. As Farfrae leaves town to emigrate to America, Henchard takes Farfrae's hand and makes a proposal more passionate than the one he makes to Susan when asking her to remarry him, telling Farfrae to set his own wages (M 49). Farfrae desires economic success, but he appears to be moved, perhaps more from vanity than from a shared attraction (Kramer 77–78), and promises to stay (M 49).

Henchard does not seek equality: "He was the kind of man to whom some human object for pouring out his heat upon—were it emotive or were it choleric—was almost a necessity" (M 95). Ironically the narrator underlines the unhealthiness of Henchard's desire by pointing out that Henchard thought of this possession of others as establishing "this tenderest human tie" (M 95). Thus the relationship between the men can be successful only as long as Farfrae accedes to Henchard's need for an object who asserts no independence. Perhaps partly because of this subduing of himself to the mayor's needs Farfrae becomes indispensable to the increase in the mayor's business (M 69).

There is no warning before Farfrae abruptly separates himself from his employer. Henchard employs Abel Whittle, a slightly retarded man. Inconvenienced by Whittle's lateness several times, Henchard responds sadistically, forcing Abel to come to work without his outer overalls. Abel was shamed, but took his oppressor's part, apologizing to Farfrae for lack of dress (M 74–76). Farfrae asserts his power as manager and demands that Abel get dressed, contravening the mayor's orders. They argue in public (M 76). Farfrae chastises Henchard, "'a man 'o your position should ken better, sir! It is tyrannical and no worthy of you'" (76). The mayor backs down, feeling shamed publicly. The imaginary fusion he had briefly enjoyed with Farfrae is over. Although Henchard retains Farfrae as an employee, he never again trusts Farfrae. Shame and stealth enter a relationship that had been free of them.

A public entertainment planned by Farfrae and some other businessmen to rival that of Henchard becomes the occasion of a public break between the men (M 78–83). Henchard's defenses have been invaded so thoroughly by his inability to handle his passion for Farfrae while maintaining a separate identity, that he loses control of himself. When he leaves his own entertainment to inspect Farfrae's more successful one, Henchard is criticized by two aldermen. Henchard does not parry their remarks, but responds to them by saying that Farfrae will soon quit his employ, publicly placing Farfrae in the same position as Farfrae had placed him by intervening on Abel's behalf (M 83). He loses both times: Farfrae quits (M 83). As if his fury had been a drunk that he had cured by sleeping it off, "in the morning" Henchard regrets "his jealous temper" but it is too late (M 83).

The many miseries that follow Henchard's experience of losing Farfrae at the entertainment could have been avoided. Donald Farfrae seems conscious of this. With his usual cold-blooded business sense, he realizes that marrying Elizabeth-Jane would resolve the estrangement between himself and her father (M 121). For her part, Elizabeth-Jane had been drawn to Farfrae when she had first seen him at The King's Arms. Her silent love for him had only increased with time.

Henchard, however, is unable to control his need for warfare and keep his rage from interfering with his business and social standing in the community. With the impossibility of legal divorce in the England of the 1840s, Farfrae would have been tethered to him as his son-in-law for the duration of their lives. Even so, a Farfrae married to Elizabeth-Jane would have remained as emotionally unavailable to Henchard as a Farfrae who owned his own business. Perhaps out of resentment that his stepdaughter rather than himself would gain the man, and certainly out of his inability to control his aggression, Henchard cannot accept this solution but focuses on obstructing Farfrae's rise rather than his own business (M 87). Emotional and financial combat coalesce.

At this juncture of the plot, Susan Henchard dies. Because the fantasy fusion with Farfrae is irrecoverable, Henchard decides to tell Elizabeth-Jane she is his daughter (M 93–95). Shortly thereafter, Henchard reads his wife's deathbed confession and discovers that the sailor to whom he had sold his wife is the father of the girl for whose sake he had remarried Susan and to whom he had now publicly given his name (M 95–98).[15]

His suffering is extreme, veering between self-hate and a wild glee at the ironic justice of the matter. He lacks the internal resources to withstand such a blow. His immense needs have been thwarted. That which he had felt would fulfill his emotional needs, this daughter, has been "snatched" (M 97) from him, and he can accept this loss as little as he can accept the loss of Farfrae. For one is but a smaller version of the other. Elizabeth-Jane was meant as a substitute Farfrae, a daughter bound to him, and unable by gender and social convention to have either contradicted his will or to have left him except by marriage.

But Henchard makes their life together miserable, coldly criticizing and mocking her. His harsh behavior is within the usage of custom and law; the patriarch had absolute control over women in his household in Victorian England (Gorham; Roberts). But the emotional beating to which he subjects her does not assuage his pain. So little can he bear the sight of her that he eats his meals at either of the more prosperous hotels with other burghers and "farmers" (M 101).

But this enforced interaction with the men of Casterbridge does not heighten his popularity. Instead, Henchard is spurned by the very men who had once elected him mayor: "Henchard, whose two years' mayoralty was ending, had been made aware that he was not to be chosen to fill a vacancy in the list of aldermen; and that Farfrae was likely to become one of the Council. . . ." (M 103). Henchard had interpreted Farfrae's leaving him as due to Farfrae's refusal "to put up with his temper any longer" (M 86). The councilmen, too, had felt the lash of Henchard's temper "on more than one occasion" (M 86). They are perhaps only too glad to side with a Farfrae who is strong enough to best the mayor.

John Paterson asserts that Henchard's possessiveness and self-destructive behaviors arise from Henchard's tragic character (353). To Giordano they express and exacerbate Henchard's suicidality. I believe that Henchard's tragic character and his suicidality arise from his alcoholism. Even though he has been sober throughout this period, his self-referential obsessions, his inability to tolerate or articulate painful feelings, and his repetition of certain destructive patterns of behavior are aspects of the illness of alcoholism, as I have discussed earlier when examining "the clinical [male] alcoholic personality" (Levin, *Introduction* 124).

As I observed previously, alcoholism may be culturally interpreted as a disease of dependency that manifests itself in human relationships and in symbolic modes of behavior. Howard Blane's speculations about patterns of alcoholic dependency suggest an explanation for much of Henchard's behavior. Henchard either relies exclusively on alcohol for sustenance and severs human ties, or he relinquishes alcohol and depends on manipulative and obsessional human entanglements. The plot of *Mayor* demonstrates Henchard's tragic affliction with the illness of alcoholism.

The concatenation of events that bring about the fall of the mayor of Casterbridge occurs only secondarily as a result of Henchard's blazing temper. As I have shown, Henchard's anger arises from his inability to manage his own feelings in response to circumstance. Henchard makes repeated mistakes in business because he responds to his obsessional attachment to Farfrae rather than to events (Langbaum 130–31).

Thomas Hardy was worried about the dependence of the serialized plot of *The Mayor of Casterbridge* on "improbabilities of incident" when it was first published in *The Graphic* (F. Hardy 231). However, he revised the novel before its publication in book form. "Most modern critics," asserts Millgate, find it to be "perhaps the most shapely of all his novels, tightly organized and structurally eloquent" (*Hardy Biography* 269). That this is the case is illustrated by Hardy's masterful timing of several interconnected climactic events.

Henchard is not felled by a malign fate; Hardy's plot strategies delineate a Henchard whose alcoholism leads him to respond so maladaptively to external events that he himself causes his fall. A series of plausible circumstances occur in combination: the alliance of his estranged stepdaughter with Lucetta, now wooed by Farfrae (M 123–25); the reappearance of Jopp, whom he had dismissed in favor of Farfrae; a spell of bad weather; and the reappearance of the furmity-woman who denounces Henchard as the drunken man who had sold his wife 20 years before.

Henchard's choices to rehire Jopp, to gamble in the corn and hay markets, to pursue Lucetta, who has come to loathe and fear him, all devolve on his rivalrous obsessional attachment to Farfrae. Confessing his past in a public court on hearing the furmity-woman's accusations does not seem on the surface to bear on Farfrae, yet it does.

When Farfrae challenged Henchard over the humiliation of Abel Whittle, Henchard believed Farfrae's motive was his ownership of "the secret o' my life" (M 77). The narrator has frequently demonstrated Henchard's superstitious nature, an aspect of himself that is allied to his inability to accept responsibility for the results of his actions. Henchard visited the weather-prophet and then feared to share a meal with him lest that put him more under the man's spell (M 140–44). Learning that Elizabeth-Jane was not his daughter, he experienced this blow as a punishment by "some sinister intelligence" (M 97). Similarly, when he has foolishly gambled on the harvest weather, he wonders whether someone is burning a waxen image of himself instead of looking to his own conduct to ascertain the reasons for his troubles (M 146). A man this superstitious would feel strongly the power of possession—that somehow his soul was entangled with Farfrae's because Henchard had confided to him what Henchard felt was the most shameful episode in his previous life. These facets of Michael Henchard, rooted in his upbringing and shared perspective with those of his time and social class, are also examples of an "external locus of control."

Henchard feels great shame about the wife sale, even after 20 years. To finally pay the social price for his action might have been a relief. The appearance of the furmity-woman gives Henchard a chance to confess this secret.

Equally important, if Henchard could tell the truth about his past, Farfrae would no longer control his "secret," his hidden self. Farfrae's power over him would be eliminated (Giordano 85; Nelson 137). Like all his other actions that devolve on the imaginary relation between the two, Henchard's actions show no common sense and recognize no social realities. If Henchard had been able to behave with the self-control and circumspection he had shown at the dinner at The King's Arms, he would have challenged the furmity-woman's story as sharply as did the second magistrate who dismissed it as drunken ravings (M 155). That Henchard admits to her story destroys him: "[T]he police-court incident . . . formed the edge or turn in the incline of Henchard's fortunes . . . the velocity of his descent . . . became accelerated every hour" (M 167).

Their encounter demonstrates the Aristotelian tragic principles of recognition and reversal.[16] The furmity-woman recognizes Henchard, not just as the drunken man who had sold his wife in her tent, but as her equal, declaring: "'he's no better than I, and has no

right to sit there in judgment upon me'" (M 155). Henchard immediately agrees that his having sold Susan "'does prove that I'm no
better than she!'" (M 155) Their recognition of their sameness is
also proleptic.

The narrative insistently demonstrates the furmity-woman's
downward alcoholic slide. From the proud owner of a stable business (M 12), by the 1840s she has become "an old woman, haggard,
wrinkled, and almost in rags" (M 17) who is "tentless, dirty," and
desperate for even the business of small boys (M 17). Soon after her
courtroom testimony, she finds a comfortable niche in Mixen Lane,
safe haven of social outcasts (M 197). Her gender is as significant as
her alcoholism, for female drunkards in Victorian England were regarded as even worse than their male counterparts (Logan 126–58).
That a female alcoholic mirroring the man he will become should
offer Henchard the means to tell the truth and in doing so destroy
himself is characteristic of Hardy's narrative patterns and their emblematic significance.

Henchard's dependence on the fantasy of fusion with Farfrae
through the ruinous pursuit of Farfrae's destruction has caused his
own. In short order, the reversals readers associate with Aristotelian
tragedy are complete. Because of his alcoholism, the mayor of Casterbridge has lost everything: his stepdaughter, his former mistress,
his business, his possessions. At the auction, Farfrae buys Henchard's house, his business, even his furniture and homely possessions. On hearing of this, Henchard wonders whether Farfrae might
try to "buy my body and soul" (M 172). In fact, Farfrae did not
have to "buy" Henchard's soul, for Henchard had already long before given it over to him by his fixation on Farfrae rather than his
own needs. His despair increases. A drink is not far ahead.

THE ALLURE OF ALCOHOL: "'HOW MUCH LONGER HAVE HE GOT TO SUFFER FROM IT?'"

Henchard's social and economic downfall is dramatized by his
change of neighborhood and social class. Poverty and unemployment
force him to move into Mixen Lane, a "notorious" neighborhood,

populated by hard drinkers, gamblers, poachers, sex workers, and those working people too poor to live anywhere else (M 195–96).

Thomas Hardy claimed that he never set out to shock his readers. Criticism depressed him. His response to critics' views of his first published novel was to "[wish] himself dead" (Millgate, *Hardy, Biography* 134; see also Page 14). Whether or not his hurt and surprise at his detractors' view of him were disingenuous,[17] Hardy's novels interrogate Victorian middle-class pieties and unexamined assumptions.

Victorian middle-class ideology insisted on the wide gulf between the working class and the middle class. Onto the working class were projected those human traits the middle classes thought least desirable, such as drunkenness, vice, and crime. One of the most important contributions Hardy made to this debate was to humanize working-class members who had problems with alcohol in the figures of minor characters such as Joseph Poorgrass, Marian, Solomon Longways, and in the towering figures of Michael Henchard and Jude Fawley. Throughout *Mayor,* Hardy seeks to endow the stereotype of the drunken worker with the three-dimensional range and verisimilitude of a complex character of the sort with whom middle-class Victorian readers had been trained to identify. To this end, by chapter 3 when Henchard has become sober and risen into the prosperous class, Hardy deepens his examination of Michael Henchard by splitting off certain aspects of Henchard. These develop a life of their own in the rustic commentators on Michael Henchard and in their friends in Mixen Lane.

Hardy began writing fiction in the 1860s when sensation novels, influenced partly by the example of later Dickensian narratives, were popular and lucrative. Urged by his first readers' reports to focus on plot (Gittings, *Young* 106–7). Hardy did so rather than rely on the omniscient narrator's minute psychological investigation of realistic characters as modeled by George Eliot.[18] As Robert Garis long ago pointed out in *The Dickens Theatre,* externalizing the unconscious of characters rather than extensively analyzing the subtleties of consciousness is an effective fictional device.

One method for such externalization is that of "splitting," of breaking off diverse aspects of a character into separate characters rather than combining these within one figure. Readers know that these "doubles" comment on each other by their motivations and interactions (Van Ghent 208–9; Bailey, "Visitants" 1161) Ironically, the use of doubling to represent characters so familiar in Victorian fiction is now valorized by the postmodernist assertion that the integrated self created by realistic modes of characterization is an inaccurate representation of the human.

As Hardy's worldview became bleaker, his use of those characters whom critics referred to as "the rustics" changed. At first, the rustics—the chorus of genial folk who served as knowing, though detached, observers of the main characters—were bucolic figures like the folk population in *Under the Greenwood Tree,* living lives safe from fortune's buffets of illness, poverty, and loss of livelihood. But by the appearance of *Far From the Madding Crowd,* Gabriel Oak the shepherd, who once would have been a secondary figure, became first the moral center of the tale and then its hero. Similarly, in *The Return of the Native,* the major character, Clym Yeobright, deliberately becomes downwardly mobile and chooses the life of the rural poor. Finally, the rustics in *Mayor* are not rustic; they are the urban poor and their commentaries, while still frequently humorous, are also apt to be rueful, bitter, and harshly ironic. "[O]ne could almost speak of the events at Mixen Lane as a sub-plot, the darkened reflection through plebeian grotesquerie of the main strand of the action" (Howe 101; see also Paterson 359–62; Nelson 126–27).

Throughout the text, Solomon Longways and Christopher Coney often comment on the middle-class characters. Consistently hard drinkers, they have an almost religious relation to alcohol. They think of it, they talk of it, they find ways to drink it daily. Whenever they appear, they are emblems of those working men whose lives are defined by what, where, when, how much they drink and with whom. Their statements echo what the mayor once stated to Farfrae was his desire to drink down to the bottom of an eight-bushel barrel of ale (M 38). Solomon and Christopher's focus on alcohol is a subtle way to keep the reader aware of the power of alcohol over human lives.

That alcohol helps kill Henchard while making Solomon's and Christopher's lives both difficult yet tolerable is significant.

Solomon and Christopher symbolize the preindustrial way of life when hard drinking was inextricable from occupation in the British Isles (Stivers 22–33). Compassionate to all three characters, Hardy seems to be examining the fine distinction between "habitual drunkenness" and the effects of "occupational drinking."

That Solomon and Christopher are physically dependent on alcohol, if not alcoholics, is implied in their earliest banter. In chapter 5 they stand with Elizabeth-Jane looking into the bow window of The King's Arms, commenting on the action. Solomon answers Elizabeth-Jane's query about the mayor's not drinking by saying, (as quoted earlier in the chapter) that Henchard had forsworn drinking, a vow most people respected "'for yer gospel oath is a serious thing'" (M 27). Grasping why the decision is "a serious thing"—because it is an impossible punishment—Christopher asks Solomon, "'[H]ow much longer have he got to suffer from it, Solomon Longways?'" (M 27). Christopher's remarks imply doubt that abstaining from drink could be a solution to problems rather than a cause of them. The inability to conceptualize a tolerable life without alcohol is an indication of probable dependence on the substance.

Solomon and Christopher are next seen drinking at the Three Mariners on Donald Farfrae's first night in Casterbridge. Farfrae's singing sentimental Scots songs moves them deeply, but they question his sincerity (M 40–41). To Christopher, this is nonsense; if the singer had loved his birthplace so much, Christopher says, then Farfrae would not have emigrated.

On the surface this scene may be amusing, but in fact, there is an undercurrent of bitterness in Christopher's remarks. His feelings arise only partly out of a self-pity enhanced by the alcohol he drinks, for his response is motivated by the effects on his life of the economics of the increasing decline of agriculture in nineteenth-century England. In 1815 more than half of the British population was rural and engaged in farm work. By 1914, this number had dwindled to such an extent due to the crisis in agriculture caused by foreign competition, that Britain imported rather than produced a considerable percentage of its food (Thompson, *Twentieth* 194–95). Thomas Hardy bitterly referred to this transformation as "the tendency of water to flow uphill when forced" (Hardy, *Personal* 188). In fact, as

Christopher knows, Farfrae had decided to leave Scotland and emigrate to America for the same reason Solomon and Christopher now live in a town in poverty rather than on farms: the economic dislocation of the movement from an agrarian, rural way of life to an industrialized, increasingly urban one caused untold suffering and havoc in the lives of the working class and rural laborers (Howe 101).

Far from mocking "the drunken worker," Hardy's careful delineation of class awareness and class struggle dignifies these workers. His narrative strategies result in making comprehensible their hard drinking as only one part of their complex reactions to the socioeconomic facts of their lives. It is also true, however, that Hardy is careful to indicate that their drinking has "a life of its own" (Vaillant, *Revisited* 366) and that that is a motivation beyond the difficulties of their lives.

The bitter undercurrent to their humorous commentary about the mayor of Casterbridge continues as Solomon and Christopher and a group of their friends are next seen observing Henchard's (re)marriage to Susan. They are unimpressed by Susan and contemptuous of the mayor for choosing her. "'[D]aze me if I ever see a man wait so long before to take so little,'" exclaims Christopher (M 64). Their humorous remarks reveal that this group has known one another from childhood and that they began their lives as poor rural people, not town folk (M 65). As the wedding party leaves, Christopher and Solomon feel they must have a drink to offset the chill produced by "'drinking nothing but small table ninepenny this last week or two . . .'" (M 66). Christopher agrees to accompany Solomon because "'I'm as clammy as a cockle-snail'" (M 66). Alcohol runs like a river (Hamill 61) through all their lives, and they see it as an accompaniment to the hard struggles and the comradeship that makes it possible to survive.

But the narrative indicates an awareness beyond their own: their relation to alcohol is not innocuous. The first proof of this occurs with the theft of the death coins placed on Susan Henchard's eyes. Mother Cuxom narrates at the town pump what her listeners "deprecate" as this "cannibal deed" (M 92). Almost immediately after Susan was buried, Christopher went to the garden where the nurse had been commanded to bury the ounce pennies: "'that man Christopher Coney, went and dug 'em up and spent 'em at the Three Mariners'" (M 92). He was joined in this by Solomon's rationalizing the deed, done on a Sunday: "'To respect the dead is sound doxology; and I wouldn't sell skellintons... to be varnished for 'natomies, except I were out of work. But money is scarce and throats get dry. Why *should* death rob life 'o fourpence? I say there was no treason in it'" (M 92; emphasis in original). Solomon's niceties of moral gradation are amusing and astute. The need to drink coupled with the need to survive is real. Solomon would rob graves only if he were unemployed; scruples are for those who can afford them.

The gruesome theft of drinking money from the middle-class dead by the lower-class needy is handled by the narrator without moralizing. Although this incident may, with Hardyean irony, allude to the story of the buried talents in one of the parables of Christ, it certainly refers to British social history. The "cannibal deed" is grave-robbing. As medical training relied increasingly on the study of anatomy, illegal disinterments increased in the eighteenth century and early nineteenth century (R. Richardson 31). Previous to this, cadavers used for medical experiment and training were many times those of the bodies of murderers put to death by the government. But the Anatomy Act of 1831 allowed the sale of the bodies of paupers and inhabitants of the workhouse "too poor to pay for their own funerals" (R. Richardson xv). The social turbulence caused by the rage of the poor at the passage of the Anatomy Act of 1831 is reflected in their peers' disapproval of Solomon's and Christopher's actions. The phrase "respectable skellintons" indicates the widespread awareness that, although the rich were as fearful as the poor of such activities, in reality, it was the graves of the poor that were easiest to rob (R. Richardson 80, 98–99). Victorian readers in 1886 might recognize the reference to illegal disinterments and probably feel a revulsion at the act of grave-robbing similar to that shared by earlier Victorians of all social classes (R. Richardson 75–99).

Readers can assume that Hardy intended the grave-robbing allusion because Hardy's work is deeply embedded in the physical and historical world. He treasured and studied local lore, both for his own satisfaction as "a Victorian antiquary," and because he wanted "to record the Wessex world as it actually *was*" (Millgate, *Hardy, Novelist* 244; emphasis in original). The deliberate historical reference to grave-robbing suggests the seriousness of Solomon's and Christopher's alcohol use. To underline its significance, Hardy has Christopher refer to Susan earlier in the text as "a skellinton" (M 64). It is unlikely the men would have stolen the pennies used to close the eyes of such a "respectable" corpse as the wife of the mayor had Solomon and Christopher not been physically dependent on alcohol. The fact that these two men stole from the woman the mayor had sold when drunk reveals that even in death, she was robbed by alcohol of her dignity. This double dishonor suggests that Solomon's and Christopher's theft of her burial coins points to the mayor's use of alcohol. His alcoholism, seemingly buried beneath his lengthy sobriety, is the "skellinton" (O'Toole 23) that rattles behind many of his behaviors and leaps forcibly from the closet with the furmity-woman's disclosure in the court.

Each time Solomon and Christopher have appeared, they have done so at formative moments in the mayor's life: his abstinence at the King's Arms; his meeting with Farfrae; the reappearance in his life of his wife and her daughter; his remarriage to Susan; Susan's death. Each appearance has contained scenes of their drinking. But the use of Susan's burial money for alcohol is menacing. Ever after this moment, the appearance of these two rustics serves to foreground the power and meaning of alcohol in Michael Henchard's life as well as theirs. Noting the bond between Michael Henchard and the working-class characters, Peter Easingwood remarks that Henchard "dies like one of the 'workfolk'" (71).

Solomon and Christopher are but two examples, and by no means the worst, of a very hard-drinking population of all social classes in Casterbridge. Their lives go on quietly, but some of their friends and acquaintances are neither so well off nor so able to contain the effects of drinking as Solomon and Christopher. These are what the Victorians would refer to as the undeserving poor, or, in Hardy's terminology, Casterbridge's "Mephistophelean Visitants," the unacknowledged double, its hidden life. Modern readers are by now familiar with this interpretation of bourgeois Victorian society:

not only Victorian fiction, but Victorian culture specialized in doubling. Underneath the staid Victorian bourgeois ideology of respectability and sexual restraint, the hidden lives of even so-called ordinary Victorians revealed extensive, often obsessive or non-normative sexual activity (McClintock 122–60).

Narrative doubling in *Mayor* inextricably connects the apparent with the hidden. The course of life in Mixen Lane moves in a continuous parallel with the lives of those in the richer sections of Casterbridge. As Mixen Lane's residents go about their lives, with the majority of Casterbridge bourgeoisie ignoring them, so the mayor's alcoholism leads its subterranean life, unseen until circumstances arise that force it into an exploding visibility.

As I already noted, Michael Henchard begins his movement to Mixen Lane long before he takes up residence there. The night he discovers that Elizabeth-Jane is not his own daughter, he crosses the bridge at the bottom of High Street and stands on a riverbank skirting the northeast limits of the town (M 97). Seething with self-pity, he has taken the first step down the road to Mixen Lane, for the bridge he had crossed had its more ominous counterpart, a stone bridge frequented by "those who had failed in business, in love, in *sobriety,* in crime" (M 170–71; emphasis added). The narrator jocularly remarks that those standing on the stone bridge often gazed for so long in the water that they found themselves floating within it (M 171–72). It was to that bridge of suicides Michael Henchard went after he lost his businesses and confessed to the furmity-woman's story.

The stone bridge serves as the literal bridge to his passage downward on the social scale. Farfrae comes to it, offering Henchard sanctuary in a back part of his former home, his own furniture, and dinner for the evening. Henchard, moved, refuses, knowing that "'we should quarrel'" (M 173–74). He does, however, seek and accept a job with Farfrae as a hay trusser, becoming "a day-labourer in the barns and granaries he formerly had owned" (M 175).

At about this time, rumors circulate that Farfrae is being considered as a possible candidate for mayor (M 175). Enviously ruminating on this news (M 176), Henchard "lapsed into moodiness"

(M 176). "[H]is former hatred of the Scotchman returned. Concurrently with this he underwent a moral change" (M 176). Henchard works with Solomon Longways, formerly in Henchard's employ but now employed by Farfrae. It was Solomon who had known exactly the amount of time Henchard had to endure until he could drink again: "'exactly two calendar years longer'" (M 27).

The representation of Henchard's alcoholism by the poor workfolk, Solomon Longways' and Christopher Coney's daily drinking, heretofore shadows seen behind the mayor, can now be dispensed with. For now, Henchard is not above Longways and Coney, but, like them, a menial laborer. Fittingly, it is to Solomon that Henchard confides his countdown of the days left until "'I shall be released from my oath . . . and then I mean to enjoy myself, please God!'" (M 176) Solomon's response is not recorded. It does not have to be. For now the two men speak the same language, the knowledge that the excruciating separation from alcohol is no longer to be borne. Henchard has become one with the man who felt that the need to drink made it alright to steal drinking money from the dead. Henchard has become the equal of working men who drink daily.

That the former mayor of Casterbridge returns to drinking on a Sunday would, for the middle-class Victorian reader, underline the loss of moral values that Henchard underwent as he moved back to drinking. Casterbridgians, too, react to Henchard's resumption of the use of alcohol. By one of those plot strategies that so annoy critics, two men happen to speak of it below Elizabeth-Jane's window, "'Michael Henchard have busted out drinking after taking nothing for twenty-one years!'" (M 176)

HENCHARD'S RETURN TO DRINKING

Late twentieth-century North American alcoholism theory posits no single explanation of relapse into drinking (Vaillant, *Revisited* 221–27). But that which might have compelled Michael Henchard's return to drinking is clear. First, he had sworn an oath to be sober for only twenty-one years, not the rest of his life. Second, the intense shame and self-hate he had felt after he sold his wife, which he had thought to banish forever with abstinence from alcohol and financial success, had returned. At the point in the narrative at which he returns to drink he may feel more shame than he had as a young man, for only a few had witnessed the sale, whereas everyone in Casterbridge has witnessed his fall from power and wealth (Bean, "Denial" 93). For these reasons, Henchard experienced a "moral change" (M 176). Henchard thought himself into a drink before he drank again, just as some contemporary alcohol theorists and treatment specialists argue is part of a relapse pattern (Gorski and Miller 139–56).

Henchard drinks again in order to numb his feelings. As Gordon Barnes points out, "[f]rom alcoholics' own accounts, it appears that alcoholics drink to alleviate a sense of subjective discomfort" (619). Vaillant noted that alcohol is "a powerful reinforcer" because it "nonspecifically alters an individual's feeling state . . . analogous to the 'trip abroad' that nineteenth-century physicians once prescribed to relieve depression in rich patients" (Vaillant, *Natural* 175; see also Vaillant, *Revisited* 222).

Social learning theorists agree that alcoholics expect that alcohol will reduce tension (Wilson 258). In G. A. Marlatt's pioneering analysis of the psychosocial impetus to return to drinking in "successfully" sober alcoholics "accounting for almost a third of the relapses studied, was the experience of frustration and anger. . . . Instead of expressing these feelings of anger or dealing with them in a constructive manner, these patients began drinking again" (qtd. in Wilson 259–60).

Michael Henchard apparently does associate drinking alcohol in large quantities with a numbing of his feelings of self-hate and low self-esteem, with release from inhibitions and tension and an invulnerability from the consequences of his behavior. Henchard associates drinking with the ability to act out his feelings at will, with a disregard for the opinions of others, with a sense of power, and with—paradoxically—the promise of his youth. These are not qualities he associates with the latter part of his sobriety, for during that period his life had become increasingly more challenging emotionally. Just as Marlatt hypothesized, the conditioned response Henchard has to drinking promises relief from overwhelming feelings that he can no longer tolerate.

Drinking, however, does not take him on an extended rest cure; it hastens his death. Rather than enabling him to flee from himself, drinking brings him closer to those aspects of himself that in 21 years of sobriety he had had only moderate success in dealing with—severe, suicidal depression, homicidal rages, intense and incessant self-hate and shame. Henchard had, even in sobriety, difficulty maintaining public self-control. Now he has none.

Within a few weeks of his return to drinking, Henchard seems to be just as publicly out of control as when he had sold his wife. This fact in the text suggests that in observing alcoholics, Thomas Hardy had noticed an aspect of what might now be called "the disease concept of alcohol," according to which there is no physiological recovery possible from addiction to alcohol. Thus, once the alcoholic drinks again, within a short time she or he progresses to the point of addiction from which relief had been gained in sobriety (Jellinek qtd. in Vaillant, *Natural* 133). Henchard's lack of control over when and how much he drinks would, in this interpretation, have less to do with his psychological motivations for escape from his present feelings and situation than with the need of his body for a powerful drug that it craved. But the inevitability of alcoholic progression is a point that remains heatedly disputed (Vaillant, *Revisited* 166). Clinicians can demonstrate that drinking patterns in alcoholics are not always linear (Ludwig 49–68; Cahalan and Clark qtd. in Vaillant *Revisited,* 163; but see S. Brown, *Treating the Alcoholic* 6–7, 76; and Vaillant, *Revisited* 163–70, 378–80). Contrary to the Jellinek model of progression, Henchard's drinking patterns changed, moving from increasing binges to sudden sobriety, to a period of daily drinking, then back to periodic if not binge drinking.

Nevertheless, in observing Antell and Moule, Hardy would have seen that merely stopping drinking did not "cure" the craving for drink as a means to alleviate a situation or a feeling, nor did having stopped for a time indicate that the drinker could control his drinking once he started again. Once Henchard starts drinking again, the quickness with which Henchard descends into shame and homicidal rage points also to Thomas Hardy's knowledge about alcoholism. Hardy appears to have speculated that there existed a causal relation between reliance on alcohol and self-destructive or homicidal behavior. Hardy could see that alcohol had been a large part of that tragic waste of the life of his former mentor Horace Moule. Similarly, Hardy observed an association between violence and heavy drinking. As I noted, his mother and maternal aunts interfered at least once to protect his aunt Mary from his uncle John Antell's attacks on her during bouts of drunkenness. Hardy had seen or had learned through family gossip the relation between drinking and disinhibition in violence, sex, and petty crime in the neighboring town of Puddletown. He shaped these observations into fiction by having his narrator chronicle what happens to Henchard once Henchard returns to drinking.

However one characterizes it—according to contemporary or Victorian alcoholism theories—it is obvious that Michael Henchard's return to drinking brings disaster to himself and those with whom he is involved. On the day of his first drinking again, he has erupted in a violent rage in The Three Mariners and threatened to harm the other pub drinkers. He locks them in the pub, threatens them with the poker, and curses them (M 174). Having begun drinking, Henchard returns to homicidal rages.

Elizabeth-Jane enters the pub in order to convince him to leave. To her Henchard rationalizes his drinking, an indication of his shame that he has begun again: "'I have kept my oath for twenty-one years and now I can drink with a good conscience'" (M 180), He confides the reasons why he wants to kill Farfrae: "'He has taken away everything from me . . .'" (M 180). As a Victorian daughter and as someone deeply concerned about propriety (M 165), Elizabeth-Jane would feel that curbing her stepfather's drinking and behavior was her duty. To some twentieth-century North American clinicians, however, Elizabeth-Jane's belief that she must rescue Henchard is another indication that Henchard's drinking is so serious it has affected those around him, for the conviction developed in those living closely with alcoholism that they must care for the loved one may become an obsession parallel to the drinker's obsession to drink (S. Brown, *Adult* 34–35, 60).

Elizabeth-Jane is deeply alarmed by his drunken threats because she knows that Henchard lacks control of his temper even when he is sober. Convinced that Henchard means what he says, she asks to work with him at his hay trussing. In an effort to control Henchard's drinking, Elizabeth-Jane brings him tea at teatime, delaying Henchard's daily drink. This is a sign of the progression of the illness, for as a young man Henchard had been a binge rather than a daily drinker.

The narrator ties Henchard's increase in alcohol consumption to his increased resentment at Farfrae, "fortifying his heart by drinking more freely at the Three Mariners every evening" (M 182). Obsessional resentment is one behavior some North American clinicians see frequently in treating alcoholism (Wallace 30–31). Henchard can neither express nor control his feelings; he cannot bear to face them, and he has no one who will reason with him about them.

Devoted as she is to him, Elizabeth-Jane is not able to assuage his pain. Henchard is alone. His sense of rejection, shame, and self-hatred are exacerbated by the very means he uses to control them. As numerous—if disputed—studies show, to a problem drinker or an alcoholic, alcohol serves to increase painful feelings and anxiety after a time, rather than numbing them (Vaillant, *Revisited* 79–80; Cox 162–63; but see Levin, *Treatment* 44 and Wilson 258–59).

Elizabeth-Jane witnesses Henchard's first attempt to kill Farfrae (M 182) and warns him of the danger. Farfrae pays attention to the information because he respects her maturity and good sense, but continues with his plan to set Henchard up in a new business in a little seed shop. But Henchard's behavior when drinking ruins the scheme (M 184–85).

Meanwhile Lucetta accidentally meets Henchard in the street and demands the return of her love letters. Henchard realizes that the letters are in Farfrae's safe, and that, if read, these will ruin Farfrae's love for Lucetta and their marriage. The next night, Farfrae is made mayor.

After "prim[ing] himself with grog, as he did very frequently now," (M 187) Henchard decides to obtain the letters from Farfrae and read them to him. Yet Henchard cannot bring himself to reveal the truth (M 188–89). Drinking again has neither extinguished his love for Farfrae nor his conscience. Remorsefully he decides to return the incriminating love letters to Lucetta by asking Jopp to deliver them, an adroit plot maneuver that enacts Henchard's hatred of the couple.

As Jopp departs on his errand, he encounters several of Long-ways' and Coney's friends whom he accompanies to Peter's Finger, "the church of Mixen Lane," its pub (M 196). Of course, all gathered (including the furmity-woman) soon read the letters. The listeners' increasingly rough responses culminate in their decision to put on a skimmington ride. In a skimmington ride, effigies resembling those being publicly shamed are paraded back to back to publicize their sexual relations and to shame the woman.

The plans of those in Peter's Finger for a skimmington ride are ironically paralleled by those of the monied community in Caster-bridge to honor "the Royal Personage" who is to stop for a few minutes in Casterbridge. The degradation brought about by Hen-chard's renewed drinking reaches its lowest point with the royal visit.

Supported by alcohol, Henchard can feel momentarily powerful again as he temporarily imprisons the town council members, demanding to march in the welcoming procession (M 201–202). At the moment of confronting the council, it is also possible that he has so lost touch with reality that he feels he belongs in the procession. Alcohol has helped him sustain the delusional system that some twentieth-century North American psychologists of alcoholism label "the grandiose self": that that which is desired and wished for exists (Levin, *Treatment* 228).

The councilmen are frightened and appalled by his audacity. Because he had just been drinking, they can probably smell the alcohol on his breath. As the current mayor of Casterbridge, Farfrae refuses Henchard's demand. Outraged, Henchard turns and walks out, the town drunkard, muttering threats (M 202).

Some critics who believe that Hardy maliciously pursues his characters object to the concatenation of events at this plot juncture. But tragedy most convincingly occurs when the hook of circumstances pierces the tragic figure at his or her weakest point. Further, Henchard responds to the complicated circumstances that occur within 36 hours of one another during "a time of emotional darkness" (M 219) and "when primed with grog" (M 187). His alcoholism is the determining factor in his choices and behavior. The Royal Personage stops briefly in Casterbridge in the morning; soon Henchard tries and fails to kill Farfrae in the granary loft Henchard had formerly owned. That night the skimmington ride takes place, causing Lucetta's miscarriage, which leads to Henchard's ludicrous attempt to return the decoyed Farfrae to his dying wife. Lucetta's death that night leads Elizabeth-Jane to Henchard's abode to bring the news early the next morning. Father and stepdaughter are reconciled; Elizabeth-Jane sleeps in the next room of Henchard's cottage when Newson reappears there. During these event-filled hours Henchard is either inebriated or but a few hours past imbibing.

One of the most poignant scenes in *Mayor* is the moment of The Royal Personage's arrival. Henchard "primed himself in the morning with a glass of rum. . . ." (M 202). Henchard apparently expects to give the man a little homemade flag he has with him. But the hostility toward himself and others that he may not be conscious of is clear in his dress: "the fretted and weather-beaten garments of bygone years" (M 203). As the royal carriage arrives, Henchard is the first to offer a greeting: " . . . removing his hat he *staggered* to the side of the slowing vehicle, waving the Union Jack to and fro with his left hand while he blandly held out his right to the Illustrious Personage. . . ." (M 203–204; emphasis added). Farfrae shoves Henchard out of the way while the Royal Personage pretends not to have noticed.

Michael Henchard has shamed himself by appearing as a nameless drunk who staggers in public, one pushed around by those in power. At this moment he startlingly resembles the drunken furmity-woman who was reported to have relieved herself against the courthouse wall (M 153). Self-hatred turned into an equal aggression against others, arrogance, and the use of a grandiose self-defense to prevent acknowledging one's actual status—all of the attributes found in some twentieth-century North American male alcoholics—are partial motivations for Michael Henchard's drunken welcoming of the Royal Personage.

The chorus of Longways and Coney is present throughout the scene. Like Henchard, they had used the visit as an excuse to drink, focusing not on the Royal visitor, but on the night's plans for the

skimmington ride. Because some of the group objects to Farfrae's
rise and his cooling toward them—his former champions—their desire to see him shamed is great. But this is not a feeling Longways
and Coney fully share. They decide to set up a ruse to get Farfrae
out of town so he will not witness the ride. But the oblique references to Henchard contained within the rustics' annoyance at Farfrae and Lucetta seem to imply an affinity to Henchard's feelings
about his position, a compassion for him in his broken state that
they may be too tactful to express (M 205). Through their connection to Longways and Coney, the downtrodden Mixen Lane inhabitants who plan and execute the skimmington ride seem to take
revenge on Lucetta and Farfrae "for" Henchard. This suggestion is
sustained by the point both the narrator and Henchard make later
in the text that the effigy of her indirectly kills Lucetta but the effigy
of Henchard saves him from suicide (M 227–29).

Henchard, too, seeks revenge, enraged at Farfrae's publicly
pushing him away from the Royal visitor (M 206–207). Henchard
gets a rope and goes to find Farfrae in the loft that Farfrae now
owns. Farfrae arrives singing and whistling, making the music that
always calms Henchard's rage. Farfrae is still angry at Henchard's
interference with the Royal visitor, and is also made harsher to the
older man by "his conviction that Henchard had been drinking" (M
208). They argue and Henchard tells Farfrae of his murderous intention (M 209).

Henchard is doubly vanquished in the fight. He has been unable
to kill and he has exposed vulnerable feelings and needs that Farfrae
understandably spurns (M 208–10).[19] When after fighting, Henchard cannot bring himself to kill the man he had loved, Farfrae
goes silently away, leaving Henchard to feel "his full measure of
shame and self-reproach" (M 210).

The narrator emphasizes the sexualized element in this surrender in a language that his Victorian readers could understand, expressing the Victorian idea that submission was by definition a
female attribute. "So thoroughly subdued was he that he remained . . . in a crouching attitude, unusual for a man, and for such
a man. Its womanliness sat tragically on the figure of so stern a piece
of virility" (M 210).

Henchard's grief increases: "'He thought highly of me once,' he murmured. 'Now he'll hate me and despise me for ever'" (M 210). But the acceptance of his assault and the probable alienation of Farfrae from him is impossible. Henchard denies the idea of it: "[H]e became possessed by an overpowering wish to see Farfrae again that night, and by some desperate pleading to attempt the well nigh impossible task of winning pardon for his late mad attack" (M 210).

The relation between problem drinking and homosexual latency has been a basic assumption of Freudian thinking about alcoholism for many years. In a letter to Otto Fleiss on January 11, 1897, Sigmund Freud suggested that "alcoholism is a substitution for a homosexual perversion" (qtd. in Barry 115; see also, Levin, *Treatment* 77).

Although it is certainly not my intention to support Freudian labeling of homosexuality as a perversion, scholarly rigor demands that Freudian speculations be mentioned when examining Henchard's passion for Farfrae and the relation of this love to Henchard's alcoholism. Henchard's obsessional relation to his imagined construct of Farfrae led Henchard to make certain choices that eventually caused the loss of his property and position. Henchard's decision to abase himself and to work for Farfrae rather than leave Casterbridge and start anew (which he later did) was tied not only to Henchard's obsession with the younger man, but became one of the rationalizations he used to flagellate himself into drinking excessively once again.

The elements of sexual longing and shame in Henchard's feelings after his attack on Farfrae, which the narrator calls "female," are apparent. The breakdown of Henchard's denial against his possible sexual feelings for Farfrae, perhaps indicated by the ellipses in the narrator's report of their battle (M 210), may be a contributing cause of Henchard's final fall. Henchard's strong dependency needs and his equally strong need to deny these are culturally normative for his time (which sanctioned male bonding without validating emotional dependency), and are also inseparable from his alcoholism.

Henchard does not expose and express his love for Farfrae only once; he does so twice. The second time occurs shortly after his trying to murder Farfrae partly out of thwarted love for him. Henchard, still stupefied (M 210) by the incidents in the hayloft, and also probably by the alcohol he had consumed, had been passed by the skimmington riders, but had only a vague sense that donkeys went by (M 217). However, as they returned, he saw them and knew instantly that the entourage presaged trouble for Farfrae, whose whereabouts Henchard knew. In his guilt, he seeks his beloved rival.

The farcical scene that ensues is deeply tragic. It is an enactment, on a miniature scale, of the relationship between the two men—Henchard, longing, Farfrae, rejecting, Henchard paying the price, once again, of his alcoholism. Henchard runs to the route to Weatherbury and does catch up with Farfrae who, of course, doubts his warnings about Lucetta (M 218). Henchard demands that Farfrae return home, although he is not at first specific about what is wrong. Farfrae, however, believes that Henchard's story is a ploy to detain and then kill him (M 218).

As the narrator reports the thoughts going through Farfrae's mind, no mention is made of Henchard's declaration of love. It is as though it had never been spoken, so great is the repression of it. But it is this obsessional love that motivates Henchard to abase himself yet again. Henchard understands Farfrae's disbelief and insists, "'O Farfrae! Don't mistrust me—I am a wretched man; but my heart is true to you still'" (M 219). The poignancy of this scene is increased by the irony that Henchard's passionate declarations strike Farfrae as words of hatred. Keeping his horse well away from the pleading Henchard, Farfrae refuses to believe Henchard and rushes to Weatherbury (M 219).

Running after Farfrae to declare his innocence, the veering between extremes of longing to kill him out of love for him, and the conviction that he could convince the man he had almost killed of the truth of his statements and thus possibly save his wife and his marriage are not the reactions of a sober man. Twentieth-century North American clinicians repeatedly point to the terrible sufferings of certain of their male alcoholic patients, sufferings caused by what to those without clinical knowledge about alcoholism might label as almost willful self-destructive behaviors. But to those with a knowledge of alcoholism, this tragicomic interaction with Farfrae might be interpreted as the result of the painful dependency needs of certain male alcoholics (Levin, *Introduction* 61–63). Further, it is arguable that had Henchard not been drinking, the impulses that propel him to abase himself before Farfrae might have been held in check or never erupted.

When Farfrae returns home, he realizes that Henchard had told him the truth, although the narrator notes no softening of his attitude to the former mayor, merely mentioning that "he was in a state bordering on distraction at his misconception of Henchard's motives" (M 220). On her deathbed, Lucetta had revealed to Farfrae the story of her past relation to Henchard (M 221). Having lost Farfrae by his actions, Henchard's obsession becomes Elizabeth-Jane once again because, once again, Farfrae is unavailable to him (M 221).

At this point in the plot Newson, the sailor, comes to Henchard's house seeking his daughter. For those readers who see the *Mayor* in terms of Aristotelian definitions of tragedy, the return of both the furmity-woman and Richard Newson results inexorably from the tragic action that sets the plot in motion, the wife sale.

As they stand face to face, Newson and Henchard are excruciatingly aware that their intimate but hostile connection is underpinned by sexual relations with the same woman and fatherly claims on Elizabeth-Jane who Henchard now knows to be Newson's daughter. Henchard announces, "'I cannot even allow that I'm the man you met then'" (M 223). Unfortunately, Henchard is more like the young man who sold his wife in a drunken fit than he can admit, as his tragicomic pursuit of Farfrae after trying to murder him demonstrates.

When faced with what Newson asks of him, he has no effective response. His immediate, instinctual reaction is unrealistic, "the impulse of a moment" (M 224). Henchard had not had a drink in about 36 hours, but surely his thinking is still clouded by the alcohol he had consumed and by all that has ensued with Farfrae. Henchard tells Newson that Elizabeth-Jane is dead (M 224). Without argument or question, Newson accepts this assertion and leaves.

Certain the man would return quickly to claim his daughter, Henchard finds Elizabeth-Jane in the next room still resting where he had left her. He is determined to keep her with him, especially now that he has a rival for her daughterly love. His changed behavior amazes and attracts her, for she is as starved for loving companionship as he is. The contemporary psychiatrist Michael Elkin has observed his alcoholic patients' ability to manipulate and charm families and friends into doing their bidding (21). Henchard does exactly that. He plays on the vulnerable Elizabeth-Jane so that her compassion is awakened. Her behavior is understandable both in light of the duty a Victorian daughter owed a father and in view of the effects of parental alcoholism on some twentieth-century North American family members. They are reconciled (M 226).[20]

Henchard expects Newson's return momentarily. As he leaves Elizabeth-Jane to go to work, he despairs as "one who has lost all that can make life interesting, or even tolerable" (M 226). Bean, among other clinicians, has referred to the drinking alcoholic's characteristic mental sufferings, including powerlessness and obsessional terror about the future and self-loathing about past losses ("Denial" 76 and Bean-Bayog, "Psychopathology" 334–35, 339–45). She could have been describing Henchard's incessant, self-punitive internal monologue after his interview with Newson.

During that day, Henchard exacerbates his depression by imagining a future in which his worst fear materializes—utter, abject loneliness in a world devoid of joy or hope (M 226). Dwelling on the miseries of the future, the excessive self-pity, and the sense of personal helplessness because one is the victim of external circumstances and other people's actions, are characteristic of the thought processes of some twentieth-century North American alcoholics (Ludwig 20–30, 78; Vaillant, *Revisited* 362–73; Bean, "Denial" 68–69, 74–79 and Bean-Bayog, "Psychopathology" 343–45; S. Brown, *Treating the Alcoholic* 79, 88, 96–100; Wallace 26–32).

Yet telling Elizabeth-Jane the truth about Susan's lie never occurs to him. As Wallace has remarked about some of his male alcoholic clients, "[e]ven in some alcoholics with considerable sobriety, there is often a curious lack of true empathy, a seeming inability to grasp the position of the other" (30). Henchard cannot relinquish his selfish grasp of Elizabeth-Jane, a perhaps unconscious choice exacerbated, if not caused, by alcoholism.

Henchard now understands that he needs relationships with other human beings whom he loves and respects in order to sustain his own humanity. Henchard can at last admit his vulnerability and dependency. But he sees no hope for human love without Elizabeth-Jane. Her value to him is increased perhaps because he knows he has no legal claim on her and that her loss is inevitable.

Without voicing it to himself, that evening Henchard decides to commit suicide. As I have noted earlier, there is a correlation among depression, alcoholism, and suicide, although the exact causal nature of the relationship is in dispute.

But Henchard is stopped from throwing himself into the weir-hole of the Blackwater by seeing as himself, the effigy used in the skimmington ride that is floating there: "he perceived with a sense of horror that it was *himself*. Not a man somewhat resembling him, but one in all respects his counterpart, his actual double, was floating as if dead in Ten Hatches Hole" (M 227; emphasis in original).

Going home, he finds that Elizabeth-Jane has returned out of renewed concern for him (M 227–28). He takes her with him to Ten Hatches Hole where she verifies that what he had seen was the effigy of him used in the skimmington ride that the participants must have thrown into the river upstream. Henchard demands to know where the other effigy is: "'Why that one only?'" And then he reveals to her what he had been going to do: "'That performance of theirs killed her, but kept me alive!'" (M 228) Elizabeth-Jane is so shaken by his admission of thoughts of suicide that she demands to return and live with him (M 228–29).

After Elizabeth-Jane's return to his domicile as his daughter, Henchard is never again shown drinking. Because he is so out of control when he does drink, the fact that he seems able to contain his impulses is reason enough to suppose he has stopped drinking, even though the narrator never mentions whether he is or is not drinking.

How can Henchard who had been drinking daily and who has been brought even lower through drinking than through bad business practices have stopped once again? The answer may be summarized, following Vaillant's formulation, as "substitute dependencies" (*Revisited* 250). In a lengthy discussion of the ways in which alcoholics can successfully stop drinking, Vaillant mentions a combination of attitudinal and behavioral changes, many of which this section of the novel illustrates. These include an ability to rely on a spiritual source outside oneself, help from others offered without judgment, structured reintegration into a community, and a new love relationship (Vaillant, *Revisited* 233–54).

Henchard has stopped drinking once before in the text, relying on a "gospel oath" to gain prolonged abstinence. Similarly, religion is the original cause of the second time he stops in the text. Henchard sees the effigy as "an appalling miracle," (M 227) evidence of Divine "interference," (M 228) indicating that he was safe "in Somebody's hand" (M 229).

This conviction of being cradled by a benign deity is much stronger than his earlier attempt to use conventional religion to underpin his oath to abstain from drinking entirely for 21 years. Then he had sought spiritual help. Now he seems to feel that such a source of help had sought him unbidden. The sense of peace and being loved in spite of his unworthiness is especially strong as he had been about to break one of the most solemn commandments of the church, the injunction against suicide.

Sober, he then transfers his dependence on this Divine presence to Elizabeth-Jane, an ideal substitute, for her remaining with him may also seem miraculous. The reassertion of his severe dependency on Elizabeth-Jane, the serenity, security, and happiness this openly acknowledged dependency brings him, seems to enable him to remain sober. Although the sense of Divine intervention is replaced by "the apparition of Newson [which] haunted him," (M 229) Henchard is nevertheless able to live another nine months in peace with his stepdaughter.

For Elizabeth-Jane's sake, Henchard accepts the gift from the town council (headed by Farfrae) of a little seed and grain shop. Is this generous gift Farfrae's unstated answer to Henchard's murderous love? More likely it results from Farfrae's need for Elizabeth-Jane to regain enough respectability so he can marry her.

Henchard and Elizabeth-Jane live above the shop and tend the business, which begins to thrive (M 231). Being dependent on Elizabeth-Jane has relieved Henchard of a number of alcohol-related behaviors. No mention is made of his drinking. The narrator characterizes him as "a netted lion" (M 231), "denaturalized" (M 233), "not now the Henchard of former days" (232). He defers to Elizabeth-Jane who is acting, if not as a mother, then certainly as an elder to the debilitated man. He is too dependent on her to risk any behaviors that might alienate her, and he is too afraid of losing her, his last link with the human community, to cross her. Sustained by his dependence, Henchard thus exhibits an unusual amount of self-control, and even occasionally tries to control his distorted thinking (M 233).

Their changed positions are noted in a sophisticated narrative touch. When Elizabeth-Jane was the powerless figure in her family and in the town, she had the project of being the eyes of the narrator (Langbaum 138–40). Now it is Henchard who is observed observing her, ever aware that she may be taken from him. He watches her to set his own mood and behavior, to match her even as she had with him and for the same reason—their relationship depends on his allowing her to dictate the terms of it (M 231).

Henchard soon realizes that Donald Farfrae may be courting her again (M 231–32). In some ways the prospect of a marriage is worse than his fear of Newson. His terrified conviction that without a reciprocal dependence on Elizabeth-Jane he can have no means or reason to live releases, momentarily, his homicidal and suicidal tendencies (M 234–35).

Henchard plays with the idea of revealing Elizabeth-Jane's illegitimacy to Farfrae in order to prevent the marriage and to tie her to him rather than to Newson, but decides against this (M 235). Now sober and able to acknowledge his dependency, he can resist such temptation.

But within the year Newson reappears. In circumstances neither explained nor dramatized, Newson allies himself to Farfrae (M 238). Henchard's characteristic self-hatred disables him from fighting for the one being he loves and on whose love he feels his continued life depends (M 238). Henchard decides to flee rather than engage in the excruciating emotional work of talking about his feelings to Elizabeth-Jane, and fighting with Newson and Farfrae over the young woman.

Contemporary clinicians E. J. Khantzian or Jerome Levin might argue that Henchard does not have the internal self-structure to manage such a fight, which would require not only verbal agility, but the direct expression of feelings. John Wallace has observed that although their behavior while drinking may suggest otherwise, "alcoholics do not thrive in situations characterized by conflict, competition, and win-lose outcomes. In fact, it is precisely in these situations that they tend to pick up a drink" (31). Henchard's "haughty" (M 238) refusal to explain that he himself was deceived as to her parentage, and then to bargain for a diminished relation to Elizabeth-Jane, seems related to these deficits in the self-structure that are either one of the predisposing causes or the results of the damage of alcoholism, depending on one's perspective. (Bean, "Denial" 76 and Bean-Bayog, "Psychopathology" 342–43; Levin, *Treatment* 219–24, 234–41; Vaillant, *Revisited* 275–77).

Henchard is uncomfortable with language. He is deeply ashamed of his feelings, no matter what these feelings are, and finds the shame of expressing feelings intolerable. The only time he has managed to convey passion for another human being was his announcement of his love for Donald Farfrae after he had been drinking. Further, he may feel shame that his lie to Newson reflected a sense that his claims on the young girl were illegitimate.

Before Farfrae has a chance to reunite Elizabeth-Jane with Newson, Henchard tells her he is leaving Casterbridge. She begs him to stay, while asking his permission to marry Donald Farfrae, which he gives (M 238). Without explaining the full causes of his departure, he tells her that "'[m]y presence might make things awkward in the future; and, in short, it is best that I go'" (M 238). Unable to present his case, Henchard says only, "'[d]on't let my sins, *when you know them all,* cause 'ee to quite forget that though I loved 'ee late I loved 'ee well'" (M 238; emphasis in original).

Elizabeth-Jane accompanies him as far as the stone bridge that has marked his downward mobility. She watches as Henchard leaves Casterbridge. Dressed in clothes similar to those he had worn on entering the town at age twenty-one (he had bought them earlier that day), he breaks out into dry sobs, already missing her. "'If I had only got her with me. . . . Hard work would be nothing to me then! . . .

I—Cain—go alone as I deserve—an outcast and a vagabond. But my punishment is *not* greater than I can bear!'" (M 239; emphasis in original) His bravado proves to be hollow, for his punishment is greater than he can bear.

Henchard predicted rightly. When Elizabeth-Jane learns that he had sent away her real father, she changes. Anger is not in her repertoire of behaviors, partly because Elizabeth-Jane is extremely conventional, an attempt to ensure the respectability she had worked so hard to acquire (M 165). But she refuses further connection to her false stepfather: "'I said I would never forget him. But O! I think I ought to forget him now!'" (M 242)

Is it likely that Elizabeth-Jane, so morbidly sensitive to others' suffering that she had worked at manual labor to keep her stepfather from drinking and had moved in with him to assuage his pain and prevent his suicide, should sever all emotional ties with the man? His unexplained selfishness in keeping her away from her father would be motive enough. Further, according to some twentieth-century North American clinicians who have worked with children of alcoholic parents, the reservoir of resentment and rage stored against the parent whose illness exacted a huge toll from the dependent child is enormous (U.S. Department of Health and Human Services, *Final Report* 30; Whitfield 66). Elizabeth-Jane's sudden and complete reversal of affect is one possible mode of separation from an alcoholic parent (S. Brown, *Adult* 120–25, 139–44, 179).

Economics are a factor as well. Financially dependent on Henchard, Elizabeth-Jane would have had to suppress resentment at his past ill-treatment. Henchard's lie about her father combined with her alliance to Donald Farfrae, a rich and powerful man who had reason to be an enemy of her stepfather's, could have provided a respectable reason to acknowledge Henchard's exploitation of her.

Unfortunately, Henchard cannot as easily rid himself of his dependence on Elizabeth-Jane as she can rid herself of her relation to him. Considering Henchard's behavior after he has left Casterbridge, the question naturally arises as to why he does not drink again? If he is an alcoholic, and if he is in despair even greater than that which had led him to drink after a dry period of 21 years, it seems unlikely that Henchard would not drink. This is not something the narrator speculates about. But unlike Henchard's drinking again after 21 years, there is no direct statement in the text to show that cravings for drink arose as Henchard's misery at being separated from his stepdaughter increased. Henchard had drunk again, the narrator had said, because he underwent a "moral change" (M 176). Filled with self-pity, he was in a state of homicidal rage at Farfrae. Henchard's attachment to Elizabeth-Jane differs from his attachment to Farfrae. It has no early childhood remembrance or sexual component, although it is as obsessional. Thus, Henchard's loss of her causes shame, loneliness, and remorse, but he is not angry at Elizabeth-Jane. He feels he has wronged her, not she him.

There is, however, one similarity in Henchard's attachments to both Farfrae and Elizabeth-Jane and in that similarity may lie a possible answer to why he does not drink again. I had argued earlier that Henchard's obsessional focus on Farfrae led Henchard to develop an imaginary relationship to the figure of the younger man that did not depend on direct interaction with Farfrae. Henchard would not respond directly to Farfrae's actions, but obliquely, often imagining motives or causes that Farfrae might have denied. In this intense one-sided relationship, all of Henchard's moves were plotted in direct reaction to his assumptions about Farfrae's behaviors. Brooding for long hours daily on Farfrae, compulsively responding to his moves served some of the same purposes as Henchard's binge drinking—and proved to be equally beyond control.

Elizabeth-Jane had long ago assumed for Henchard the position in his internal life that Farfrae had once occupied. So great was his dependence on her that he had changed his behaviors, as I noted earlier. The dependence continues in imagination, for Elizabeth-Jane is the object of continued speculation, longing, and of his very movements: "his wandering . . . became part of a circle of which Casterbridge formed the centre" (M 244).

Henchard thinks of her continually: "every few minutes—[he] conjectured her actions. . . . And then he would say . . . 'O you fool! All this about a daughter who is no daughter of thine!'" (M 244)

The mental processes evident in these quotations illustrate Henchard's distorted thinking. His obsessional thinking about Elizabeth-Jane turns into grandiose vistas of human life from which he is excluded (M 245). His either/or thinking embroidered by grandiose self-pity is characteristic of some twentieth-century male alcoholics (Bean, "Denial" 69; See also S. Brown, *Treating the Alcoholic* 79, 88, 96–100; S. Brown, *Adult* 108–9; Ludwig 19, 78; Wallace 28; Kinney and Leaton 160–61).

He struggles with himself; partly because he wants to live: "To make one more attempt to be near her: to go back; to see her, to plead his cause before her, to ask forgiveness for his fraud, to endeavor strenuously to hold his own in her love; it was worth the risk of repulse, ay, of life itself" (M 245).

This statement indicates that Henchard has a fantasy and an agenda. He believes that he can convince Elizabeth-Jane of his point of view. Although it is true that he had successfully persuaded Farfrae to stay in town, he had been able to offer a great deal of money and an excellent job to back his pleas. Similarly, he had pleaded his case before the returned Susan, but she was desperate and had no other means of economic support besides himself.

Henchard has never successfully argued against his own self-hate when facing anyone he feels has a right to be angry at him. The telltale characteristic of his thinking is that if he fails in this scheme he has the right to die. In other words, working himself into the emotional conviction that he will be able to win Elizabeth-Jane is partly a way to prepare himself to take his own life.

Henchard's denial of reality, of the past, of his own limitations mingled with a sense of omnipotence based on the distortions resulting from severe depression—though by no means limited to those suffering with the illness of alcoholism—represents the kind of thinking process that clinicians, such as John Wallace, have written about when describing their clinical work with alcoholic patients: "drinking alcoholics (as well as recently sober ones) can maintain views of reality in the face of even massively disconfirming feedback. . . . the characteristic blindness of the alcoholic . . . is [psycho]dynamically linked to chronically low self-esteem, feelings of worthlessness, guilt, fear, and what might otherwise prove to be overwhelming anxiety" (30). (For a different explanation of Henchard's suicidality, see Giordano 93–97.)

Against everything that he knows about Elizabeth-Jane's tenacious character, and her morality and sense of propriety, he becomes convinced that his desire for her love is really her desire for his presence at her wedding (M 246). This unbidden compulsion that skews Henchard's thinking resembles many other ideas that have overtaken him without his conscious assent—to sell his wife, to demand that Farfrae become his partner, to gamble on the weather-prophet, to decide the weather-prophet was wrong, to torture Lucetta emotionally, to greet the Royal Personage, to try to kill Farfrae. And like these other rash decisions it is without regard for the realities of his actual situation and that of others. As I have demonstrated, these ideas are inseparable from Henchard's alcoholism.

Henchard had planned the trip sensibly, but the self-destructiveness of the plan soon becomes evident. Suggesting that it is a compulsive idea and not one that he has much control over, Henchard becomes unable to function rationally once in Casterbridge (M 247). At his approach to his former home, now owned by Farfrae, he is overwhelmed by self-hatred and regret, going around to the back entrance where a servant lets him in (M 248). Henchard has not planned for the onrush of feelings he will experience once he sees Elizabeth-Jane (M 249). Henchard realizes at that moment that he is not equal to the occasion (M 249). Unfortunately at the precise moment, Elizabeth-Jane is brought into the back parlor by the servant.

Elizabeth-Jane treats Henchard exactly as he had known she would before the wild desire of seeing her again had overcome him. She is coldly furious. But instead of launching into an apology or defense, all he can manage to utter is "'[t]hen you know all; but don't give all your thought to him!'" He finishes lamely, "'[d]o ye save a little room for me!'" (M 249)

This characteristic self-centered demand intensifies her fury. She lashes out at Henchard with a powerful bitterness such as she has never before exhibited: she would have loved him "always," but he has "bitterly deceived" her. She then describes Newson's suffering from Henchard's lie about her death in a way that he surely found particularly galling, including speaking of them as an "us," as fused, the very relation he himself had sought. Her passionate denunciation of him culminates in her cry, "'O how can I love as I once did a man who has served us like this!'" (M 249) It seems that time away from Henchard, surrounded by two non alcoholic men who loved her, has allowed Elizabeth-Jane to acknowledge her resentment against the often emotionally savage treatment by her false stepfather (O'Toole 20). His fantasy dies and with it, any hope of presenting the justice of his case to her (M 250).

Henchard takes her part against himself, and his self-hatred takes a characteristic form. He defends himself by an assumed haughtiness and moves to evoke her pity (M 250). But Elizabeth-Jane is no longer to be manipulated by Henchard's posturing.

Although it is unfortunate for him, her changed behavior indicates that she has separated herself from the effects of living with an alcoholic parental figure. She neither follows him out of the house, which he leaves immediately upon uttering his response, nor sends someone after him.

So resolutely had she turned from Henchard that Elizabeth-Jane becomes conscious of him again only after learning that he had brought the bird that the servants had found starved to death in its cage. Her feelings for the bird are greater than those for Henchard. But she understands intuitively that the bird represents her stepfather; the terrible suffering it must have endured reminds her of him (M 251).

Compassionately, Elizabeth-Jane determines to "make her peace with [Henchard]; try to do something to render his life less that of an outcast and more tolerable to him" (M 251). It is only at this point of forgiveness that she can allow herself to become conscious of the fact that Henchard is suicidal (M 251). Enacting the hostility that he has never openly spoken, Farfrae reluctantly assents to her proposal to seek Henchard. Finally their inquiries reveal Henchard's whereabouts, but they travel such a distance that Farfrae becomes anxious lest they have to stay overnight in an inn and spend money (M 253). They are about to turn back when they recognize Abel Whittle, who coincidentally appears just at that moment and takes them to Henchard's dwelling.

But they are too late. Michael Henchard had starved himself to death after Elizabeth-Jane has rejected him. Abel had followed Henchard out of town on the night of the wedding because of his former kindness to Mrs. Whittle, caring for his former employer (M 254).

Michael Henchard dies the death of an alcoholic. No, he did not die by alcohol poisoning, but he did die as a direct result of behavior resulting from the mental distortions characteristic of some male alcoholics. His last will and testament is the document of one so self-loathing. Feelings of self-abnegation and shame so great as to cause Henchard to feel unworthy of burial in holy ground (M 254) seem to arise from those beliefs about themselves that some North American clinicians such as Margaret Bean, George Vaillant, Arnold Ludwig, Jerome Levin, John Wallace, and Stephanie Brown find in some of their alcoholic patients.

But Henchard's will is also a manipulative act. His first request is that Elizabeth-Jane not be told of his death. But in a countryside so full of closely intertwined lives in small communities where all are known, where the movements of everyone are seen and eventually reported by others, it is impossible that Elizabeth-Jane would have remained ignorant of Henchard's death.

In this chapter I have analyzed aspects of Henchard's behaviors to Farfrae and Elizabeth-Jane that demonstrate a loss of self so extreme that Henchard seems to disappear into his fantasy affiliations with Farfrae and his stepdaughter. Elizabeth-Jane's and Donald Farfrae's forceful repudiations of Henchard contrast sharply with his obsessional attachments to them. His own life with him at the center of it becomes submerged without his conscious consent into his imagined relations to the lives of others. In so analyzing Henchard's attachments and concomitant loss of self, I have suggested aspects of an argument I will fully explore in my treatment of *To the Lighthouse:* several of Michael Henchard's relationships might fruitfully be considered codependent.

But the Elizabeth-Jane who rejected Henchard gradually got over his death. Her apparent relief at his absence from her life may indicate the strong effect that less than a decade of life in the (false) position of stepchild to an alcoholic parental figure had had on her. In the next chapter, I will explore the power of this connection between alcoholic parent and child, focusing on the transformation into art of the rage and survival strategies of some who are children of alcoholics.

CHAPTER TWO

THE "GREAT STONE JAR"

The Art of Escape in
James Joyce's *A Portrait of the
Artist as a Young Man*

SCHOLARS HAVE PROVEN THAT THE FATHER in Stanislaus Joyce's *Complete Dublin Diary* is intertextually inseparable from James Joyce's composing process in the creation of Simon Dedalus, the father in James Joyce's *A Portrait of the Artist as a Young Man* (Healey, *Complete Dublin Diary* vii).[1] Simon Dedalus is perceived from the point of view of his helpless son Stephen in *Portrait,* a depiction consistent with Stanislaus Joyce's representation of his powerless entrapment in the alcoholic family of *The Complete Dublin Diary* (Cixous 131–45).

Indeed, *A Portrait of the Artist as a Young Man* as redrafted from *Stephen Hero* alludes to many aspects of the life that Stanislaus Joyce recorded in his diary, with one obvious absence: alcohol itself seems to be missing from the alcoholic home in *A Portrait of the Artist as a Young Man.* But the visible absence of alcohol is significant. James Joyce deliberately submerged an alcoholism narrative inside *A Portrait of the Artist as a Young Man.*

Stanislaus Joyce's *Complete Dublin Diary* is usefully read as alcoholism literature, insisting as it does that John Joyce's (James

Joyce's father) drinking caused the suffering of his family, deforming
the daily life of his wife and children. Stanislaus's diary uses what is
now called the medical model to demonstrate that alcohol is the
focus of John Joyce's life, the causal agent in the family's decline and
the father's progressive alcoholic disintegration. But lacunae and cir-
cumstantial evidence—not the novel's manifest plot—are the only
markers of drinking in *Portrait*. Yet many Joyce critics insist on the
autobiographical origins of Joyce's art. I conclude from the discrepancy between the novel's manifest narrative and critical emphasis on
the novel's autobiographical origin that in this novel James Joyce deliberately disguised Simon Dedalus's alcoholism as influencing motive and characterization. Drinking is a suppressed narrative
referent that helps make sense of disparate events and paralipses in
the text. In *Portrait*, the narrative method and the characterization
of Stephen Dedalus in relation to his father reveal the hidden presence of alcoholism.

Generations of divergent readings by Joyce critics have established certain key points. Mimetic readings of Stephen Dedalus have
investigated the novel as bildungsroman, demonstrating the complex psychological causes of Stephen's adolescent angst, posturing,
and sexual sufferings (Epstein, "Joyce" and *Ordeal;* Rossman,
"Spiritual" and "Villanelle"; Naremore, "Consciousness"; Norris,
Web; Kershner, *Bakhtin*). Critics' explorations of Stephen's Catholic
guilt and his tortured relation to the feminine have problematized
his division of women into whores and madonnas (Kenner, "Portrait"; Henke, "Narcissist"; Rossman, "Spiritual"). Frances L.
Restuccia has linked Stephen's masochism with Stephen's complex
feelings for his father and his substitution of himself in the female
sexual position.

Critics have investigated the Christian, the Byronic, the Shel-
leyan, the satanic, the romantic (Norris, *Web;* Kershner, *Bakhtin*),
and the fin-de-siècle origins of Stephen's view of the artist (Scholes
and Kain). Critics have argued inconclusively for decades about the
aesthetic value of Stephen's writing, debating as well the conflict between psychological realism and authorial irony in the portrait of
Stephen's artistry (Norris, *Web;* Dettmar; Booth; Scholes). Even so,
many critics agree that psychological suffering is inseparable from

Stephen's artistic products (Rossman, "Spiritual," "Villanelle"; Friedman, "Self"; Benstock; Wright).

Critics have become increasingly adept at explicating Joyce's narrative methods, thus influencing interpretive methodologies applied to many other modernist and postmodernist texts (J. H. Miller, "Narrative" 3–4). Critics have investigated Joyce's masterful manipulation of indirect interior monologue, building an important guide to reading strategies (Kenner, *Joyce's;* Tindall; Booth; Riquelme; Dettmar; Norris, *Web*). William York Tindall argued that repeated symbols in each novel form a narrative, accruing increasing—though disputed—meanings with each appearance and transformation (85–93). John Paul Riquelme refined this insight, noting that the reading process enables the reader to absorb this narrative of symbols as the reader's own memory (54, 80). Hence the reader recognizes and incorporates the increasingly freighted symbolic narrative into the reading process, thus understanding and identifying with Stephen Dedalus and his life story.[2]

More recently, Joyce critics have established that Joycean narratives deny repressed material while making it manifest. Although Hugh Kenner was one of the first critics to prove that devious denial was a crucial Joycean strategy (*Joyce's* 102–108), Susan Stanford Friedman's work synthesized psychological investigation and narratology ("Self"). By examining what Gérard Genette labels paralipsis (material deliberately excised from the text [Genette 51–54]) Hans Walter Gabler discovered important lacunae in *Portrait*. Gabler's and Friedman's revealing the existence of narrative denial in *Portrait* has provided me with one strategy central to making visible an alcoholism narrative. Margot Norris has situated Joyce's narrative methods in cultural and historical context, modeling methodologies I use, although in doing so I depart from her argument and objectives.

My reading is built on this superstructure of Joyce critics' insights and strategies, which has provided the tools I use to apply the biopsychosocial model of alcoholism to character and narrative in *Portrait*.

The turn to cultural studies, though by no means universal in Joyce criticism, has decentered if not displaced postmodernist, poststructuralist, language-focused approaches to the writer and his texts. I, too, use those critical approaches that reattach texts to cultural systems of gender, socioeconomics, and historical interpretation to authorize my methods of analysis and point of view.

The biopsychosocial approach to alcoholism incorporates aspects of the culture into its analysis. Even so, my reading is not a cultural studies approach. Alcoholism is a complex illness the symptoms of which include the conviction by the alcoholic and members of his or her family that the drinker is not an alcoholic, but drinks by choice. Denial of the non-willed compulsion to drink may be exhibited not just by the drinker but by his or her culture. I argue that Simon Dedalus's drinking is certainly culturally-normative and gender-specific, but, although I see it as the result of illness—and thus non-willed—I do not see it as benign. Simon's drinking causes problems for him, his family, and influences Stephen's artistic choices.[3]

Symbolic readings of language and culture may inadvertently collude with the narratives of denied disclosure in *Portrait*. The biopsychosocial theor(ies) of alcoholism as a reading strategy avoid(s) those approaches that may mimic the denial of alcoholism, which I will argue is present in *Portrait*'s modes of character creation and narrative. Of necessity I will focus on the mimetic level of the text, reading the family dynamic and the trajectory of child development through the lens of alcoholism discourse.

Mimetic readings of *Portrait* have been challenged but not displaced by postmodernist interpretations. Feminists have explored the psychological complexity of Stephen Dedalus's misogyny (Scott, "Emma"; Henke, "Misogynist," "Narcissist"). From its publication, readers have constructed Stephen in *Portrait* as a psychologically realistic character (Rossman, "Villanelle," "Spiritual"; Epstein, "Joyce," *Ordeal*; Scholes, "Poet"; Klein).

Currently critics are increasingly citing drinking behaviors in Joyce's texts. Richard Pearce takes Simon Dedalus's alcoholism as a given ("Simon's" 130–32), for example. B. K. Kershner's *Joyce, Bakhtin, and Popular Literature* notes Simon Dedalus's heavy drinking (183–84). Recently Kershner has stated that Simon is "an alcoholic" and "an ineffectual father," ("History" 35) an assertion my argument will substantiate. Critical assent to the fact of drinking is not infrequent, but its meaning in terms of characterization and narrative procedure (Hofheinz; Voelker, *Joyce/Lowry*) has only recently begun to be articulated.

Few biographers and critics in 1999 deny John Joyce's problem with alcohol. The recent publication of *The Voluminous Life and Genius of James Joyce's Father, John Stanislaus Joyce* acknowledges the father's alcoholism without the bitterness of his son Stanislaus Joyce's *Complete Dublin Diary*.[4] Among James Joyce's biographers, Richard Ellman and Helene Cixous (40–47) foreground John Joyce's drinking.[5] However, Stanislaus Joyce is the only commentator on the Joyce family who repeatedly draws explicit connections between John Joyce's drinking, his behavior, and the family's downward mobility.

This lack of connection is particularly significant in Joyce studies where it is almost universally the case that Joyce scholars acknowledge the connection of James Joyce's fiction to his biography, drawing parallels between events and people and their fictional transformations in Joyce's narratives. Rarely, however, do critics connect John Joyce's drinking as a problem to the textual ramifications of that problem as seen in light of a biopsychosocial explanation of alcoholism. If critics make such connections, however, they explain these in reference to Dublin pub culture (for example, Pearce, "Simon's" 137) or mass-market commodifications (Rocco). The cultural studies methodologies that are deeply respectful of other cultures' views of themselves, for that reason may be inadvertently complicitous with the denial consequent to alcoholism. My biopsychosocial reading may appear to some to be reductive; nevertheless, I have chosen this interpretive strategy because its so-called reductiveness foregrounds the ramifications of alcoholism as these affect character and narrative.

Scholars question the accuracy of Stanislaus's *Complete Dublin Diary,* a major source for information about John Joyce's problematic drinking. George H. Healey, the editor of *The Complete Dublin Diary,* questions Stanislaus's aggressive bias against his father (vii). Arnold Goldman's more nuanced reading acknowledges the impact of John Joyce's drunkenness on his sons, but stresses instead a psychoanalytic focus on the siblings' rivalry for the father.[6] Joseph Kelly quotes Healey, Ellman, and Goldman to disprove that *The Complete Dublin Diary* was contemporaneous with events, suggesting that parts of it may have been rewritten as late as the 1940s (167).[7]

Kelly's understanding of Healey's acknowledgment differs from my own. Healey carefully notes that *The Complete Dublin Diary* he edited is based on a previous document, apparently the draft of the volume on which the book Healey edited is based (ix). Healey regards *The Complete Dublin Diary* as the product of a "young [Stanislaus]" (ix). Although Richard Ellman in 1969 told George H. Healey that parts of *The Complete Dublin Diary* had been modified (Kelly 250 n 113), Healey appeared confident in 1971 that the preponderance of the document he edited accurately records some of the events from 1903 to 1905.

Joseph Kelly views Stanislaus Joyce as "eccentric" as his brother James (157). He interrogates Stanislaus's claims of James's selfishness by showing that Stanislaus's caretaking of his brother during the Trieste years suffocated the older brother who had to escape from it and him (157), a behavior often found in children of alcoholic and drug-dependent parents, as I will demonstrate in my discussion of Virginia Woolf's mother. But never once does Kelly dispute Stanislaus's view of John Joyce's drinking.

Joseph Kelly's thoughtful criticisms do not destabilize the power of Stanislaus's subjective experience of parental alcoholism in *The Complete Dublin Diary,* nor the fact of James Joyce's reliance on that material in his creation of *Stephen Hero.* Even had time only deepened Stanislaus's bitterness toward his father, that does not necessarily mean that his description of parental brutality and progressive alcoholism are undermined, for what Joyce scholars dispute are Stanislaus's claims about James Joyce's opinions and artistic growth (Kelly 154–68), not John Joyce's drinking.

Richard Ellman's account of the early years of James Joyce in his canonical biography (Kelly 172–73) is based on Stanislaus's version of events (Kelly 156). Recently, Joyce scholars have challenged Richard Ellman's biography. Ira Nadel questions Ellman's interpretations of many of his sources, and the reliance for much of his information on Stanislaus Joyce (89), a significant problem as Stanislaus's texts are for Ellman and thus for Joyce studies the basis of much biographical interpretation of the writer. Expanding Nadel's critique, Joseph Kelly disputes Ellman's *James Joyce* because it fashions Joyce after his fictions, refuses to historicize Joyce, avoids "counterchecking" (157) to ensure accuracy, creating a figure of the artist as a new critic would define the term.

Nevertheless, neither Kelly nor Nadel questions the extent of John Joyce's drinking; in fact, Kelly concurs, calling him "his [Stanislaus's] drunk father" (157). Interestingly, Ira Nadel suggests that James Joyce's problem with alcohol (95) should become a topic of critical discussion (98). Allegations about James Joyce's drinking, especially in light of the increasing evidence for its genetic origin (Noble 216; Sigvardsson, Bohman, [and] Cloninger, "Replication"), are not my concern, however; I focus on the impact on *Portrait* of the author's growing up within a family structured to enable the father's alcoholism.

Joseph Kelly notes that Ellman's biographical account in chapters 2 through 10 of "the Dublin years" is based on Stanislaus's version of events (156). Ellman apparently follows Stanislaus's view of John Joyce's drinking, noting that it was progressive and not under rational control. Ellman also enumerates what Stanislaus Joyce felt were the consequences of John Joyce's drinking, though Ellman does not present them as directly due to the drinking. Chaos in the family's daily life (*James Joyce,* rev. ed. 37; 41),[8] frequent moves to increasingly poorer neighborhoods and accommodations (*JJII* 43; 68–9), food bought increasingly on credit (*JJII* 69), verbal and physical violence against May Joyce, his wife, and his children (*JJII* 41), and verbal violence, full of epithets, blame, and profanity (also noted by Kearney 57) duly appear in Ellman's biography of James Joyce. However, there are major differences in emphasis and inclusion between Stanislaus's *Complete Dublin Diary* and Ellman's biography.

Ellman's intent was apparently to present the Joyce story with as little admixture of judgment as possible.[9] Further, although the second edition was issued in 1982, the original book had first been published in 1959. The educated American's thinking about families and addiction in the 1950s was entirely different from such thinking in the 1980s, and it is the earlier audience's viewpoint that might have influenced Ellman's presentation of John Joyce.

Ellman, therefore, seems to have chosen to call John Joyce's drinking "excessive" rather than alcoholic (*JJII* 132, 136, 851). It is apparent to a reader familiar with the medical and biopsychosocial models of alcoholism theory, however, that although he does not use the language of addiction, Ellman follows Stanislaus's view of John Joyce's progressive disintegration. On page 18 Ellman notes that at the time of John's marriage to May Murray, he was "already a heavy drinker." Ellman describes John's behavior in the year of James's birth: he would meet his friends at the railway station, and "sing and drink all evening in the drawing-room on the second floor" (*JJII* 24). Ellman seems to suggest the role played by increasing alcohol addiction in leading to what he describes as John Joyce's "fall": "For John Joyce, the fall of [Charles Stewart] Parnell, closely synchronized with a fall in his own fortunes, was the dividing line between the stale present and the good old days" (*JJII* 33).[10] Interwoven with his description of the father's increasingly hostile refusal to take care of his growing family, Ellman states, "[John Joyce] blamed his misfortunes on imaginary 'enemies,' and turned on his family, rancorous because their support curtailed his consumption of alcohol, though it did not do so very much" (*JJII* 34). However, Ellman balances his view—as Stanislaus did not—by remarking that John Joyce's passionate support of Charles Stewart Parnell almost cost him his pension (*JJII* 34) and perhaps other means of employment as well, an insight thoroughly substantiated by John Wyse Jackson and Peter Costello.

Ellman's phrase "imaginary 'enemies'" suggests an aspect of alcoholism I analyzed in discussing Michael Henchard. One of the characteristics of alcoholism that twentieth-century North American treatment specialists note frequently is the issue of the "locus of control." Thus for the alcoholic, the "enemy," the blameability factor, is usually someone or something outside the self; the alcoholic rarely accepts responsibility for his or her problematic circumstances. Chapter 1 cites evidence that an alcoholic may go to great lengths of rationalization simultaneously to justify and deny problematic drinking. In the quotation cited earlier, Ellman makes clear that what motivated John Joyce's rage was that supporting his family threatened his drinking money. The dailiness of John Joyce's drinking, what the medical model would explain as his "having to drink," is clear in Ellman's masterly use of a nonrestrictive clause: "and at election times he could always depend upon the usual small jobs to make him momentarily affluent and, necessarily, drunk" (*JJII* 39), implying that John Joyce could make no rational choice; drinking was a necessary behavior.

Thus it appears to me that in the 1982 edition of the standard biography, Ellman is pointing to John Joyce's addiction to alcohol. His decision not to use the term perhaps arose because Ellman chose to tell the story from James Joyce's point of view. As Ellman makes explicit, James Joyce either refused or was unable to separate himself from his father's self-assessment (*JJII* 640–47). As James Joyce aged, he seems to have deliberately chosen to become more like his father rather than risk facing what separation would have required.

Ellman, too, was understandably wary of the stereotypical view of alcohol addiction as being endemic in the lives of the Irish family (McGoldrick, "Irish" 318–19, 328–29). He most probably wanted to avoid reductive cultural stereotyping. Further, according to John, James, and Stanislaus Joyce, John Joyce's drinking did not exceed cultural norms. Stanislaus assessed his father's drinking as culturally normative (*My Brother's* 63, 74, 98) as part of "that hard-drinking generation['s behavior]" (*My Brother's* 60). Similarly, one of the things James Joyce most admired about his father (and, as Brenda Maddox's biography of Nora Joyce makes clear, James Joyce tried to imitate [Maddox 68–69, 181, 185–86]) was the elder's sociability, the linkage of his drinking to male bonding in the pub around liquor, song, and storytelling. Further, as Vincent Cheng has proven, James Joyce energetically rejected negative racialized depictions of the Irish. A more overt narrative of alcoholism by Ellman in 1982 might have seemed to encourage misreadings that connected stereotypical Irishness (animality, stupidity, dissipation) with drunkenness (Cheng 32–34, 47–49; see also Platt 78–79).[11]

Ellman's focus on the particular locale and wider culture outside the family as James Joyce's formative arena expands the focus and avoids reductive stereotyping. Certainly James Joyce's life was not limited to that of his family's struggles, but that these and their effect on him were considerably worse than Ellman's rational and exhaustive account suggests has been made clear by other scholars. For example, Ruth Bauerle's careful movement from the biographical origins of family drinking and violence through the transformations of the fictionalization process into such stories as "The Dead," suggests that in her opinion James Joyce's family of origin induced extensive suffering and consequent deformations of character (119–21).

Biographers have long noted that James Joyce's younger brother Stanislaus did not idealize his father, as did James, although this divergence of view might have been partially prompted by the fact that Stanislaus Joyce defined himself oppositionally against his brother, and envied the fact that John Joyce favored James (Ellman, *JJII* 44, 75). Sociologists of the family know that children do not experience family life in the same way, and that birth order determines, to some extent, how the child perceives his or her parents and siblings. In a family organized around parental alcoholism, the birth order of children, the age at which the children leave the family, or what share they receive of the family resources, is crucial to their selfhood as well as to their views of their families (Keltner, McIntyre, and Gee).

Scholarly scrutiny of Stanislaus Joyce's viewpoint has corrected much of Stanislaus's bias. But I have not found any Joyce scholar who disputes the accuracy of Stanislaus's view of John Joyce's drinking. Therefore to substantiate my discussion of the submerged alcoholism narrative in *Portrait*, I will first analyze Stanislaus Joyce's *Complete Dublin Diary* as a document recording the emotional life of a son of an alcoholic.

I believe that such a claim can be made without eliciting charges of ahistoricizing alcoholism and its results for the alcoholic and his or her family. I would be willing to discount these similarities if I were a deconstructionist or postmodernist, if I thought poverty were the cause of and not the result of John Joyce's drinking, and if I thought that the insufficiency of reference to alcoholism in *Portrait* ruled it out as one probable cause of Simon's problems. In fact, however, I am convinced that the narrative methods of suppressing alcohol in *Portrait* and its narrative reappearance in disguised forms attests to its probable causality in Simon's failures.

I acknowledge that a poverty-stricken family in turn-of-the-century Ireland is not an alcoholic family in white middle-class North America, the source of many clients of the therapists on whose works I rely. Nor can I assert that people are emotionally constituted the same way in all cultures and in all times, for certainly there is no agreement theoretically on this issue and it remains a contested site in both history and anthropology. Nevertheless, I find sufficient social, cultural, and economic similarities to warrant making comparisons. Biological responses to addictive substances are universal, although cultural constructions of addiction are not (Berridge and Edwards 278–81; but see Barrows and Room, "Introduction" 4–19). Each country is a patriarchal one; in each country children are legally subject to their parents' guardianship; each country sustains and supports the male use of alcohol as a defining aspect of the social construction of "manhood"; and in each country a wide variety of alcoholic beverages are readily available and relatively cheap; and each circumstance includes life in an urban context.

In light of these similarities, I believe it is not inaccurate to suggest that the emotional responses to a parent's alcoholism that therapists have noted in twentieth-century North American clients, who are mostly middle class, may be used to investigate the emotional responses of a son who believes his father is an alcoholic in a late-nineteenth-century downwardly mobile Irish family.

The evidence amassed by twentieth-century North American clinicians whose research has demonstrated the emotional damage suffered by children of alcoholic parents is now under review.[12] The extensive body of material about the damage created by alcoholism in families documents the experiential consequences of growing up with alcoholism, consequences recorded in psychometric tests, but also noted by clinicians working therapeutically with many clients.

Although much of this data supports the "personality theory" that children of alcoholics suffer from intrapsychic and interpersonal difficulties—such as low self-esteem and conduct disorders, among other problems—other data seems to contradict these findings (Windle and Searles, *Children* 1–5). Suggesting a struggle between competing groups to control this discourse, Heather J. Gotham and Kenneth J. Sher note dryly that "there is some discrepancy between popular or clinical literature and empirical research regarding COAs" (34).

Current debates about the type and extent of emotional damage suffered by children of alcoholics have not disproved the substantial evidence that some children growing up in homes distorted by parental alcoholism suffer severe consequences: "[d]espite the uncertainties that prevail, there is a general consensus that children of alcoholics are a population at risk. They are overrepresented in the caseloads of medical, psychiatric, and child guidance clinics; in the juvenile justice system; and in cases of child abuse" (Seilhamer and Jacob 169). Therefore, although I acknowledge those arguments that question the accuracy of the category "adult child of an alcoholic," I am convinced that enough evidence of consistent damage from alcoholism in families exists in some children of alcoholic parents to warrant continued use of the concept of "adult children of alcoholics."

Biopsychosocial theories based on studies of children from alcoholic homes can usefully illuminate both *The Complete Dublin Diary* and the denied alcoholism narrative of *Portrait*. The methods and conclusions of such theories will therefore supply part of the theoretical grounding on which my own study rests. First examining *The Complete Dublin Diary* as the testament of a son of an alcoholic, I will then study Stephen Dedalus (older brother of Maurice, the fictionalized Stanislaus Joyce in *Stephen Hero*) as the son of an alcoholic father. I will examine Stephen Dedalus in context of family systems theory and current ideas about the chronic trauma parental alcoholism may produce in some children in order to investigate specific aspects of *Portrait*'s narrative and methods of characterization.

As is evident in *The Complete Dublin Diary,* the brothers' experience of their father's drinking differed greatly. James Joyce did not experience his father's alcoholic progression in the way recorded by his younger brother (Ellman, *JJII* 69).

Stanislaus Joyce was born on December 17, 1884, into a home where he would not be the favorite son. Stanislaus did not, as did his elder brother, receive the gift of (an albeit brief) boarding school education with its further privilege of even a short absence from the home. Attending school while living at home, he observed without a break the effects on his mother and siblings of family violence and diminishing resources for food and shelter. He saw clearly his father's descent down the scale in social class, self-respect, job opportunities, and impulse control. His portrait of John Joyce presents the complex truth about the father that some of the elder son's letters and a close reading of the novels substantiates. Many Joyce scholars in fact acknowledge that, as Cixous phrased it, "the sinister father [in *Portrait*] is John as seen by Stannie (37) . . . Stephen Dedalus' dislike for his father in *Portrait* is that of Stannie, not of Jim, for the father in real life" (136; see also Goldman 68–70).

George H. Healey disconnects Stanislaus Joyce's record of his family's chaotic life from his father's alcoholism. Introducing Stanislaus Joyce's *Complete Dublin Diary*, Healey states: "[t]his diary was recorded with great care by a sensitive and intelligent boy, eighteen years old at its opening, twenty at its close, who knew that something was dismally wrong with his life, who reacted by lashing out savagely at almost everything around him, who was often injudicious and unjust, but who was trying to be reasonable and honest" (*CDD* vii).

Healey's judgment that Stanislaus is unjust and injudicious is interrogated by the very judiciousness that Stanislaus struggles to maintain. Constantly he questions himself about his fairness to his father (*CDD* 15, 23, 31, 47, 71, 75, 135, 142–43, 152–53, 168–70). He repeatedly readjusts his view, trying to see his father without contempt or hatred, or, failing that, to honor him. But he cannot, and to his credit, he does not, deny how often his father drinks, nor what alcohol does to John Joyce and hence to the family.

Stanislaus is able to separate himself emotionally and intellectually from the family environment, even while physically within it, partially by recording in writing what he sees and feels. Even should the reader think that Stanislaus Joyce is irrationally phobic about alcohol, the reason for this phobia is evident in the circumstances that the drinking led to and maintained. To a reader versed in alcoholism theory, it is the negative consequences of the father's drinking, not the narrator's talking about it, which appear "injudicious and unjust." The material in *The Complete Dublin Diary* records the intersection of chaos, violence, and poverty with parental alcoholism as documented in much clinical literature about the environments of many twentieth-century North American children who grew up in middle- and working-class alcoholic families.

Were John Joyce's consistent drunkenness and brutality as Stanislaus Joyce recorded them from 1903 to 1905 the result of his grief over his wife's death? Although the medical model would castigate such a suggestion as denial, the biopsychosocial model would consider it, as I will now do. Although his wife's death may certainly have exacerbated his sense of needing to drink, the chronicity of John Joyce's drinking and his behaviors indicate something much more severe than situational drinking. Stanislaus's subsequent portraits of his father reveal that John Joyce's drinking did not taper off as his grief lessened. If anything, the drinking got worse.

What Stephanie Brown calls "the family atmosphere" (*Adult* 21) is similar to what *The Complete Dublin Diary* describes: "Chaos is one of the most prominent features of this [alcoholic family] atmosphere" (S. Brown, *Adult* 49). S. M. Baker stated that "family life of the children of alcoholics may be described as chaotic and isolated with an abundance of inconsistency . . . with the presence of emotional turmoil a constant factor" (qtd. in S. Brown, *Adult* 24). R. Fox suggested that the emotional and physical chaos in alcoholic families produces an "inconsistency [that] makes it difficult for the child to develop consistent standards of behavior, and that the emotional warmth and support needed for the development of a sense of self-worth are seriously lacking" (qtd. in S. Brown, *Adult* 23). These clinicians agree that "family disruption impedes becoming a socialized adult" (S. Brown, *Adult* 17).

Those clinicians cited by Brown note frequently that the roles of children and parents in alcoholic families are reversed, "with the father assuming the role of naughty child" (Jackson qtd. in S. Brown, *Adult* 23). Repeatedly Stanislaus criticizes John Joyce's refusal to take adult responsibility for himself or his numerous children.

The consistently inconsistent behavior of John Joyce and Stanislaus's constant shifts of attitude in trying to understand his father and to establish a stable relation with his father are similar to N.

Newell's clients' experiences: in periods of sobriety the alcoholic father "[i]nspires the natural love of his offspring, who build there-
from an ideal father image of omnipotence and loving kindness. The
disillusionment of the drunken episode is shattering to the . . . child
who is subjected to alternating experiences of exalted hopes and
blighting disappointments" (Newell qtd. in S. Brown, *Adult* 22).
Stanislaus Joyce records in his *Complete Dublin Diary* his own
shifts of attitude and attachment; these appear similar to those experienced by Newell's clients. Stanislaus reports "watching [John
Joyce] drunk, watching him sober, watching him when he has
money and when he has not, when he is on friendly terms with me
and when he is not, and as a result I find I do not like him" (*CDD*
143).

The *Complete Dublin Diary* insists upon John Joyce's alcoholic
"progression," tracing a steady deterioration in his self-control, behavior to family, ability to work, and the kind of companionship he
sought outside of the house. Inadvertently, Stanislaus Joyce's chronicle of his father's alcoholic decline documents one of the tenets of
the medical model of alcoholism, that at a certain point, the alcoholic enters and cannot by force of will withdraw from, a downward financial, emotional, and physical spiral.[13] Although
inevitable deterioration is not a tenet of the biopyschosocial view of
alcoholism, that downward spiral is explicit in The *Complete
Dublin Diary* and observable in *Portrait*. Whether or not it were inevitable, Stanislaus does not argue; that it occurred and that he observed it closely, he documents scrupulously.

The *Complete Dublin Diary* establishes as its basic premise the
chronicity to which John Joyce's drinking had progressed during the
years 1903 to 1905 (Cixous 136–142). On September 26, 1904,
Stanislaus asserts that his father "has become a crazy drunkard"
(*CDD* 6). While short, infrequent episodes of sobriety do occur,
Stanislaus asserts that John Joyce needs to drink daily. "When there
is money he will spend all he can and reel home drunk in the
evening, and when there is not he will blame everyone but himself"
(*CDD* 69). The *Complete Dublin Diary* repeatedly connects the entrapment of the father in drinking with the resulting suffering of his
children (133, 177).

Stanislaus Joyce holds his father responsible for the misery in the household, for the family's ill health, blighted prospects, and their mother's death (*CDD* 175–76). As I have argued about the fictional daughter of an alcoholic, Elizabeth-Jane in *Mayor*, "the blameability factor" is complex in some children of alcoholics. In many cases, the alcoholic parent may be the originating cause of his or her children's range of troubles. However, an alcoholic parent may set the pattern for seeking to blame others for that for which one might oneself be partially responsible. Some, though not all, children of alcoholics do focus on the parent rather than on themselves as sole cause of any familial problems, while nevertheless continuing to look to the afflicted parent for rescue. Stanislaus is self-aware, acknowledging that he blames his family for his focus on their unhappiness (*CDD* 170).

Within this dual pattern of blaming, John Joyce blaming the children and everyone else (*CDD* 69), and Stanislaus Joyce blaming his father, *The Complete Dublin Diary* chronicles the results for the children of the father's seemingly constant drunkenness in the years 1903 to 1905. For instance, on September 26, 1903, Stanislaus notes the emotional and financial chaos characteristic of John Joyce's household (*CDD* 17). The entry of April 20, 1904, records that "[w]hen there is money in this house it is impossible to do anything because of Pappie's drunkenness and quarrelling. When there is no money it is impossible to do anything because of the hunger and cold and want of light" (*CDD* 27–28).

Apparently John Joyce regarded his children, particularly his daughters, as "encumbrance[s]" (*CDD* 7) to be battered and used. Stanislaus remarks on March 24, 1904 that "[w]e—Jim, Charlie and I—relieve one another in the house like policemen as the girls are not safe in it with Pappie. A few nights ago . . . he attempted to strike some of them. . . . If the children see two of us preparing to go out, they run up to the third to ask him to stay in" (*CDD* 24). Summarizing this passage, Helene Cixous observes that "John Joyce was criminally irresponsible; he was The Enemy [*sic*] to his family, and his sons mounted guard against him" (139).

Verbal violence usually accompanied physical violence (*CDD* 28). Part of the violence directed against the children seems caused by John Joyce's sense that all resources in the house are to be his alone; hence, none of the children's personal possessions are safe. On April 16, 1904, his sister Poppie gave their father his bootlaces, leaving Stanislaus without usable boots (*CDD* 29–30). (Stanislaus notes that he pawned his own clothes to use the money for food [*CDD* 77].)

On July 18, 1904, Stanislaus Joyce adds up the cumulative assessment of his father's drinking and its deleterious effects on the Joyce family (*CDD* 175–76). Stanislaus blames John Joyce for the children's bad health, including their serious dental problems, due in part to the father's having drunk up the family's small income, rather than paying for nourishment and medical care. The son also accuses his father of causing his children's entrapment in a lower social class than that of their own father's at his birth. Most seriously, Stanislaus views his father as a killer. Stanislaus blames his father for the early death of his brother Georgie, and also holds his father responsible for the miserable life of his mother, May Joyce, whom he continued to treat badly even as she died an agonizing death from cancer. With mordant humor, Helene Cixous agrees: "[t]his delightful list is still an underestimate" (138). To buttress Stanislaus's accusations, Cixous elaborates on them: "[i]t is unfortunately true that the father's drinking and absenteeism were responsible for a great deal of suffering. Charlie died of tuberculosis in hospital, for instance, and out of eight children surviving, four died young, undernourished, ill cared for, not looked after at all" (138).

Stanislaus then requotes himself, ending this accusatory entry by appending to it a copy of an earlier entry from an earlier journal (Healey, *CDD* ix) dated April 27, 1902: "[a]fter ten Pappie came in with few pence left. We—and the children—had fasted 14 hours. I heard his drunken intonations in the dark downstairs . . . This is a true portrait of my progenitor: the leading one a dance and then the disappointing, baffling, baulking and turning up drunk—the business of breaking hearts" (*CDD* 178).

The harrowing experience of reading *The Complete Dublin Diary* is all the more powerful because of Stanislaus Joyce's struggle to be honest and fair-minded. The intensity of his gaze illuminates not just his father, but himself. George H. Healey uses the word "enmeshed" (*CDD* vii) to describe the Joyce children's experience of being mired in the complex human relationships recorded in *The Complete Dublin Diary*. One instance of such enmeshment is the fact that James Joyce read[14] and used portions of his brother's diary in the composing process of writing *Stephen Hero* (Healey, *CDD* vii).

Joseph Voelker suggested further proof of such linkage, connecting the ending of *The Complete Dublin Diary* (176–77) to that of the prayer to "Old Father, Old Artificer," with which *Portrait* ends by means of their similar dates—April 27. April 27th was payday for John Joyce, a time inextricable from John Joyce's drinking (Voelker, "April" 325): "On the 27th of the month, when he was paid, [my father] was usually up very early, in a state of high agitation at the thought of all the whiskey in view for that day" (S. Joyce, *My Brother's* qtd. in Voelker, "April" 325). The novel's conclusion is ironic: a prayer to such a drunkard would hardly stand one in good stead "now" or "forever."

As George H. Healey notes, "James read these minutes [the material Stanislaus refashioned into *The Complete Dublin Diary*] while they were being written, asked to have them sent to him after he left Ireland, and borrowed from them [when composing *Stephen Hero*]" ("Preface" vii). Helene Cixous explores the importance of *The Complete Dublin Diary* to James Joyce's work (131–45), asserting that Simon Dedalus in *A Portrait of the Artist as a Young Man* greatly resembles Stanislaus's portrait of John Joyce in *The Complete Dublin Diary* (136). In the argument that follows, I will demonstrate that Simon Dedalus is an alcoholic whose illness adversely affects Stephen Dedalus's psychological development, a situation replicated by narrative behaviors which simultaneously represent and deny alcoholism.

INTERPRETIVE STRATEGIES

In *Joyce's Web: The Social Unraveling of Modernism,* Margot Norris rereads *Portrait* from the vantage of *Finnegans Wake*. Norris argues that critical tradition misreads Stephen's response to his loss of class status as a "heroicizing of the artist," by ignoring Joycean irony which denies "the apotheosis of the artist—the individual's rational self-liberation from the mythologizings of religion, state, and home" (*Web* 183).

In an article later revised when incorporated into *Joyce's Web,* Norris summarizes while interrogating the standard view of *Portrait* as a combination of bildungsroman and küntslerroman ("Politics" 61–63), noting that "Joyce gives us both the lie and its mystification" ("Politics" 65). She deflates Stephen Dedalus's view, arguing that, like many Irish, Stephen left home because "he has no material or social prospects there. He transforms emigration into exile, and cloaks his *Deklasierung,* his loss of class, in the bohemian imperatives of heresy, freethinking and art" ("Politics" 70–71; emphasis in original).

But what is the cause of Stephen's loss of class status? Reading from the double vantage of alcoholism and narrative theories, I will argue that the narrative discloses that Simon Dedalus's drinking is one of the causal if not the single causal agent for the fall from comfortable class status (See also Naremore, "Consciousness" 132).

The physical decline of the Dedalus family is trivialized by Stephen in an elegantly ironic list. Toward the close of the novel, Stephen answers his close friend Cranly's question about his family's class status by enumerating Simon Dedalus's countless jobs. Out of a total of fourteen, two concern alcohol, though the mention of these is buried in the middle of the list which includes the phrase, "something in a distillery . . ." (*P* 241). Cranly notes Stephen's minimizing of the alcohol by his equally ironic response, "[t]he distillery is damn good." (*P* 241). In miniature, this simultaneous narrative insistence on and denial of the problem is an example of what I call denied disclosure.

The physical setting of the novel offers a series of metaphors for life in an alcoholic home. Hell, the topic of the sermon in chapter 3 of the novel, seems an excellent commentary on this life. The descriptions of the Dedaluses' many homes seem to embody the process of alcoholic disintegration, and to parallel and symbolize the father's increasing loss of mature human capacity. At first the Dedaluses inhabit a large home with imposing furniture. They have a maid and are able to serve in an elegant and festive room a luxurious Christmas meal (*P* 29–30). Alcohol, however, looms large. Mr. Dedalus "brought forth a great stone jar of whisky [*sic*] from the [sideboard] and filled the decanter slowly . . ." (*P* 28). Mr. Dedalus pours himself and Mr. Casey the liquor that, as I will suggest later, is shown to be inextricably implicated in their verbally abusive shouting match with Mrs. Riordan over Parnell. I will return to the Christmas party, but for now I note that when Mr. Dedalus pulls forth the whiskey jar, he is not shown as removing its cork or even that there is a plug in it. An unattached c/Cork later surfaces in important moments in the text, a silent yet textually marked tribute to the uncontained power of alcohol.

Alcohol and financial loss clearly intersect in chapter 2, offering an overt but not highlighted suggestion as to why the Dedalus family's physical circumstances are so consistently at peril. It is in chapter 2 that Mr. Dedalus journeys to Cork to pay the price for his inability to stop drinking. Stephen and the other Dedalus children are powerless to escape and to speak about their situation.

Placing the reader as well as the schoolboys on retreat in hell, the narrative in chapter 3 reinforces the emotional torture Stephen experiences even as he is its powerless witness. The harrowing physical and mental tortures of the damned occur in an inferno into which all the evil of the world collects in "a vast reeking sewer . . ." (*P* 120). Thus, living in hell for all eternity is not only the topic of the priest's sermon on the Retreat; it is an apt metaphor for the lives of some children whose parents have trouble with alcohol. Hell, however, never changes, whereas life in the Dedalus home steadily worsens.

When Stephen returns home cleansed by his confession in chapter 3, the impoverished breakfast—glaringly different from the Christmas dinner—looks to him like the pure offerings of a communion table. Within one chapter even these simple foods have become desecrated (*P* 174). Comparing the meal described in chapter 1 (*P* 29–30) to the tea leavings in chapter 4 (*P* 162–63) reveals a piercing yet subtle image of just how much Mr. Dedalus's drinking has cost his six children, his wife, and himself. At that point in the narrative, the family has once again been evicted as the younger children tell Stephen in pig Latin *(P 163)*. The failure of the pig Latin to obscure the eviction is similar to the insistence of the narrative on simultaneously making plain and denying the implication of alcohol in the increasing degradation of the family's life.

Chapter 4 marks Stephen's choice of his father's way of life rather than the priesthood. His father's home, located on marshy ground, is disorderly and unstable *(P 162)*. The cow dung-filled fields of chapter 2 are recalled in the kitchen gardens now effulgent with "vegetable" decay *(P 162)*.

In chapter 5 the home abuts onto a "waterlogged" "lane" awash in "wet rubbish" and "mouldering offal," *(P 175)* images clearly alluding to the sewage in chapter 3 and the rotting vegetables of chapter 4. Inside the home, few of the grand trappings remain of the status and comfort present at the Christmas dinner in chapter 1. They lack orderly meals of adequate and healthy food *(P 174)*. The Dedaluses, who appear to live in or near the drains of Hell *(P 120)*, have fallen from feast to hunger, an image invoked as Stephen is writing the villanelle *(P 218)*.

Little could be more indicative of the complete overturn of their class privilege than the horrifying picture of family disintegration apparent from the first paragraphs of the final chapter of the book. The father is omnipotent but invisible, a force so threatening that he has but to whistle to force the women in the family to tremble with fear and almost knock one another over as they rush to do his bidding. The beautifully dressed mother in chapter 1 now is an exhausted slattern, living in abject fear of the once-monied husband.

The picture reveals much more than the disordered squalor of the father's home *(P 162)* alluded to in chapter 4. It reveals a brutalized and socially impotent family. It is unlikely that the shocking difference between this group of people and the mother and father pictured by Stephen in chapter 1 was caused by loss of money alone; the fear of the father is too extreme. This paralyzing fear suggests to me that financial and status loss were symptoms of and not the cause of the family's downfall.

During his impoverished breakfast Stephen had idly read the numerous pawn tickets near him on the scarred kitchen table. They were kept in a box whose lid was dotted by "lousemarks" *(P 174)*.

These indications of poverty impact the women more than the men: a system of servitude sustains the position of relative privilege to which Stephen's status as firstborn son entitles him. He orders his mother to get his bath ready and orders are passed down the line from mother to sister to sister (*P* 174–75).

Irish family life at the turn of the century reflected a specific social system. As borne out by Florence L. Walzl's essay, "Dubliners: Women in Irish Society," such a home was under the control of the father whose whim was law, but whose authority was often enforced by the mother. Sex-role stereotyping was extreme, a fact exacerbating the division of labor whereby the females cooked, cleaned, and serviced the physical life of the family. The majority of women were not educated, although sons were; women were second-class citizens.

The mother and sisters' relations here, however, indicate something more than the usual hierarchy of servitude to the patriarch, whereby the more powerful passes on onerous tasks to the one beneath her in the family system (*P* 174–75). They are terrified of doing anything that might provoke the father. The nameless girl (perhaps deliberately nameless to underline the eclipse of female identity in such a family) who goes to the foot of the stairs to answer the father's whistle as if they were dogs not even worth addressing by language (*P* 174–75), will do anything to appease him. Stephen hastens out of the house while his sister assures the father that Stephen has already left. Bellowing curses on his eldest son, Simon seems unable to get downstairs to prove her wrong, but clearly remains suspicious that he is not getting his needs met—the need to insult his eldest son to his face.

More is going on here than financial ruin. Implied in this scene is an explosive father whom all fear, one who is able to rule through this implicit threat of a violent temper. Explicating the rage, hunger, and pain complicating the multifaceted ironies of Joyce's narrative dialogic, Norris states that "[t]he brutal Irish father, we are reminded, is the colonial father caught in the impossible situation of making a home safe when his nation is not safe" (*Web* 209). Privileged by gender and social convention, Mr. Dedalus may be mimicking the exercise of imperial state power in his "Home Rule," (Cheng

58) but such an analogy need not deny the narrative embedding of Mr. Dedalus's "courage" in alcohol or the results of that abusive power for the women of his household.

The cowed, almost paralyzed, women who do his bidding are not aided by the brother. While he may think of himself as heroic because he appears to laugh at the father, it is noteworthy that Stephen does not go to the foot of the stairs to take on the older man. His imperial heroism is illusory, thus, and is, like his father's on whom it is modeled, enacted at the expense of his sisters and mother. This family dynamic is extreme even when measured by the traditional sex-role divisions in families of this social class during this time period.

Comment on the father's behavior is silenced. Why is he upstairs when everyone else is awake and going about the tasks of the day? Why does he not go to work? Why does he whistle and curse instead of speaking in civil language? What is the matter with him, and why does no one refer to this? Why does no one take any action to state or to change the situation? The fact that nothing is said or done, that all goes on as if the situation were other than it is, or simply a natural fact of existence, may be the result of what many twentieth-century North American alcohologists term a family system of denial (Whitfield 75–77; Steinglass, et al., 143–45, 263–92; S. Brown, *Adult* 36–41, 43, 106, 172). I will argue that the Dedalus family's denial both highlights and is an enactment of the denial of the obvious, which is a crucial narrative technique in this novel.

The denial narrative of chapter 1 is examined in the behaviors of the narrative in chapter 2, the chapter that, when closely examined, obscures yet exposes the alcoholism which is complexly portrayed in the novel.

THE DENIAL NARRATIVE

My argument depends on my analysis of chapter 2 of *Portrait*. I read this chapter through the prism of previous Joyce critics' insights and methodologies combined with my analysis of alcoholism as a biopsychosocial illness.

I argue that paralipsis, the deliberate excision of material from a narrative, in chapter 2 is an objective correlative for the denial process inherent in alcoholism as a biopsychosocial illness. Hans Walter Gabler has demonstrated that reconstructing material obscured by a paralipsis is crucial to understanding Stephen Dedalus's writing in *Portrait*. Gabler realized that Stephen's first poem to E. C. about the tram ride home, presented in a prose summary, replaced Stephen's never-written poem about Parnell ("Christmas" 32).

Critics have thoroughly investigated the biographical and textual importance of Charles Stewart Parnell in Stephen and Simon Dedalus's lives and in John's and James Joyce's lives (Kelly 40–41; Manganiello 3–9, 14–23, 49–50, 212–14; Cheng 48, 59, 69, 72–73; Spoo 43). Assuming that Parnell is a textual marker for a constellation of meanings, I argue that the novel embeds Parnell in the representation and denial of Simon Dedalus's alcoholism.

A much larger paralipsis than the suppressed poem to Parnell occurs in chapter 2. A story of bar drinking is told in place of the excised narrative of the sale of Simon Dedalus's Cork property. The narrative suppression of the sale of the property has similarities to the psychological phenomena of "splitting," dissociation, and alcoholic denial. These textual "blackouts" are not physiological, but serve as an "unconscious" narrative response that can eliminate Stephen's, Simon's, and the reader's recognition of Simon's increasing dependence on alcohol and the havoc it causes in his life and that of his family.

Hence I argue that chapter 2 denies while representing alcoholic denial as a strategy of both character and plot. Further, I demonstrate that chapter 2 has the fullest mimetic representation of the impact of Simon Dedalus's increasing alcoholism on Stephen's psychological development.

Simon deteriorates dramatically during chapter 2. His ineffectual incoherence and rage, his blaming external forces, his refusal of the adult role toward his wife and son are similar to behaviors exhibited by Michael Henchard that I have discussed in chapter 1.

The equally dramatic changes in Stephen mirror the changes in his father, again in ways reflective of a parent's increasing alcoholism. Stephen's feelings become constricted, numbed, or increas-

ingly flat, although he can occasionally feel anger. That he is not
angry at his father but is instead angry at himself suggests that the
denial process of alcoholism occurs in the son in a way that mirrors
the denial process in his father. Increasingly Stephen withdraws, observing rather than participating in the world around him. With-
drawing from children his own age, he takes refuge in fantasy.

None of these characteristics is unique to the Dedalus family.
They have been repeatedly reported by those therapists who treat
families where alcohol is a problem. Closely scrutinizing chapter 2
of *Portrait*, I will document these changes in Simon and Stephen
Dedalus and connect them to Simon's problem with alcohol.

I believe that such a connection can be made without eliciting
charges of ahistoricizing alcoholism and its results for the alcoholic
and his or her family, as I discussed. To interpret Stephen Dedalus as
the son of an alcoholic, I will rely on psychological studies of the
emotional responses to a parent's alcoholism that therapists have
noted in twentieth-century North American male and female middle-
class white clients. For reasons I have explained earlier, I do not believe it is inappropriate to use such materials as a way to investigate
the emotional responses of the fictional Stephen Dedalus.

THE CONTINUING CRITICAL PROBLEM OF THE AUTHORIAL VOICE/PRESENCE IN *PORTRAIT*

Joyce critics have helped pioneer the increasingly widespread scholarly recognition of what in Bakhtin's terminology is a dialogic, the
many-voiced quality of narrative. Hugh Kenner was among the first
to recognize that this polyvocality, which he named *Joyce's Voices*,
derived in part from Joyce's stunningly complex manipulation of
free indirect discourse. Naming it "the Uncle Charles principle,"
Kenner demonstrated that "his fictions tend not to have a detached
narrator, though they seem to have. His words are in such delicate
equilibrium . . . that they detect the gravitational field of the nearest
person . . . the narrative idiom need not be the narrator's" (*Joyce's*
16–18). Narratologist Shlomith Rimmon-Kenan's characterizes
what Kenner names "the Uncle Charles principle" as the peculiar

"double-edged" nature of free indirect discourse that originates in its ability to "[enhance] the bivocality or polyvocality of the text by bringing into play a plurality of speakers or attitudes" (Rimmon-Kenan 113). Because of the complexity of narrative voice in Joyce's novels, few critics agree on which voice proceeds from whom in *Portrait*—the character or the narrator's view of the character. Additionally, critics disagree about the identity and location of the narrator (Gillespie 85–90). Thus critics still struggle to develop effective methods and terminology by which to analyze and interpret tone and speaker in any given passage of *Portrait*'s free indirect discourse.

Margot Norris formulated a many-layered analysis of Joycean dialogic in "Stifled Back Answers: The Gender Politics of Art in Joyce's 'The Dead,'" a series of reading strategies she explored fully in *Joyce's Web*.[15]

In "Stifled 'Back Answers'" Norris models a methodology of reading that has directly influenced my use of the concept (originally found in the work of Jameson [Jameson 88]) of a narrative that behaves as a subject with a consciousness and an intentionality. Norris's reading strategy reveals and interprets what she names "'back answer[s]'" ("Stifled" 480). This is a language embodied in the text that is an active force in structuring both the narration and the reader's reading of that narration, but a language that does not have the stated assent of the narration, the narrator, or "the narrative voice" ("Stifled" 479). This latter term Norris uses for that part of the narration that delivers truths and information seemingly at variance with the surface deployment of the meaning of the text ("Stifled" 484). Describing "'back answers,'" Norris clarifies that they take the form of denied disclosure: they are "both blatant and discounted, unmistakable and invisible at the same time" ("Stifled" 482). In summary, James Joyce "inscrib[es] in his disavowing narration a series of linked and analogous 'back answers' or protests that trouble the text and cause it to stifle them in collusion with characters who do the same" (Norris, "Stifled" 502). In making her argument about textual reverberations that interrogate the narrative, Margot Norris has explained the method by which *A Portrait of the Artist as a Young Man* represents alcoholic denial.

Norris catalogues the mechanisms by which the "'back answers'" function as "a kind of shadow text," ("Stifled" 492) including but not limited to narrative behaviors, narrative imitations, narrative doublings, and narrative enactments ("Stifled" 483, 495–98, 500) of the unspoken, ironic interpretations of people and ideas, events that the surface text would appear to discount.

Norris's active rereading of "stifled 'back answers'" is vigorously feminist, an active political stance against a conservative reading of Joyce as a purveyor of apolitical aesthetics ("Stifled" 480–82). Norris refuses to support what she characterizes as critical collusion with surface narrative denials of a meaning that the textual "'back answers' make clear" ("Stifled" 494). Her methodology gives new resonance to the extensive critical discourse on Joycean irony ("Stifled" 484, 486), recuperating that irony for an active, political engagement with the text and its implications.

The manifest narrative and the free indirect discourse of Stephen Dedalus do not seem to acknowledge the possibility that alcohol is a problem for Simon Dedalus. Nevertheless, there does exist in *Portrait,* a "stifled back" yet ever-present critical analysis of surface narrative content that demonstrates Simon Dedalus's alcoholism.

One such textual interrogation operates by abrupt juxtaposition.[16] The use of juxtapositions is an especially effective kind of denial, for no explanation about the implied connections such juxtapositions would suggest is supplied, either within the manifest narrative or within the free indirect discourse. Because of the linear nature of the reading process itself, I experience several juxtapositions in *Portrait* as authorizing my readings of implied causality. Such implied causality is part of what I read as the "stifled back" alcoholism narrative of *Portrait.* It is there I will locate that which led me to read alcohol as a problem in the representation of the Dedalus family.

FAMILIAL ALCOHOLISM AND TRAUMA

As the son of an alcoholic Stephen Dedalus demonstrates those characteristics that some twentieth-century North American clinicians suggest can sometimes result from both the chronic and the acute traumas of growing up with severe parental alcoholism.

Some specialists see similarities between the experiences of children who suffer trauma and those of children living daily in homes affected by alcoholism. The chronic strain of daily chaos, parental mood swings, and uncertainties about financial and emotional resources are constant in many homes where parental alcoholism is a problem.

A child living in such family circumstances is under daily, unremitting stress. In fact, it is the chronicity of childhood fear, powerlessness over the alcoholic parent, and resulting stress that clinicians point to as causing trauma. H. Krystal has suggested that trauma may be of two kinds, "acute," a trauma that happens once, and "strain," a chronic trauma that continues over a period of time (qtd. in S. Brown, *Adult* 96). Stephanie Brown and Timmen L. Cermak speculate that both kinds of traumatic events occur in households dominated by alcoholism (S. Brown, *Adult* 96). I will argue that the narrative of chapter 2 of *Portrait* demonstrates both "chronic" and "acute" trauma.

Chapters 1 and 2 of *Portrait* depict mounting stressors on the Dedalus family. Notice of these stressors is not authorized by a covert authorial presence or a character's explicitly reported thoughts, but the reader witnesses them.

Psychologists agree that traumatic occurrences follow specific patterns. As the overwhelming life experience occurs that becomes a trauma, the survivor is "flooded," perhaps paralyzed with fear. At that moment, all senses become so overloaded that the survivor is sometimes unable to think or react. In other cases, the survivor enters a state of hyperarousal and hyperactivity (van der Kolk, *Psychological* 3–4; Rieker and Carmen, 362–63).

Stephanie Brown explains that in growing up with parental alcoholism, many of her clients experienced both "acute" trauma and traumatic "strain" that predisposed them

> to respond excessively and maladaptively to intense affects, manifested by a sense of being "dead" or by a variety of dissociative reactions ... [including] "defensive exclusion," the ability ... to

exclude, redefine, or distort information or events. . . . [to] range from the most extreme anhedonia—the absence of any affect or memories and a very limited cognitive range in adulthood—to severe chronic anxiety and depersonalization. (*Adult* 96–97)

I will argue below that Stephen Dedalus experiences many of these affective states.

"Splitting" is one of the responses of a child in a chronic traumatic situation, one noted by twentieth-century psychologists across a wide spectrum of treatment approaches. As my analysis of Stephen's four-paged response to seeing the word *Foetus* may suggest (see pp. 120–125) the mechanism of "splitting" is one of the principle mechanisms by which the narrative is advanced in chapter 2. Emotional "splitting" can be manifested in part by "anxious attachment," that can occur "when the parent is unable or unwilling to respond to the child's needs. Although it may have many different causes, the most common are commensurate with a traumatic history. It is associated . . . with narcissistic unavailability, depression, *alcoholism,* and somatic preoccupation. . . ." (Krugman 133; emphasis added). Nevertheless, to maintain connection to unavailable or abusive parents, the child "splits" his or her internal self-structure (Krugman 131–33; Rieker and Carmen 364). The split between ideal parent and the "bad" self of the child can serve a positive purpose; it can provide "an illusion of security because it leaves the parents intact as available and caring figures and places the responsibility for problems on the child" (S. Brown, *Adult* 132).

Stephanie Brown points out that, developmentally, the young child cannot conceptualize cause and effect relations, hence, "children . . . see themselves as the cause agent" (*Adult* 176). The "splitting" also may reflect "a sense of omnipotence, often adopted early by children to ward off recognition of helplessness and fear" (S. Brown, *Adult* 132). Stephen is still a young boy when Simon's drinking begins to affect his family life. Brown's insight is pertinent to the events in chapter 2 when Stephen unconsciously foregrounds his sense of sinfulness rather than respond more directly to the changes in his father.

Brown's analyses of children's cognitive splitting may clarify some of the process that Stephen undergoes in chapter 2: "When children assume responsibility, they may develop a pattern of self-hatred, self-criticism, and self-abuse in response to the conflict of having caused the problem and then being unable to solve it. They may become . . . high achievers but impoverished in their range of cognitive and emotional development" (S. Brown, *Adult* 176).[17]

As I stated earlier, in my reading of chapter 2 I will argue that both chronic and acute trauma occur early in Stephen's life. I will demonstrate that Stephen's free indirect discourse reveals his cognitive "splitting." I will show that narrative juxtaposition rather than overt statements of causality may reflect the results of trauma, for the narrative may at times seem to mimic the inadvertent denial processes the characters undergo in order to function.

Traumatic experiences may necessitate methods of escape. If no physical escape is possible, mental escape becomes essential. One of the methods of such escape is cognitive dissociation, the unconscious avoidance of feelings or perception of one's own experiences and material circumstances.

Varied kinds of dissociative experiences occur in chapter 2. For example, when in Cork, Stephen undergoes an annihilating experience of depersonalization, a disappearance of self that recapitulates the painful response Simon Dedalus might be unable to experience directly at the loss of his own patrimony.

Stephen demonstrates "numbing," a gradual loss of feeling, most notably an increasing inability to feel and to express anger even when doing so is warranted *(P* 64, 77, 82). Increasingly he withdraws into a haughty superiority, relieved by fantasy and masturbation. He assumes a mask of imperturbability. This division between his public and private selves is exemplified, too, in the increasing frequency of his moments of dissociation and fantasies during which he sometimes uses himself as the recipient of displaced rage, exemplifying the process of "splitting."

In my analysis of the Cork sequences, I will argue that trauma occurs both as experience for the character Stephen Dedalus, who is an ineffective witness to his father's destruction, and as an experience disrupting—seemingly traumatizing—the narrative itself. I will discuss what I will call the fetus narrative as an example of traumatic "splitting" during which the overwhelmed Stephen substitutes himself for his father as the mental recipient of emotional assault.

Alcoholism is sometimes described by the metaphor of escape. Certainly chapter 2 demonstrates modes of escape. Simon Dedalus and Uncle Charles meander while exploring their new surroundings *(P* 61), a behavior Stephen adopts once the family moves to Dublin. Simon Dedalus's retreat into alcohol is juxtaposed to and in fact, the narrative suggests, may mirror Stephen's flights from self into varied kinds of dissociative experiences. The narrative itself crafts an ellipsis that denies to the reader crucial information about the impact of alcoholism on Simon Dedalus's choices and behaviors. Superimposed on this ellipsis, Stephen's denial process reaches its crescendo in the passages set in Cork just as the narrative denial process reaches its crescendo in Cork.

However, the effect of this breakdown of the character's and the narrative's denial depends on the reader's having recognized associations between events, images, ideas, and feelings while the characters have escaped into alcohol or by dissociation. Simon and Stephen Dedalus are in denial; the reader, on the other hand, experiences recognition by reading retrospectively, making connections that father and son cannot seem to tolerate.

To make this argument, I will build upon suggestions by John Paul Riquelme and Michael Gillespie about the reading process by which James Joyce guides the reader to construct the novel. Riquelme is correct when he states that "[t]he narrator has been making a persona for the reader as well as for himself in his portrayal of Stephen. The reader has learned the conventions of the literary techniques that the author uses" (57). Discussing chapter 2, Riquelme argues that the reading process enables the reader to absorb and interpret Stephen's memories (80).

PREVIEW TO CORK EPISODES: THE CHRISTMAS DINNER

Critics have thoroughly investigated the biographical and textual importance of Parnell in Stephen and Simon Dedalus's lives and in

John and James Joyce's lives (Kelly 40–41; Manganiello 3–9, 14–23, 49–50, 212–14; Cheng 48, 59, 69, 72–3; Spoo 43) suggesting that Parnell is a textual marker for a constellation of meanings. I will argue that the novel's complex presentation of Parnell also embeds Parnell in the narrative's methods of representing and denying Simon Dedalus's alcoholism.

The Cork sequence in the narrative presupposes that the reader recalls the Christmas dinner party. Stephen's role as the heroic elder son, his terror of the argument between Mr. Casey, Aunt Dante, and his father, and the importance of Parnell to both son and father during the Christmas dinner are recapitulated and reformulated in the Cork sequences. The name of the city of Cork itself supplies a pun connected to the "great stone jar" (P 28) from which Simon Dedalus's Christmas whiskey flows. Exploring Dublin Stephen noticed in the harbor a "multitude of corks that lay bobbing . . . in a thick yellow scum . . ." (P 66), a possible allusion to the unstoppered whiskey container (P 28) from which the Dedalus's present troubles may have begun to flow. As Simon Dedalus replaces the whiskey jug in the locker, he is not shown to replace the stopper (P 28). Uncorked, the liquor becomes the alcohol he drinks from his "pocketflask" (P 87) and then the flood of tears he weeps in self-pity on the train ride to the city; unstoppered, the liquor flows over the narrative, covering the space where the story of the sale of the property might have been.

At the Christmas dinner Mr. Dedalus identifies himself with Parnell. Later he tells his son he is hounded by foes (P 65) whom he cannot regroup enough to attack, as Parnell could not. Even at the time of the sale of the Cork property, Simon could still think of himself as similar in circumstance and nobility to his vision of Parnell, a victim of forces outside himself.

Stephen, too, is a figurative stand-in for Parnell. This identification occurs by implication, for during chapter 1 Stephen had experienced his own illness as causing not only his imagined, but Parnell's actual death (P 23–24, 27). In chapter 2 this merger by imagery of father/son/Parnell suggests as one of its meanings the fusion of father and son, perhaps a sign of alcoholism's boundary invasion experienced by some children of alcoholic parents.

The Christmas dinner ends with Simon's sobbing (*P* 39). Some North American psychologists have documented that alcoholic behavior in families escalates during certain social rituals, notably at Christmas (S. Brown, *Adult* 21, 54–55). Peter Steinglass and his co-authors have suggested that the way alcohol is or is not allowed to influence relationships and behavior during many contemporary North Americans' Christmas holidays with the family is an important indicator of the extent of the incorporation of the alcoholic's drinking into the life of the family (131–33).

Although late-nineteenth-century Dublin differs from urban life in twentieth-century North America, it appears true that Christmas is a significant holiday for the Dedalus family and their guests. Furthermore Christmas had been a time of excess in European drinking customs for centuries (Stivers 17; Bales 166), a pattern that continued in somewhat modified form as part of European urban life in the nineteenth century (B. Harrison 40, 43–45).

Hence Mr. Casey's and Simon Dedalus's drinking whiskey before the Christmas dinner is culturally normative. Simon Dedalus's anticlericalism is exacerbated by the Christian holiday, increasing his rage against the priests' treatment of Parnell. What is noteworthy is that Simon Dedalus's mounting rage and grief over Parnell and his inability to control his feelings occur at Christmas. His ugly reprisals against Aunt Dante would never be considered gentlemanly (Toolan 296–97). Such behaviors are part of patterns of loss of control at other times in the text when he is shown to be drinking. Returning to the Christmas dinner after having read the later book chapters, and recognizing that this first scene occurs at Christmas, readers may then speculate about Simon's drinking as a contributing factor to the increasingly disrupted family meals in the Dedalus family.

Before receiving his teary eulogy at the Christmas dinner, Parnell dies many deaths in this novel. One occurs while Stephen is in the infirmary in Clongowes Wood School (*P* 27), a death Stephen remembers when he is in Cork. There, reciting his own history to himself in the acutely traumatic moment of the fetus narrative, Stephen recalls "[b]ut he had not died then. Parnell had died." (*P* 93). At that moment, Stephen realizes that the little boy he had been had disappeared, "fad[ed] out . . . lost and forgotten" *(P* 93). This little boy had been emotionally abandoned by his parents, themselves unable to control the events obliquely reported in chapter 2. The interconnection of Stephen's memory of Parnell's death with his dissociative experience when in Cork reinscribes Parnell as a sign for the father's drinking and the price the son pays for that drinking. The narrative iteration of Parnell's death also symbolizes Stephen's sense of being emotionally deadened, which I have discussed earlier.

CORK EPISODES

The narrative of Stephen's and Simon's Cork experiences reveals, while at the same time obscuring, Simon Dedalus's alcoholic drinking.

Twenty-six pages of text in the Anderson edition of the novel occur in chapter 2 before the trip to Cork. Those twenty-six pages encompass the passage of narrative time during which Simon Dedalus's troubles affect his life and that of his family. However, only on the journey to Cork and in Cork does the narrative overtly implicate alcohol as a factor in those troubles. The narrative does this in a series of brilliant maneuvers that "censor" (Genette 53) the sale of the father's patrimony by superimposing upon its narrated absence the father's continuous drinking.

Significantly the narrative does not ascribe to Stephen the making of a connection between alcohol and his father's incoherent stories of "enemies" (*P* 65), or his father's loud talking to Uncle Charles before dinner (*P* 66). But the second paragraph reveals Simon Dedalus nervously drinking from a small, portable liquor container as they travel by rail to Cork (*P* 86–87). Coldly watching his father drink during this trip, Stephen listens to his father's self-pitying reminiscences of Simon's young manhood, "a tale broken by sighs or draughts from his pocketflask whenever the image of some dead friend appeared in it or whenever the evoker remembered suddenly the purpose of his actual visit." (*P* 87). Simon's sentimental speeches cannot, however, obscure Stephen's knowledge "that his father's property was going to be sold by auction and in the manner of his own dispossession he felt the world give the lie rudely to his phantasy." (*P* 87).

By being affectless Stephen can better resist his father's manipulation. He will allow himself to feel no "sympathy" or "pity" (*P* 87), a very different response to his earlier interest in his father and Uncle Charles's tales (*P* 62). Now these stories are revealed by circumstance as fabrications. Stephen understands that his father has lost his inheritance to such an extent that he has no control over the disposition of funds; the auction will net profits for others. The mingling of unclear pronoun references in the last line of the passage points to a deliberate blurring of boundaries between father and son.

As his father passes out, Stephen experiences a frantic anxiety, the first tinge of feelings that mount into his later annihilation panic. Stephen's survival skills enable him to try to conquer this terror by "a trail of foolish words" that is first a prayer and then becomes patterned phrases to fit what Stephen hears in a specific meter, as "the insistent rhythm of the train . . . [t]his furious music allayed his dread . . ." (*P* 87). Stephen's use of poetic meter as a means of escape from the pain of unbearable knowledge has one of its origins in this scene.

Once in Cork, Stephen shifts between fusion with his father to intolerance of him. In their hotel room the morning after their night train ride, father and son experience a moment of strange intimacy. Significantly this suspension of ordinary relations occurs while Simon examines himself in the mirror (*P* 88).

This picture of a father focused on surface appearance rather than the reality of financial disaster and its possible causes is hardly a sympathetic one. It suggests through narrative retrospection (Genette 53) Stephen staring at himself in his mother's mirror after finishing his poem about E. C. and their tram ride (*P* 70–71). Stephen's mirror-gazing as part of the poetic process marks what Genette calls an "*explicit* ellipsis" (106; emphasis in original), for Stephen's first poem, one about Parnell that Stephen had begun the day after the Christmas dinner, is never completed and is never presented in the narrative (Gabler, "Christmas" 32). Simon's stance before the mirror when in Cork also recalls that just before the start of the Christmas dinner party, Simon studied his dress and appearance "in the pierglass above the mantlepiece . . ." (*P* 27). Through the repetition of specific words, phrases, and images, the narrative thus suggests a connection between the argument during the Christmas dinner, Stephen's first and second poems, and Simon's troubles.

Simon leads his son to the campus of the medical college that he had once attended in Cork. Stephen feels only agitated "restlessness" (*P* 89). He is ashamed of Simon's mistaking as sincere the porter's feigned interest (*P* 89). Perhaps he was hungover from drinking on the train; perhaps Simon may be displaying the loss of self-respect often characteristic of alcoholism (Bean-Bayog, "Psychopathology" 342 and Bean, "Denial" 67–69; Wallace 26).

At that moment of annoyance with his father, Stephen spies the word *Foetus* carved into the desk (*P* 89; emphasis in original). He is fortunate that his survivor's mind can manufacture some external sign to distance his feelings of contempt and dread about his inheritance.

This wood-carved word becomes first a mirror, then an opening into memory, and then seems to become an intricate wood cut in which is inscribed a story. This resonant word thus takes on a life of its own, a language and story strong enough to obscure both Simon Dedalus and the loss of the family property. From the carved word comes another narrative rather than the sale of the property or the father's reliance on alcohol to get through the experience.

In characterizing narrative occurrences of exactly this type, Genette names the deliberate excision from narrative of important moments as paralipsis, a "[systematic] concealing. . . . Here the narrative does not skip over a moment in time, as in an ellipsis, but it *sidesteps* a given element" (52; emphasis in original). These are events that might be important to a deeper understanding of the character's "affective life," and yet both the narrative and the narrator suppress information about them (Genette 52). Characterizing some paralipses as "implied ellipses," or as narrative moments of "opaque silence," Genette defines these as ellipses "whose very presence is not announced in the text and which the reader can infer only from some chronological lacuna or gap in narrative continuity . . . we will never, even retrospectively, know anything of what [that experience was like]" (Genette 108).

The detail narrated in response to Stephen's shock at the sight of the word *"Foetus"* serves as a paralipsis. This implied ellipsis covers two concurrent but never-written narratives, one of the auction, and the other of his father's activities during the auction. Where is the property that is sold? How much is it worth? Who attends the auction? Who buys the property? The denied disclosure, however, is replaced by suggested causality. For not only is a narrative of the sale "censored"—to use Genette's word (53)—but Simon's use of alcohol is foregrounded in the narrative position where readers might expect the sale to have been.

Thus the deliberate narrative paralipsis may be read as an implied causality, a tale of alcohol told in place of the sale of the property. The narrative's refusal to represent the sale resembles Stephen's disconnecting his father's behaviors from Stephen's annihilating anxieties, his disconnecting the significance of his father's trips to the bar from Simon's financial losses.

At Stephen's sight of the word carved into the desk, Simon Dedalus recedes from Stephen's indirect interior monologue. Stephen visualizes a crowd of male students carving the word (P 89–90) imagining one with a mustache, an image recovering his father (P 27, 88). He is astonished to discover that other young men may have been both aroused and repulsed by the medical vocabulary of procreation (P 90).

Stephen's shame and hatred center not on his father's loss of their money and its possible connection to alcohol, but instead on his own sexual guilt. Armed with the wood-carved word and the images that burst from it, he can now direct rage at himself: "The letters cut in the stained wood of the desk stared upon him . . . making him loathe himself for his own mad and filthy orgies." (P 91). As a boy raised in a patriarchal Catholic family, educated by priests in Catholic schools in turn-of-the-century Ireland, it is not surprising that he does not find confirmation in the fact that other young men think about sex and procreation. Instead, seeing the word carved in the desk seems to make him feel more isolated and ashamed of his masturbation and sexuality (Henke, "Misogynist" 90).

I read this substitution of Stephen for Simon as a symbolic representation similar to the denial process inherent in alcoholism.

Focusing on Stephen's guilty sense of sexuality and on Stephen as the figure in his own story, neither Stephen nor the manifest narrative has to report the sale of the property, nor its causes. They do not have to suggest that Stephen might reasonably feel that his father is the problem or that his father's drinking may have contributed to, if not caused, the financial problems. The narrative mimics Stephen's behavior by focusing on the son not the father. Stephen and the narrative share in the creation of a denial process. Stephen's focus on his "bad self" rather than on his father demonstrates the cognitive "splitting" that is often a result of acute and chronic trauma, discussed earlier. What I call the fetus narrative extends through the text until the moment father and son enter the bar (P 90–93).

As he issues advice that would be comical if the circumstances were not tragic (P 91), Simon rationalizes his current behaviors. The European use by the parent of the child was changing by the century's end, leading to sons' resentment of fatherly exploitation (Epstein, "Joyce" 28–29). Contemporary clinicians point to the exploitation of the child by the alcoholic parent as one of the most difficult of behaviors for the child to deal with. It indicates a reversal of roles often seen between eldest children and alcoholic parents (S. Brown, *Adult* 140, 148–51; Davis 113; O'Gorman 84).

His father rambles on about his own father until "Stephen heard his father's voice break into a laugh which was almost a sob." (P 92). Simon's self-pity recalls for readers and possibly for Stephen that Simon's public drinking on the train to Cork had accompanied his sobs, suggesting that drinking may have exacerbated if not caused his feelings.

Understandably, the embarrassment, rage, and shame produced by his father's cries are difficult for the son to accept. Responses fail him. He suffers an acute traumatic moment that encapsulates within it images of the chronic trauma with which he has lived. The narrative constricts itself as does Stephen's mind. His usually ready wit fails him. He can no longer function cognitively. He experiences an annihilating anxiety attack. His senses become overloaded. He almost blacks out. However, Stephen does not think of Simon as the problem, but of himself as the culprit, guilty of masturbation (P 92–93).

This moment of Stephen's imagined death represents an "acute" trauma. Traumatic experiences follow specific patterns, as I noted earlier (van der Kolk 3–4; Rieker and Carmen 362–63). What Stephen experiences as the crescendo of the fetus narrative appears to fit this pattern.

This traumatic moment is the culmination, not just of the walk, but of the narrative of chapter 2. It is the moment when Stephen Dedalus feels himself almost die rather than consciously face the meaning of why he and his father are in Cork. It summarizes the increasing constriction of Stephen's emotional life in response to Simon's worsening financial and social situation, either as part of or as caused by his problem with alcohol. Stephen's anxiety attack suggests alcohol's part in the immediate moment. When he becomes unable to block out the reality of what is happening by shaming himself, Stephen cannot think. Words lose meaning. The boy feels disconnected from people, seasons, emotions. He ceases to exist and has to rebirth his fetal self through language. His simple declarative sentences reestablish his connection to his father and their place on the physical earth (P 92–93).

His masturbation and its concomitant fantasies, however, have not killed him as he reminds himself; though Parnell was dead; he was alive (P 93). Stephen's shame over masturbation, convincing in context of a male adolescence in the Dublin of that day, is additionally a device of substitution, a brilliant if unconscious narrative denial mechanism. Stephen's difficult puberty coincides with the elided fact of this father's troubles and the relation these may have to drinking. It is of this series of troubles that the little Stephen of Clongowes Wood School has symbolically died. His childhood has died. He attends Belvedere Day School as a charity boy. He becomes a walled-off observer. Stephen redirects adolescent sexuality into the service of escape from the pain of his father's alcoholism and its consequences.

The narrative paralipsis has succeeded. Because of the shifting between past and present, father and son, memory and present moment (P 92–93), focus has been displaced from the loss of the property and Simon Dedalus and shifted to his anxious son. By the time when what Stephen might call "the real world" (P 65) intrudes, the sale of the property is over.

Another story is told in place of the excised story of the sale of the property, a story of drinking. The sentence immediately following Stephen's story of the death and remembrance of the little Stephen in the Cork sequence begins, "[o]n the evening of the day on which the property was sold Stephen followed his father meekly about the city from bar to bar." (*P* 93). The next paragraph uses time unclearly: "They had set out early in the morning . . ." (*P* 93). Which drinking episode took place when? When do the scenes with Johnny Cashman occur—the day of the sale of the property, or the day after? Are there two days of hard drinking, or one?

The narrative replaces the sale by foregrounding the drinking. Thus the covert authorial narrative presence gets to suggest causality without seeming to do so, denying a disclosure, disclosing denial, exhibiting what Norris might call a "stifled 'back answer.'" The narrative's use of time suggests a slight similarity to the amnesia of alcoholic drinking, where the drinker returns to consciousness, unsure how much time has passed, unaware of what she or he has done during the lost time (Levin, *Introduction* 52).

Knowledge of the possible connection of the Dedalus family's troubles to alcohol bursts into the narrative at the same time it may burst into the consciousness of the main character. That is, the narrative suppresses but emphasizes a connection that the character cannot name, thus reenacting a denied denial. This eruption into narrative consciousness is itself an objective correlative of an acute traumatic event.

The consequences of his father's drinking are inescapable, no matter how much the narrative imitates an inadvertent swerve from traumatic consciousness. Stephen Dedalus will have no patrimony, no position, no future of the sort he had been lead to expect he would have. Stephen's annihilation panic deflects this information. Nor can he focus on his father as its cause.

What I have called the fetus narrative in chapter 2 might thus serve as a fictionalized replica of two kinds of trauma, an acute trauma grounded in a life of chronic trauma in the shadow of a father's alcoholism. When this occurs, the child witnessing the alcohol problem "splits" himself or herself, blaming him or herself, while denying parental behavior and its consequences.

THE BAR NARRATIVE IN CORK

The fetus narrative occurs during the narrative time in which Simon walks with Stephen to a bar in Cork. Their trek had started soon after breakfast in a coffee shop "where Mr. Dedalus's cup had rattled noisily against its saucer, and Stephen had tried to cover that shameful sign of his father's drinkingbout of the night before by moving his chair and coughing. One humiliation had succeeded another . . ." (P 93). It is difficult for a reader knowledgeable about the physical facts about alcoholism to believe that the effects of Simon's drinking have suddenly appeared as a problem. The morning shakes come late rather than early in alcohol addiction; they do not show up simply after one or two nights of excess (Levin, *Treatment* 25). Further, Stephen appears practiced in covering up for his father's hangover symptoms.

Similarly, Simon's hostility, which is passed off as camaradely joviality, does not seem the simple result of one or two night's overindulgence in situational drinking. Stephen's response to his father's indirect handling of Simon's own pain and his unbidden, seemingly unconscious substitution of himself for his father as the butt of the son's rage, indicates at the least a disturbed family dynamic. Mr. Dedalus's erratic and frequent mood swings in the bar, additionally, are not different in kind, just in intensity, from behaviors glimpsed earlier in chapters 1 and 2. But it is in the bar that readers can focus on the deterioration of the relationship between father and son.

Simon Dedalus displays little self-respect. He is overly familiar with the waitresses (P 93). Like his son, he focuses his attentions on Stephen. He exposes Stephen (and hence indirectly himself) to the ridicule of the men in the bar who tease the boy about his accent, ask him to compare the rivers of Dublin and Cork, to translate passages from the Latin, and to compare girls in Cork to those in Dublin (P 94). Although such joking may seem loving in contexts of socialization practices in Dublin pub culture, read from a twentieth-century clinical perspective that recognizes the alcoholic parent's use of the child as the focus of blame, such joking takes on a more problematic implication (Stivers 82–90, 97–100; Davis 113–14; O'Gorman 84).

Johnny Cashman and the nameless observers at the bar reveal more than the rivalry Mr. Dedalus feels for his son. The bar cronies make visible Mr. Dedalus's flight from reality; they name his class origin and social position and so underline his decline from those origins to whose symbolism he clings more fiercely with each successive fall down the financial scale. Mr. Dedalus is now a gentleman in fantasy only, a poor man in fact. Cashman remarks casually that he had seen "your grandfather [presumably Mr. Dedalus's father] in his red coat riding out to hounds." (*P* 94). Johnny also knew Mr. Dedalus's grandfather, "John Stephen Dedalus, and a fierce old fireeater he was." (*P* 95). Simon has lost his own patrimony, the property of the men he and Johnny praise. The red coat is gone; Simon is now on a level with the colonized.

Johnny jests that in spite of having known four generations of Dedaluses, he remains a young man still; Mr. Dedalus agrees, requesting another round of drinks, adding, "[t]here's that son of mine there not half my age and I'm a better man than he is any day of the week." (*P* 95). The ironic narration of Simon and Johnny's chat signifies more, in my reading, than that treating others to drinks was an integral aspect of Irish pub culture at this time (Bales 168, 171; Stivers 31, 86–87). Generous Mr. Dedalus stands the boys another round of drinks at the bar to insist upon his status at the very moment that he is in Cork to sell the property of his fathers.

Interestingly, Stivers's analysis of Dublin pub cultural practices notes that the male role was constructed according to rules guiding male behavior while in the pub, not according to rules of adulthood external to the pub (Stivers 87). Simon's deflecting attention by jest onto his son as less of a man than himself is significant, too, in light of a biopsychosocial analysis. In some North American families where alcohol is the problem, the alcoholic parent tells the children they are the cause of problems, not the parental drinking (S. Brown, *Adult* 162). Mr. Dedalus's jests about Stephen recall the boy's focusing on hatred of himself rather than allowing himself to feel anger at his father during their visit to the medical college.

Stephen may be enacting Simon's unconscious self-hatred. Twentieth-century North American clinicians who treat alcoholic patients attest to the nagging guilt some clients feel, even in the midst of their denial (Bean-Bayog, "Psychopathology 340; Bean, "Denial" 67–69; Wallace 26). Certainly such guilt and shame influenced Michael Henchard's behavior after he sold his wife when drunk, after he told Farfrae about the sale and his return to menial labor having lost ownership of his business. That Simon has become so ill that he mocks rather than respects his favorite child is a poignant testimony to the unwilled nature of the biopsychosocial sickness of alcoholism. A purely social construction of Simon's behavior, however, would read it as helping his son become socialized as a male member of Dublin pub culture rituals of manhood.

One of the bar drinkers responds to Simon's teasing Stephen, saying that Simon should yield his paternal place to his own son. Now in his cups, poor Mr. Dedalus refuses by boasting that he can beat Stephen at song, at sport, at fox hunting, or at cross country racing, as if the broken man regularly engaged in these pursuits, cultural emblems of class status (*P* 95). In the tragicomedy of these guzzling old geezers, the reader sees displayed in public what Stephen had hoped to hide from his fellow students and masters, one of the possible causes of his "squalid way of life." (*P* 78).

Further irony results when Simon Dedalus and Johnny Cashman congratulate themselves on how their behavior has affected no one. Simon expresses gratitude to his creator "that we lived so long and did so little harm." Not to be outdone, his crony Cashman adds, "b]ut did so much good, Simon . . ." (*P* 95). This alcohol-inspired self-regard would be humorous if the reader is not emotionally invested in the boy who is watching it.

The men in the bar repeatedly shift their sympathy to and away from Simon. Because of the "disinhibiting effects" of alcohol in cultural context (which I discussed in chapter 1), readers might expect that aggressive behavior would be displayed in bar scenes. This scene recalls Michael Henchard in the Furmity tent, and the taunts of the other men (but not the women) that eventually embolden him to sell his wife. The hostile joking in the Cork bar recalls the sometimes vicious undercurrents of hostility of contemporary male bonding in North American bars (McClleland, et al. 142–61).

Richard Stivers in his study of pub culture in Ireland has discovered that aggressive male jockeying for position is a part of how younger men were socialized for adulthood in "bachelor groups" within the pub, overtly in opposition to familial roles that are remapped onto the male alternate "family" in the pub. In such settings, older men set the pattern for the younger men to emulate (76–80). This suggestion is corroborated by Robert F. Bales (171).

Stephen detached emotionally by floating above the bar scene (P 95–96), feeling "sundered" (P 95) from the men. The appearance of the word "sundered" reminds the reader of the time when "[t]he gang [which Stephen and Aubrey Mills led] fell asunder . . ." (P 64), the emotional fragmentation of Stephen's world at the move from Blackrock (P 60–68). It is a narrative signal that this bar scene in Cork, a paralipsis covering the representation of the sale of the Cork property, is tied inextricably back through chapter 2 to the earlier loss of status and financial security.

With little affect, Stephen observes the older men who appear to him like children in their drunkenness. His intellectual prowess and curiosity that could probe anything other than what was immediately before him now enables him to become both the moon (female) in a fragment of Shelley's poetry that he recalls, and the poet as well (P 95–96). Shelley—that rebellious upper class British heir to his father's estate who abandoned position to become an atheist and revolutionary freethinker and womanizer—is a helpful role model for this proud boy who defensively believes himself superior, but whose father's fall will destroy his inheritance (Spoo 59–63). Stephen's soothing himself by remembering lines of the poet Shelley, too, may recall another Romantic poet, Byron (W. Carpenter; Kershner, *Bakhtin* 190, 211). Passionately standing up for Byron was one of the last times the narrative shows Stephen experiencing direct anger. In defending Byron, Stephen refused to acknowledge shame about his father and family (P 78–82).

R. B. Kershner interprets Stephen's imperturbability as a pose he learned from *The Count of Monte Christo,* but does not read this pose as a response to parental alcoholism (*Bakhtin* 203–206). Some twentieth-century clinicians note that those from alcoholic families experience difficulty in directing anger at the alcoholic (S. Brown, *Adult* 121–25; Whitfield 67). Deflection of anger is one of the affective responses to acute or chronic trauma, as I discussed earlier. I connect Stephen's suppressed anger to his need to survive daily life in an alcoholic family.

Though childish in their beery camaraderie, the men Stephen observes do seem to him to bond in a community of male peers. Male and female lives were lived in entirely different ways in Dublin during Stephen's youth, where much male bonding went on in barrooms. In contrast, Stephen had not experienced such comradeship (*P* 95–96). Never once is Stephen shown bringing peers home with him. This behavior, a precaution followed by some contemporary American children of alcoholic parents (Kinney and Leaton 178; B. Robinson 33), is shown, although the causes are elided. Stephen will never know such companionship now. He is incapable of trusting other boys or mingling with them as his father can still so easily do with his cronies in the bar. It is not just that Stephen is smarter than his father or his peers. Like the moon in Shelley's poem he is coldly watchful. He must be in order to survive.

Stephen's withdrawal to observe the men from a distance above them is a metaphor for a dissociative state, less severe but of the same traumatic origin as Stephen's sense of his own death during the fetus narrative. Traumatic, the onslaught of overwhelming experience in Cork leads to Stephen's blockage of feeling, the somatization of his panic, and emotional sense that he has died. Indeed, it is true that after his visit to Cork, Stephen's "childhood was dead or lost . . ." (*P* 96).

Prize Money for the Family's Use

As I have noted, the juxtaposition of events or insights without authorial intervention or guidance is a frequent modernist narrative method. The linearity of the reading process allows readers to draw a causal connection between events that are narrated in a sequence. Arising from the reading process, this inadvertent coupling of that which may not at first appear to be connected, is a powerful tool of suggestion without direct authorial intervention. Such implied causality links the fetus narrative and the bar scenes in Cork to those events that immediately follow the sale of the Cork property.

Immediately after the Cork sequence, Stephen assumes financial responsibility for his family. He supports them for a short and chaotic time on the 33 pounds he received for his excellent work at Belvedere preparatory school.

The fact that a young boy can be allowed to use money to care for his family that might have been put aside for his own later use indicates that though Simon Dedalus may claim to be a gentleman, he acts now more like a poor man who sensibly wants to obtain financial help wherever he can. That this is at the expense of his favorite son is not significantly different from other behaviors Simon has engaged in in this chapter. His use of Stephen's money is similar to his taking Stephen to witness the events in Cork, and then having the boy accompany him to the barroom. It is similar to his making a confidant of the boy, and urging on him myths and stories about nameless opponents who caused the older man's downfall (P 65–66). To a late-twentieth-century middle-class American reader such parental behavior may seem exploitative, but the use of the child by the parent, especially the poorer parent, was a well-established fact of family life in nineteenth-century Europe. However, Edward Epstein has noted that a new view of this kind of parental exploitation of children was becoming culturally available at this time, and suggests that Samuel Butler was a possible source for Joyce's ability to fictionalize the war between the generations in Portrait (Epstein, Ordeal 2–3).

Stephen knew that he should probably buy his mother an overcoat, but instead he spends his money frivolously and quickly (P 97–98). In doing so, Stephen is following his father's example, for readers have seen this improvidence in Simon's buying drinks for his bar cronies while in Cork to auction his property.

As I have noted when discussing Stephen's responses during the fetus narrative, a not infrequent reaction to having an alcoholic parent is a series of reactions that prevents the child from blaming the parent. Some children blame themselves, and try through various means to accept responsibility for the parent's drinking (DiCiccio 50; Davis 114; S. Brown, Adult 131, 133–34, 162, 178–79; B. Robinson 41). A part of this process is the reliance of the alcoholic parent on the child as a caretaker, either physically, financially, or emotionally. Partly this is the result of some alcoholic parents' inability to provide financial support or caretaking due to the crippling of faculties and earning capacity that result from alcoholism. Such lapses are frequently noted by clinicians (see, for example, Davis 113; O'Gorman 84; S. Brown, *Adult* 140, 148, 179), as a sometimes subtle, sometimes glaring consequence of alcoholic parents' child-rearing behaviors. Reversals of the roles of parent and child are frequent in many twentieth-century North American alcoholic families (DiCiccio 50; Davis 114; S. Brown, *Adult* 131, 133–34, 162, 178–79). Perhaps fear of such a reversal motivates Simon's boozy boasts of his superiority to his son during the bar scene in Cork.

Stephen's desire to please his all too-willing parents and his childish improvidence are tragic however these behaviors are explained. Looked at in context of some frequent contemporary responses to parental alcoholism, the behaviors illuminate further the deforming of his potential and character that the narrative suggests Stephen's father's troubles and their relation to alcohol cause in the son's life.

Assuming the parental role, Stephen attempts to use his prize money to impose order on the family's chaotic life. Stephen first reorganized his room. Then he set aside a fund from which he doled out carefully recorded loans, assuming briefly the role of provider that his father no longer fulfilled. Yet Stephen felt that his attempts to create order were misguided (*P* 98).

Stephanie Brown and other North American psychologists note that the rigid imposition of order, and the search for consistent boundaries between the self and the trauma-producing world is a frequent response to a parent's alcoholic drinking (See, for example, S. Brown, *Adult* 115–31). However, Stephen faults himself for trying to help his family, imputing his motives to his desperate need to build walls against the tumultuous currents of his lust (*P* 98). His overly critical assessment of his behavior recalls his harsh self-criticism displayed during the fetus narrative. Both responses reveal the same shift of focus from his father's behavior to self-blame.

The belief that one is not really a member of one's family is a staple of the myth of the birth of the hero. That myth enables

Stephen to see himself as both Dedalus and the son of Daedalus, "the great artificer" (*P* 170), not pub drinking Simon Dedalus. The fantasy that one's parents are not really one's parents comforts some twentieth-century children in alcoholic families (S. Brown, *Adult* 161–62).[18] Understandably, Stephen wishes to disown his father and family: he experienced them as of a different lineage, related to him "rather in the mystical kinship of fosterage, fosterchild and foster-brother." (*P* 98).

Chapter 2 culminates in Stephen's loss of virginity, partially motivated by Simon's drinking and its consequences.

Stephen does not seem to experience the pain and rage of his family's downward mobility directly, narrowing his shamed focus to his sexual needs. Stephen's visit to the prostitute allows Stephen to enact "badness," to identify himself as deviant instead of recognizing that Simon Dedalus is an increasingly incapable father. Some North American twentieth-century psychologists note that sexual acting-out may be a component of the conduct disorders of some sons in families where alcohol is a problem (O'Gorman 83, 86; Windle 131–35).

Partly in response to his family's troubles, he had begun to run to the red-light district of Dublin for relief (*P* 86). When his father's drinking or its consequences become hardest to deny, Stephen "bad selfs" himself, thus screening out his father's troubles and their possible relation to drinking. Hence Stephen's visit to the prostitute mimics while deflecting several of Simon's alcoholic behaviors. Stephen can flee into sex as Simon can flee to the pub. Focused on his guilty sexuality, Stephen can avoid the fact that alcohol is implicated in the sale of the Cork property.

Stephen's motives and needs are complex and interwoven. First is the sexual relief Stephen experiences. The prostitute is young, beautiful, willing, and experienced (*P* 101). On a less positive note, however, sinking into the beautiful young prostitute's arms enables Stephen to reexperience a complex recapitulation of the annihilation of aspects of himself first apparent in the Cork episode.

Stephen's fantasy is that in making love to the prostitute, he would become "strong," confident, and courageous. However she has to make love to him while he remains passive (*P* 101).

This is not an exact replication of that loss of self Stephen experienced in Cork at the sight of the provocative word carved in the desk. But there are interesting resonances. As part of his dissociative removal from the scene during the fetus narrative, Stephen experienced sensory overload in Cork that blocked out the weather, the light, the meaning of language, and his sense of connection to the outer world (*P* 92–93). With the prostitute, too, he loses consciousness of self, aware only of his body's response to her kiss. Language becomes sexual desire and movement. To recall himself to himself in Cork, Stephen had told himself the story of his life. With the prostitute, her "softly parting lips . . ." become "the vehicle" whereby the language of desire is written on his brain in "a vague speech." The passage ends with the submergence of what the narrative represents as Stephen's consciousness into sex (*P* 101).

Numerous critics have suggested that the rendering of Stephen's consciousness through the parodic language of the fin-de-siècle poetic excesses is deliberate.[19] The fact that Joyce did not choose to use a more original language for Stephen's sexual experience with the prostitute may indicate Stephen's inability to comprehend his experience clearly. By explicating Stephen's experience through cultural clichés, the narrative implies that the experience of sexual intercourse with the prostitute substitutes for Stephen's voice. Rereading the anxiety attack in Cork through the depiction of the loss of Stephen's virginity, the reader sees another similarity between the experiences: sensory overload replaces consciousness.

The disclosed denial of the denial narrative of chapter 2 is extensive and complex. Simon Dedalus's problem with money is foregrounded; the probable relation of the money problem to his alcoholism is artfully submerged but not eliminated. The imposition of Stephen's adolescent crisis about sexuality on top of the father's problems with alcohol also serves as an effective narrative denial mechanism. The extensive passages of Stephen's dissociative experiences, too, take the focus off of Simon's behaviors in order to refocus attention on Stephen's pain, guilt, remorse, and fear, all those aspects of the emotional life of the alcoholic—here experienced by the child of an alcoholic—which I have examined in chapter 1. *Portrait*'s narrative's bursts through the denial by inserting a trip to the bar over the paralipsis of the sale of the property,[20] and is an effective device to disclose these denial processes when the passages in Cork are read through the lens of a biopsychosocial view of alcoholism.

STEPHEN THE ARTIST

Methodologies of Reading

Just as Stephen's development of an artistic sensibility seems to have some relation to parental alcoholism, so his writing process appears to be textually connected to the consequences of Simon Dedalus's drinking.

Within *Portrait* and *Ulysses,* Stephen Dedalus fails to become a successful literary artist. The villanelle Stephen writes at the end of *Portrait* has embarrassed generations of Joyce critics. Because few scholars view Stephen Dedalus's literary products as art, that his poetry is a compensatory activity has gained critical assent, if only by default. I agree with Charles Rossman's assessments that the pain Stephen Dedalus feels causes him to adopt the pose of an artist, to transform the dross of his impoverished Dublin life to the gold of immortal artifacts, a view substantiated by the more recent work of Susan Stanford Friedman ("Self") and Alberto Moreiras.

That his artistic theorizing and writing process are compensatory is further suggested by those critics who use the process of Stephen's creation of the female figure as a gage to measure his maturation. The "masturbation argument" by Doris T. Wright, Bernard Benstock, and Charles Rossman seeks to demonstrate that Stephen moves beyond immobilizing guilt about his body and sexuality in writing the villanelle.

I believe that the text embeds Stephen Dedalus's writing process and his pose as an artist firmly within his reactions to his father's alcoholism. The successful outcome of Stephen Dedalus's artistic activities may be first, to survive life in his father's house and then to leave Dublin and to separate from his family, not his villanelle or the momentary balance he achieves in writing it between the heretofore immobilizing divisions he experiences between body/self, whore/Madonna, guilt/acceptance of sexuality.

My approach is indirectly authorized by Margot Norris's arguments, which establish James Joyce's complex repudiation of the politics of Stephen Dedalus's aesthetic theories, although Norris's interpretation makes no reference to alcoholism. However, in *Joyce's Web* Margot Norris suggests that James Joyce's embedding of Stephen Dedalus's writing processes and product in squalor is a deliberately crafted narrative code (17–24, 54). Rereading Stephen Dedalus as a modernist artist through the postmodernism of Shem, the Penman, in *Finnegans Wake*, Norris suggests that James Joyce critiqued a modernism that suppressed the complex oppressions of working-class Dublin life in an art that transcended and obliterated these by beauty (*Web* 184–91).

Recuperating the squalor underpinning *Portrait*, Norris has found a way to reconnect Joyce's insistence on hardship and dirt with his ironic re-creations of Stephen's fin-de-siècle literary tropes and images (*Web* 82–85). My reading connects Simon's drinking to the chaotic tumult and miseries of life in the Dedalus household. I see Stephen's writing process as grounded in his father's alcoholism.

I have previously demonstrated that the narrative dissociates Simon Dedalus's failures from his drinking while offering a counternarrative that ties these together. Now I will argue that although the narrative appears to deny that Stephen's artistic aspirations and his poetry are inextricably tied to Simon Dedalus's alcoholism, the narrative nevertheless consistently grounds Stephen's writing process and products in the context of Simon's drinking. The evidence for the relationship between Simon's drinking and Stephen's aspirations and writing products is thus not apparent at first reading.

My argument examines several recurring narrative components. I will analyze a pattern of narrative reversals. Doing so I will demonstrate that the dissociation of Stephen's annihilation panic in Cork turns into Stephen's creative use of dissociation as he imagines Daedalus's/Icarus's flight above the Strand (P 169–70; Anderson 519 n 169.01–169.05). I will examine Stephen's movement from compensatory wordplay to a coherent arrangement of words. I will suggest connections between patterns of suppressed materials such as the poem about Parnell, the first poem to E. C., and the sale of the Cork properties. These patterns arise from narrative behaviors that consistently seek to deny yet reveal Simon's alcoholism.[21]

SIMON DEDALUS THE DRINKER
AND STEPHEN DEDALUS THE ARTIST

Stephen Dedalus's art begins in suffering. His suffering leads him to dissociate himself from what is happening to him by creative uses of fantasy, an activity at first not always under his control.

To manage his alienation while attending Clongowes Wood School, Stephen depends on escape via language, a strategy that he adopts to survive his worsening circumstances when he cannot return to Clongowes, but must live at home and attend Belvedere. Stephen uses stories, analogical thinking, mnemonic devices, prewriting, chanting, obsessional devotion to words for sound and music rather than connotative material (P 10–11). Through absorption in and by language, Stephen simultaneously makes sense of and escapes his physical and emotional surroundings.

By the time of chapter 2, Stephen's production of the fetus narrative is a positive use of fantasy, a spontaneous result of the necessary survival skill of dissociation. The fetus narrative is superimposed on a paralipsis that suppresses crucial information. It obscures both the sale of the Cork property and the connection of that sale to Simon's alcoholism, a connection suggested by the superimposition of the bar scenes over the "censored" (Genette 53) property sale. Because dissociation is inseparable from Stephen Dedalus's use of fantasy, it is inextricably implicated in his developing abilities as a writer. Thus Stephen Dedalus's creative process is embedded by narrative fiat in the complex implications of the fetus narrative.

Artistry as Compensation
in the Alcoholic Home

It is a cliché of twentieth-century psychoanalytic thinking that childhood trauma is a fertile ground for the production of artists (A.
Miller). Charles Rossman suggests that Stephen Dedalus's art is
compensatory when he argues that "many of Stephen's . . . problems
find resolution or perpetuation in aesthetic experience" ("Spiritual"
102). I agree with Rossman's view of the causes of Stephen's art, and
with Rossman's connecting Stephen's increasingly inaccessible pain
to Stephen's rich fantasy life.

However, although the methods of narrativity in *Portrait* may
indicate the origins of Stephen's art, these deliberately do not indicate its worth. The polyvocatilty of Stephen's indirect interior
monologues ironically deflates Stephen's poetic posing and products. The result of such complex narrative manipulations is that,
since the publication of *Portrait,* there has been little critical agreement on the attitude of the polyvocal narrative voice(s) toward
Stephen's poems.

Are these to be valued as serious works of art, as masturbatory
fantasies, as an earnest adolescent boy's imitations of fin-de-siècle
poems (Scholes and Kain 250–65; Scholes, "Poet"; Centola; Tindall
99)? From whom is the language emanating? What is the narratorial voice's judgment of the content (J. H. Miller, "Narrative" 3–4;
Norris, *Web,* 54–55; Dettmar 119–21)? The answers remain unde-
cidable because readers are implicated in the construction of the
narrative, and because the narrative is deliberately crafted to render
the answer ambiguous (Rimmon-Kenan 41, 68–69, 72–74, 83–85;
Genette 198–207).

I read Stephen's poetic creations as inseparable from his inherited attitudes toward women and also as inextricably connected to
the survival skills of children of alcoholics such as dissociation,
"splitting," and projection, some of whose representations in the
text I have already interpreted. I see a connection between the origin of Stephen's art in his complex relation to his Catholic sense of
sin, which helps to obscure his feelings about his father's difficulties
and their relation to alcoholism.

Parnell

Hence I argue that representations of Stephen's artistic process are textually interwoven with Simon Dedalus's problem with alcohol.

Stephen's earliest attempts to write poetry occur before the trip to Cork in chapter 2. Just as the narrative suppresses the sale of the property in Cork, it suppresses Stephen's first two poems (Gabler, "Christmas" 32). One poem is excised from the text and the other is presented in a prose summary. The fact of narrative suppression and substitution is significant. The reader may be led to draw connections between the excised parts of the text and that which is written over the excised passages.

The narrative reveals Stephen's writing process but not his poetry. As Stephen sits down to write his poem to E. C., he remembers his earlier attempt to write a poem about Parnell, but the text of that work is excised. As Gabler has suggested, the elided poem about E. C. may in fact be "a substitute for the writing of the poem about Parnell . . ." ("Christmas" 32).

Critics have established the narrative and political resonance of the figure of Parnell around whom are constellated complex images. The figure of Parnell suggests death, suffering, betrayal, and manhood, as I noted earlier. Because Simon's behavior about Parnell at the Christmas dinner party terrifies Stephen, and because Simon's excesses are connected by the image of the unstoppered whiskey container (*P* 28), that is, to his drinking and its effects on him, when the figure of Parnell recurs in instances of "incremental repetition" (Kershner, *Bakhtin* 157), alcoholism is suggested. The fact that Stephen could not write his first poem about Parnell indicates to me that he was too young to master the complex of terrifying experiences he associates with Parnell.[22]

Generations of Joyce critics have drawn the parallel between Simon's storytelling on the first page of the text and Stephen's developing artistry. Stephen's writing is connected to his father, yes, but additionally to Simon's drinking at the Christmas dinner.

Gabler's insight and my own reading of the embedding of Parnell in Simon's alcoholism suggests to me that there exists a causal connection between the narrative excision of the sale of the property and the suppressed first poem about Parnell: "When he had written this title and drawn an ornamental line underneath he fell into a daydream and began to draw diagrams on the cover of the book. He saw himself sitting at his table in Bray the morning [they have moved from Bray to Blackrock] after the discussion at the Christmas dinnertable, trying to write a poem about Parnell on the back of one of his father's second moiety notices. But his brain had then refused to grapple with the theme . . ." (P 70).

In writing a poem about Parnell, Stephen may have tried to make sense of several reactions he had during the Christmas dinner, among them, terror (P 39) and identification with his father and Parnell. He is not represented as mastering the experience by writing about it. Instead Stephen flees it by "daydreaming," suggesting that flight into fantasy is integral to his writing processes. Perhaps another reason he cannot finish the poem is that due to the family's strained finances he uses as his writing paper "one of the second moiety notices" of his father. Chester Anderson suggests that this moiety notice is not a bill sent by Simon, but a bill to him, a second notice at that (504 n 70.21).[23] Stephen uses proof of his father's financial failure as the material for writing, thus connecting the act of writing to his father's eviction, later alluded to in Simon's auctioning the patrimony in Cork. By its process of superimposing the bar narrative over the sale of the property, the narrative has tied that eviction and the sale of the patrimony to the same cause, Simon's drinking. Parnell is connected to the father's drinking behavior at the Christmas dinner, and to Stephen's panic during the fetus narrative, and thus, ever after, is embedded in the occasion of writing.

Though fearing to fail like the first time, Stephen manages his discomfort sufficiently to draft his poem about E. C. (P 70–1). The narrative foregrounds Stephen's fitful, difficult process of creation. It insists that the reader's knowledge about the elided poem concerning Parnell must precede any representation of the process of writing the poem about E. C.

The prose summary of Stephen's first poem about E. C. tells a story that did not occur. Because all information comes from Stephen, however, there is no objective evidence that what he had experienced as Emma's motivation is what actually happened. He and Emma had taken a tram home, and she had appeared to him to be flirting with him. According to the narrative, she keeps approaching him; he keeps fleeing. He thinks she wants him to kiss her. He withholds his kiss (*P* 69). Through juxtaposition, the narrative suggests that his flight from E. C. is partially located in his increasing loss of affect, a loss that I have suggested grows out of Stephen's inadvertent flight from the problems of his family and father. For Stephen and E. C. had taken the tram home after the children's party in which Stephen had sat, isolated, enjoying his alienation, judging his peers as immature and himself as superior (*P* 68).

The undisclosed poem as summarized in the text has distorted the facts. It had made Stephen appear to be in control, had depicted a woman as needing him, not him as afraid of her. It voiced Stephen's pain and grief, "[s]ome undefined sorrow" (*P* 70), and had located that sorrow in the implied love between the boy and girl. Hence it had named and normalized an unspoken feeling, transforming it into something culturally recognizable The reported imagery of the poem to E. C. is clichéd—thus resembling the hackneyed phrases in which are couched what appear to be Stephen's thoughts on his first visit to the prostitute (*P* 100–101). The lack of pertinent realistic details is in keeping with Edwardian verse of the era. Mood, aura, vague emotions of sorrow and loss were in vogue, and Edwardian verse reflected these (Centola 103; Scholes and Kain 258–63).

Stephen could have written a political poem. For, as Kershner has proved, Stephen had culturally available many stories of sacrificial male heroism in which a great man is forced from his position by female betrayal and suffers nobly as a result (*Bakhtin* 189–215). Because of the existence of such materials, Stephen might have crafted a derivative poem about Parnell as such a betrayed hero, imagining Kitty O'Shea as temptress rather than sustaining lover. But he did not.

The figure of the failed father whose fall is caused by drink is not widely disseminated through cultural stereotypes and respectable images that make such a figure available for poetry. Stephen Dedalus might have known of Hogarth's and Bruegel's drunkards, and possibly of Irish temperance narratives (Stivers 35–49; see also B. Harrison 128–30) but none of these images and stories could be readily translated into poetry.

Stephen's writing method elides the male or alcohol, and blames the female as the cause of pain. Stephen did not have at hand a socially recognizable language whereby he could link his pain to his father's drinking or decline. However, if the female is removed from the narrative's prose summary of Stephen's poem, and the father substituted, one arrives at a poem about a boy whose father is emotionally unavailable, hurtful, and whose motives are mysterious, facts that the text has revealed as part of Stephen's life story.

Thus the earliest representations of Stephen's artistic creation in the narrative are textually interwoven with Simon Dedalus's problem with alcohol. Both poems (the one Stephen wants to write but cannot, and the one he does write) appear to be inextricably connected to the increasing example of Simon's flight from responsibility and his family. Stephen's first completed poem is shown as a story that is the opposite of factual experience, a story in service of adolescent ego gratification, not an achievement of an independent, perfectly crafted artifact, Stephen's later definition of great art (*P* 215). For Stephen at this point in the narrative, the act of creation, of writing about a woman, is to write about himself while using the figure of a woman to do so (Rossman, "Villanelle" 188).

After finishing his poem about E. C., Stephen entered "his mother's bedroom" and stared fixedly at himself reflected "in the mirror" perched above the "dressingtable" (*P* 71). This is proleptic. On the trip to Cork when Stephen and his father are leaving the hotel the morning of the sale of the property, Stephen is again seen looking in the mirror. At that time, he watches his father compose himself for public view (*P* 88). It is also possible that the wood-carved word in the desk of the medical college which becomes a mirror contemplating and revealing Stephen's guilt-inducing masturbatory fantasy life (*P* 92) may be implied here.

But the connection of his first completed poem to the complicated issue of his father's drinking is more heavily remarked in the text even than the repetition of the word *dressingtable* (*P* 71) and actions of male mirror gazing. The pun on the glass/pierglass and its

connection to his father's drinking becomes clearer in chapter 2. On
the first page of the text Simon's monocle is remarked by his son:
"his father looked at him through a glass . . ." (*P* 7). By chapter 2,
the glass of Simon's perception has become foggy, transformed during the trip to Cork into a glass of alcohol.

ESCAPE FROM SIMON DEDALUS:
REVERSALS OF ANNIHILATION PANIC

In chapter 4, Stephen's dissociative abilities enable him to divest
himself of Simon Dedalus as his father. As Stephen identifies with
both Daedalus/Icarus flying over the Strand (*P* 168–69) his fantasy
and his somatization of his fantasy offer a direct reversal of his
deathlike annihilation panic experienced during the fetus narrative.
This dramatic reversal of a trauma is the gateway experience
through which Stephen must pass in order to create his poetry and
his poetic theory.

The creative reversal in which Stephen Dedalus spontaneously
dissociates from himself as Stephen Dedalus and doubles himself,
becoming aspiring, high-flying Icarus—the "hawklike man"—
rejecting his father, while also becoming "the fabulous artificer"
D[a]edaulus, his own father, is a healing, though ambiguous, triumph of Stephen's imagination (*P* 169; Anderson 519 n 169.01–
169.05). To make these connections, Stephen needed years of practice fantasizing and dissociating. Walking on the Strand, Stephen begins to use his methods of escape in the service of healing, not
self-denigration.

I do not believe that Simon is benign, but I agree with Edward
Epstein that Stephen cannot rebel overtly. Stephen's revolt cannot
safely be conscious, as I have argued earlier, for this would threaten
his ideal view of the father and force his son to confront the extent
of parental alcoholism and consequent narcissism.

After he rejects the offer to become a Jesuit, Stephen returns
home, crossing the bridge over the stream of the Tolka, having, so he
thinks, chosen the chaos and emotional disarray of his family home
(*P* 162). Safely his father's son once again, Stephen soon wanders on

the Strand when he hears his boyish colleagues call his name in Greek (*P* 168). They had named him thus before, but "[n]ow . . . his strange name seemed to him a prophecy. . . . he seemed to . . . see a winged form flying above the waves and slowly climbing the air, . . . a symbol of the artist forging anew in his workshop out of the sluggish matter of the earth a new soaring impalpable imperishable being . . ." (*P* 168–69). The name Dedalus thus becomes Daedalus, the name of the Greek artist who had fashioned the wings that allowed him to escape from the labyrinth of the Minotaur (Bulfinch 156–58). In Stephen's vision "the fabulous artificer" (*P* 169) is here imagined as a being who can fashion a new life out of the matter in which Simon is mired. The artistry of D[a]edalus transforms "the faint sour stink of rotted cabbages . . ." (*P* 162) into immortality.

Having imagined for himself a new father while still unable to reject Simon directly, Stephen experiences himself as free. But even imagined autonomy is threatening to Stephen's denial of his father's problems and their relation to drinking. Sensing that he may be both D[a]edalus and Icarus, the son whose hubristic rejection of his father's example causes his death, Stephen experiences many of the physical symptoms of his previous dissociations during annihilation episodes at the Christmas dinner and in Cork, both episodes, as I have argued, tied to Simon's drinking and Simon's resulting lack of impulse control.

Making dissociation serve his creative needs, Stephen becomes able to reconceptualize these physical experiences as freedom, not impending death:

> His heart trembled; his breath came faster and a wild spirit passed over his limbs as though he were soaring sunward. . . . This was the call of life to his soul . . . What were they now . . . the fear he had walked in night and day . . . the shame that had abased him within and without—cerements, the linens of the grave? (*P* 169–70)

Stephen can throw off terror and humiliation, the emotions seeming to underlie the fetus narrative, because he now recognizes that these were shrouds. He can also reject his family who seem to him to embody the dreary material world of emotionally difficult obligations (*P* 169).

The language reverses the language of the Cork annihilation episode, Stephen's moment of symbolic near-death during his panic in Cork. There he had had the same physical responses as in the Icarus experience: panic, shortness of breath, fear, dizziness, a feeling of leaving his body (*P* 92). There the sunlight's "sombre masses" weighed on him physically; here the sunlight is inviting. There he could not interpret reality, his thinking felt sluggish, then stymied (*P* 92). Here he reinvents the reality he sees. There is no "hawklike man" (*P* 169) in the sky, but Stephen experiences the man as being there and then interprets his own vision. In Cork he felt he had "put himself beyond the limits of reality." (*P* 92). Here he has certainly done so, but he feels exultation rather than fear. There he "could respond to no earthly or human appeal . . ." (*P* 92). Here he is called to this vision by the boys' bantering use of his now-magical name. There he was not physically present to the weather; here he can feel the season as he sees the boys bathing and the figure flying. There his body was disgusting, home to masturbation fantasies—"his monstrous way of life" (*P* 92). Here his body is a temple of the purified, reborn spirit. Although Stephen's physical feelings are similar, Stephen's response to this dissociative experience is the opposite of his response in Cork.

This flying shape is also one sign of an "unsubstantial image" that he had been "seek[ing" (*P* 65) "through the mists of childhood and boyhood" (*P* 169). Whether the passage is to be read as an ironic deflation of the adolescent boy's passionate thoughts, or an ironic recasting of modernist art's claims about the artist's cultural role (Norris, *Web* 51–67, 183–84), its grandiosity serves an emotional purpose. The imagined figure shares the ability of Simon and Johnny in the bar in Cork to fly through alcohol above circumstances, as this flying man hovers and glides in the sky above Dublin. The figure embodies, too, the flights of those popular heroes like the Count of Monte Christo who can escape from degrading circumstance (Kershner, *Bakhtin* 189–215).

Stephen's imagined episode as the doubled Icarus/D[a]edalus provides the finale to his many imaginary flights away from his daily life. For instance, in chapter 2 Stephen had been able to dissociate from Heron and his cronies' beating him for heresy, to flee into refuge with the beautiful prostitute, to escape his sense of sin through renewed entrance into a rigid, holy life at the beginning of chapter 4. Now Stephen begins to prepare for a flight that is not imaginary, but is an escape from the life in his father's house that had made him want to flee in the first place.

Stephen's extensive practice of dissociative flight into fantasy has enabled him to craft a more effective use of these abilities. This is a clear narrative suggestion that the complex uses of fantasy, which Stephen developed in response to the impact of Simon Dedalus's failures and the relation of those to alcohol, will be inseparable from his view of himself as a creative artist.

Three annihilation experiences have occurred before Stephen successfully transforms them. The fact that he can do so is a tribute to his practice in rising above squalor (Norris, *Web* 83) provided by his many flights of escape, a method he learned from his father, but was fortunate to be able to put to more positive use. In chapter 4, Stephen physically reexperiences the trauma he underwent in Cork during the fetus narrative (*P* 91–96) while reconceptualizing it not as death, but as rebirth. He is born to a new father who is yet the old father. Thus Stephen has begun to imagine himself free.

Some North American twentieth-century psychologists who theorize that some children of alcoholic parents are, when trapped by childhood in the alcoholic home, hence subject to ongoing trauma, recognize that the unconscious re-creation of the traumatic situation is one of the proofs that one has been traumatized. In order to "undo" the trauma, the self is drawn to repeat it in various guises (van der Kolk and Greenberg 72–73).

The successful reversal of trauma is apparent in Stephen's encounters with the young woman on the Strand whom critics call the Bird-Girl. Stephen's representation of the Bird-Girl as both pure and impure momentarily integrates within one figure those divergent qualities that Stephen had been unable to conceptualize as belonging to one person (Steinberg 149–52; Henke, "Narcissist" 74; Lilienfeld, "Flesh" 174–75). His ability to conceive of the Bird-Girl as simultaneously both pure and debauched may be an analogue for a momentary respite to Stephen's previous cognitive splitting of Ideal Father versus Bad Son. This recuperation of the split between bad self/ideal father echoes Stephen's transformation of a dissociative experience from symbolic death to symbolic rebirth as he observes "a hawklike man" in flight (*P* 169).

He emerges from his dissociated state after witnessing the flying man and the Bird-Girl unsure of the time or his exact location. Quickly gaining his bearings, Stephen moves further inland, finds a grassy spot and rests (*P* 172). Awakening, he feels exhilarated hope, and his relief is phrased as a reversal of the moon imagery with which the Cork bar episode ended.

As a watcher in the bar in Cork, Stephen had withdrawn like the moon in Shelley's fragment, an experience that "chilled him" enough so that he went numb and "forgot his own human and ineffectual grieving." (*P* 96). Here the experience reimmerses him in earthly life. Now instead of death, he "trembled" sensing "the strange light of some new world." (*P* 172), an experience of "rapture" he recalls as he wakens from his purifying sleep.

Here the narrative repeats linguistic echoes in order to suggest the undoing of a trauma sequence. It is not an easy experience physically or emotionally. Stephen does somatize it and has moments of fear about it. But it is transformative and as such it repeats the previous suggestion that in seeing the figure of the imagined Daedalus as his father, Stephen can reshape the symbolic death experienced during the fetus narrative in Cork.

Slowly developing a method of dissociative experience through which he can leave his body in service of creation, not self-hatred, Stephen makes himself ready to write the villanelle. That writing experience will enable him to move from the use of the figure of the female as a substitute for his use of himself as the scapegoat for his rage at his father, to a more creative use of those materials of art that are inseparable from his having grown up in a home where alcohol was a problem.

PARENTAL ALCOHOLISM AND STEPHEN DEDALUS'S VILLANELLE

My limited objective in what follows is to clarify the connections between Stephen Dedalus's successful completion of the villanelle with

Stephen's complex and often unconscious interactions with his father's alcoholism. My reading does not seek to write over that of other critics. I intend it as but one among the collective critical speculations on the origins of Stephen's creativity.

Critical debate has identified and examined two crucial sources of the pain and problems in Stephen's writing the villanelle: the grief, loss, and mourning over his parents (Friedman, "Self"; and Moreiras) and the disputed relation of masturbation to Stephen's acceptance of his body and female sexuality (Benstock 35; Wright 223; Rossman, "Villanelle" 291). But no one to my knowledge has located the origin of the villanelle in relation to Stephen Dedalus's response to Simon Dedalus's problems with alcohol. To establish this connection I will focus on the mimetic narrative level of the text, analyzing the emotional and physical aspects of Stephen's writing process.

The first verse of the villanelle comes to Stephen in the brightening stillness of early morning. He has awakened from what many critics regard as a wet dream, reported in the text in an ambiguous language which is both passionately earnest and grandiose (*P* 216–17). Previous to his dream, he had been speculating on his vision of E. C. on the library steps.

If I turn from the dispute about its intended audience (Scholes, "Poet" 478; Wright 220; Rossman, "Villanelle" 287) and the critical questions of irony and distance, I can see that the process of the poem's evolution shows the healthy use of Stephen's imagination. He is not murmuring words as he did on the train at Cork to drown out unbearable reality (*P* 87). He is not flagellating himself (*P* 92–93). He hears a rhyme and masters it, for the words lead to a poem, not to immobilizing self-hatred. Further, his dream differs from his father's dreams of past glory, which lead Simon Dedalus to wayside pubs and then to the bar in Cork.

Murmuring the rhyme scheme of the villanelle, Stephen soon crafts two more verses. Momentarily his creativity becomes blocked and the immediate present in the form of "dull white light" (*P* 217–218) begins to enter his consciousness, an image suggesting the hurtful father who would prevent Stephen's successful completion of his psychological developmental tasks (Epstein, *Ordeal* 38–40, 142).

The disarray of Stephen's room interrupts both the narrative and the poetic sequence. As Stephen looks for writing paper, he spies the remains of "the soupplate he had eaten the rice from for supper . . ." (P 218). This now empty bowl suggests the family's decline resulting from Simon's failure due to alcoholism. Did Stephen eat the rice in his room and not at the table with the family? Were there no longer family meals? Given the paucity of the tea and the fear in the household with which the chapter starts, this is a possibility.[24]

Without writing paper, Stephen writes the poem on the back of his cigarette packet, an action recalling his trying to write the elided first poem about Parnell on the back of the creditors' second bill to his father (P 70). The reader's memory thus locates the villanelle in context of Simon's eviction notice, itself a textual reference to the sale of the Cork patrimony and Simon's pub drinking there. And yet Stephen only momentarily falters, crafting these external circumstances into a poem and not into a focus on his own inadequacy or sinfulness.

Stephen re-enters the creative space by writing down the first three stanzas of the villanelle. Then he leans back in bed, recalling visits to E. C.'s home. He projects his sense of his own inadequacy into contempt for her, she who comes from a "house where young men are called by their christian names a little too soon." (P 219). Norris suggests that in these passages "we can see the extent to which Stephen's relationship with Emma Clery is troubled by class" (Web 206–207). But since the narrative has suggested that Stephen's class status is inextricably tied to his father's alcoholism, possibly his relation to Emma is troubled as well by the consequences of his father's drinking. His sarcasm hides the fact that Stephen has never had an honest relation with E. C. Strikingly, his contempt for her resembles his father's contempt for Mrs. Dedalus and his daughters.

His reverie about the visit soon leads first to his jealous recollection of E. C. flirting with Father Moran. Stephen's disgust and outrage are among his few direct expressions of anger. However, Stephen's contemptuous dismissal of "a church which was the scullerymaid of christendom." (P 219–20), may recall Mr. Dedalus's derisive dismissal at the Christmas dinner, and his saying "[w]e are an unfortunate priestridden race and always were and always will be . . ." (*P* 37).

That both traumatic replay and blocked rage at his father are part of Stephen's creative process becomes clear at Stephen's response to his own sentence stating that the church is a female servant to Christianity. At this idea, "[r]ude brutal anger . . . broke up violently her fair image . . . On all sides distorted reflections of her image started from his memory . . ." (*P* 220).

The shattered image of E. C. reflects many figures of women whom Stephen has briefly encountered. They are all working-class women, sexually attractive, and one of them is openly hostile when she sees Stephen trip (*P* 220). The demeaning laughter of that young girl is a transmutation of Stephen's self-hatred. These impoverished women may represent the Dedalus family's poverty (Norris, *Web* 206) and hence, as I have argued, suggest the location of that poverty in Simon Dedalus's problems with alcohol.

Nevertheless, in so imaging these contemptuous female figures, Stephen is not shaming himself in response to his adolescent sexuality. Making women responsible for a feeling inside himself, Stephen shifts contempt for himself to contempt for women, a culturally sanctioned behavior. Further, the moment of rage at others to avoid pain about oneself suggests the son's enactment of his father's moments of bewildered paranoia. Simon's rages have increasingly centered on those he considers his foes (*P* 65), on others, in an alcoholic projection of the "locus of control."

Further, Stephen is not immobilized in a somatized panic that paralyzes him by mental floods of visual and emotional stimuli as he had been during the trip to Cork and during his creation of the fetus narrative. In writing the villanelle, Stephen makes potentially hurtful material available for other kinds of transmutation. Hence it is understandable that at the end of this mental flow of images Stephen senses that "his anger was also a form of homage." (*P* 220), although he does not consciously acknowledge that it may be indirect homage to his father.

The crucial moment of the villanelle for some critics is the movement from the fifth to the final stanza (Wright 222; Rossman, "Villanelle" 290). Rossman has argued that Stephen's art is an escape from the body and from the difficult realities of human life ("Spiritual" 115–17; "Villanelle" 281–82). Yet it is difficult to read Stephen's responses at this point in the text as "symbolic masturbation" (Rossman, "Spiritual" 127). As Bernard Benstock and Doris T. Wright argue, the masturbation is not only real, it is a healthy necessity (see also Riquelme 77). Hence as relief spreads "along his spine," Stephen notices that he is responding to its warmth and "seeing himself as he lay, smiled. Soon he would sleep." (*P* 222). Stephen's use of the word "himself" to include his penis, which in his earlier self-hate he had thought of as a snake (*P* 139–40) with a life detached from his body, suggests an increase in his self-integration.

The integration of body and self Stephen momentarily achieves when writing the villanelle suggests a hope that Stephen's splitting might diminish. In dealing with Simon's alcoholism, Stephen had split into "bad Stephen" and "good Simon." Focused on his "badself," Stephen had located that badself within his Catholic sense of sexual sin. Acceptance of masturbation with relief and without guilt moves Stephen away from self-hate.

Stephen reviews E. C. and his poem once more. He recognizes that this almost completed poem is the successful conclusion to the poem he had previously tried to write about her (*P* 222).

Ten years before Stephen had written a poem about Emma in place of a poem about Parnell (*P* 70). He had accompanied Emma home on the tram from the party where he shrank from other children; behavior I have argued that is one of the first signs of the effects on him of his father's alcoholism. For the reader any return to that poem may also return to the textual suppression, the self-censored poem Stephen did not write, and hence to his father shouting and crying, feelings exacerbated by alcohol poured from the crockery whiskey container (*P* 28). The reader's memory and the textual recall of the suppressed poem might allude to Stephen's terror at witnessing what was happening to his father.

Central to such recall is Parnell and all that Parnell has meant in this text. Stephen's memory appears to suppress that connection. He does not note the poem to Parnell, which he had been unable to complete, but seems to regard the original poem to E. C. as the only poem he was trying to write ten years ago.

This excision is a textual marker of the absent figure of Parnell, a symbol containing Simon's use of Parnell as a vehicle of the wrongly-sacrificed savior figure, a substitute in degradation by which to avoid examining Simon's reliance on alcohol. The figure of Parnell also contains within it Stephen's deathlike annihilation panics and his merger into the dying leader, tying the son to the father's fall as well as to that of the "dead king" (P 39). Because of the workings of memory, allusion, and imagery in the narrative textually Stephen's repression is noted by the narrative and the reader if not by the character.

Earlier the narrative had followed a similar process. It had not disclosed the sale of the Cork property but had written over it the episodes in the Cork bar.

Each instance of narrative denial alludes to Simon's alcoholism. I conclude from these congruences that one origin of Stephen's successful completing of the villanelle is his use of art to deflect the pain of his father's drinking, Simon's subsequent destruction, and the impact on Stephen of these tragic events.

Stephen thinks of sending Emma his poem, but decides that her relative, an urbane prelate, would mock it and its writer (P 222). Then his feelings for E. C. soften, although she remains an object of his pity and of his construction of her. In writing his villanelle, Stephen has not healed the immobilizing split in his response to women whereby they are either whores or madonnas. As a young man raised in a Catholic patriarchal household and culture, Stephen expresses received opinions about women.

Hence Stephen's "temptress" recapitulates images of the prostitute in chapter 2 (Wright 216). When the prostitute had kissed him, he had understood that the language of sexuality had been written on his brain, but he did not write the language (P 101). Here he commands "the liquid letters of speech . . . [which pour] forth over his brain." (P 223; see also Wright 223). In control of language, he writes in his imagination the final stanza of the villanelle (Riquelme 77–78). In his writing process Stephen interpolates memories, reformulating these obsessive images into the exacting poetic formula of the villanelle.

Stephen has accomplished more than the writing of a poem. Masturbatory revels had served as the vehicle of extreme self-hatred for Stephen until this moment in the text (*P* 90, 99, 115–16). As such they recall the annihilation panic Stephen experienced on seeing the carved word *Foetus* (*P* 92) gazing back at him, forming a shaming mirror in which he views his sexual behaviors, a degradation whose effects obscure the sale of his father's Cork property (*P* 91–93). Hence this villanelle does not accidentally conclude with Stephen's being so roused that he must masturbate for relief. The act of masturbation is neither defiant nor imagined as groveling shame, but is natural and healthy (Wright 223).

Writing the villanelle Stephen may have come closer to recognizing painful truths about his father. His disordered, filthy room reflects the squalid emotional disarray of the Simon Dedalus household (*P* 162). Enough of his father's use of women remains in Stephen's approach to them to indicate that he has not separated fully from Simon Dedalus, ensuring a sense of psychic safety. But he is also now a poet in competition with priests (*P* 221; Epstein, *Ordeal* 4–5, 38–41, 156).

That Stephen himself is proud of his completion of a process that took him ten years indicates to me that the villanelle is not just a coming to terms with Emma, though it certainly is that. Having written it at last, even briefly thinking it good enough to send to Emma, indicates that Stephen has completed that task. No longer blocked by the undisclosed poem to E. C., the self-censored poem to Parnell may now have room to emerge. Perhaps in returning to his poem to E. C., Stephen has returned as well to his first use of writing to avoid and to reframe his father's behavior at the Christmas dinner. Possibly doing so is the start of his coming to terms with the complex impact of alcoholism on the family, the father, himself, and, beyond that, to his views of Irish politics.

Certainly he has circled close to some of the circumstances of his earliest attempt to write a poem to E. C. (*P* 222) without fleeing, or experiencing dread, shame, panic, or continuous artistic blockage. He can tolerate experiencing some memories long enough to transform these into literature rather than paralyzing self-flagellation. Creating the villanelle, Stephen flies above imprisoning circumstance in imagination like Icarus/Daedalus, not like drunken Johnny Cashman and Simon Dedalus in the bar in Cork.

However, there are things he has not achieved. Although he is in command of the language of creation, Stephen retains culturally mandated symbols and hackneyed language and images, recalling his formulation of his first kiss in the prostitute's haven. He has not returned to the original point of creation, to writing about Parnell, a figure for the failed father. Stephen has not formulated a language or plot by which to represent the wounding he observed and experienced. Sexuality is written over a narrative of political devastation and alcoholic disintegration.

If, however, one accepts Riquelme's argument that the text of *Portrait* verbalizes itself as the author's creation, then the villanelle suggests James Joyce's refusal of denial, if not Stephen Dedalus's. As such, the narrative has suggested a connection between Simon's drinking—possibly a failed means of assuaging political and personal loss—and Stephen's need to write. Read through Riquelme's argument, then, Stephen, through his apprenticeship as an artist, has undone some of the circumstances of the original trauma caused by the results of his father's drinking, imagining and transforming them through the writing process.

LEAVING THE ALCOHOLIC HOME

Some twentieth-century North American clinicians like Celia Dulfano and Stephanie Brown, among others, have discovered that many of their clients who grew up in families affected by alcoholism have great difficulty separating from such families (Dulfano 119–40; S. Brown, *Adult* 306–11). The riskiness of separation from an alcoholic family is brilliantly encapsulated in imagery in *A Portrait of the Artist as a Young Man*. Stephen's imaginative reversal of traumatic annihilation is couched in ambiguous imagery, as I noted earlier. For the mythological figure in flight above the Strand (*P* 168–69) with whom Stephen identifies is a composite of a successful father and a doomed son. According to the Greek myth, although Daedalus escapes from his imprisonment, his son Icarus dies in the attempt (Bulfinch 157–59). Against the advice and the example of his father, who pleads with his son to be careful, Icarus—hubristically flying too near the sun—thus melts the wax holding together the wings crafted for him by his father, and plunges to his death in the sea. On the other hand, rejecting Simon Dedalus's example, though doing so may feel psychologically life-threatening, is actually life-sustaining. Imagination and artistry are surer mechanisms than alcoholism for escape from imprisoning circumstances. The rich ambiguities in these allusions are deliberate and significant. The ambivalent imagery continues into *Ulysses,* where Stephen ruefully reviews Icarus's fall and his own as part of Stephen's shaming return to his father's house: "Fabulous artificer, the hawklike man. You flew. Whereto? Newhaven-Dieppe, steerage passenger. Paris and back. Lapwing. Icarus. *Pater, ait.* Seabedabbled, fallen, weltering. Lapwing you are. Lapwing he" (*U* 210; emphasis in original).

Clinical findings reveal similar complexity. For as Stephanie Brown points out, "individuals must face repeatedly intense feelings of guilt for leaving the still sick family behind. Primitive ties to the family of origin are maintained long into adulthood" (*Adult* 306). To read Stephen Dedalus's flight from home as motivated by the need to escape an alcoholic father may question the "liberal legitimation narrative of the artist" (Norris, *Web* 184). His departure indicates that Stephen is determined to survive the crippling circumstance of his relation to his family. But as his responses to Cranly show, he is deeply damaged. His mother is correct; he does not know "what the heart is and what it feels." (*P* 252). His misconstruction of Cranly's intentions and meaning and his resulting conviction that Cranly desires him sexually and/or that Cranly is pursuing E. C. is one indication that when presented with a close confidant (*P* 247) Stephen cannot trust or bond with others, either men or women.[25]

It would, in fact, be odd if he could, given his upbringing. Some affected by parental alcoholism have severe problems with trust and attachment (Brown, *Adult* 248). Characterizing the behavior of some of her patients, Brown might be describing the fictional figure set in late-nineteenth-century Dublin, Stephen Dedalus: "lack of trust is defensive, a constant factor in regulating intimacy as is a vigilant stance and . . . suspicion of the motives of others" (*Adult* 248). Indeed, in his journal, Stephen describes his defenses as his "spiritual-heroic refrigerating apparatus" (*P* 252). Not to love and not to trust for Stephen were sensible survival strategies that enabled him to arrive at the point where he could leave the home.

Stephen is convinced that he must leave Dublin in order to achieve artistic freedom. Even if these are rationalizations suggested by the culturally sanctioned figure of the heroic artist, that he becomes free enough to leave his home by the end of the book is the important point.

SIMON THE ALCOHOLIC

The denial narrative in *Portrait* is so successful that only narrative gaps and behaviors circumstantially suggest that Simon Dedalus is an alcoholic. The superimposition of the drinking scenes onto the paralipsis of the sale of the Cork patrimony makes a veiled causal statement that drinking cost Simon his wealth and Stephen his inheritance, class status, and secure future. Other measures of parental alcoholism are more covert than that which is displayed in the Cork scenes. Stephen's damaged emotional life, his dissociative episodes during which he slowly and courageously transforms pain into artistic creativity, and his indirect (in fact, timid) rebellion against his father, suggest the effects on his son of Simon Dedalus's alcoholism.

Simon's voicelessness is a deliberate fabrication of the novel's narrative choices. Like Donald Farfrae, Simon Dedalus's consciousness is never rendered. His behavior is visible; his motivation and his feelings are opaque.

Thus even if the reader does acknowledge that Stephen's varied survival strategies resemble those of some twentieth-century survivors of North American alcoholic families, there is no consecutive narrative sequence depicting Simon's fall into alcoholism. Of Simon's own story, the reader has only snippets. The suppressed narrative life of Simon's drinking in *Portrait* takes clearer form at the mimetic level in *Ulysses*.

Like Naremore, who sees only finances as Simon's problem, the narrative foregrounds financial hardship as the cause of Simon's behaviors and his son's suffering. Stephanie Brown points out, however, "that alcohol is a means to cope with something else that is identified as the major problem" (*Adult* 35) is often one proof of denial in an alcoholic family. Because of its focus on financial reversal, *Portrait* encourages readers to find an alternative narrative to its suppressed utterance of an alcoholism narrative. However, read through the lens of the biopsychosocial model of alcoholism, the text's deliberate disclosures of character's and narrative's denial suggest that Simon's alcoholism affected both father and son in *Portrait*.

Because Stephen Dedalus is a central figure in *Ulysses,* it would seem that that novel may serve as a commentary on *Portrait* (Centola 105 n6; Epstein, *Ordeal* 97–98; Norris, *Web* 184). Reading segments of *Portrait* and *Ulysses* at the mimetic level from the vantage of alcoholism theory may suggest facets other approaches may have obscured.

Stanislaus Joyce's view of John Joyce in *The Complete Dublin Diary* was that his father's alcoholism was progressive. As I have noted, James Joyce made use of the materials of Stanislaus's *Complete Dublin Diary* when crafting *Stephen Hero,* the novel that Joyce transformed into *Portrait*. The influence of Stanislaus's interpretation of John Joyce is apparent in Simon's transformation: readers can easily see that the jaunty father telling stories to little Stephen on page 1 of *Portrait* has become an irascible, irresponsible alcoholic in *Ulysses*.

Studying pages 237 to 239 of chapter 10 of *Ulysses* ("Wandering Rocks"), the reader familiar with twentieth-century medical discussion of alcoholism might conclude that the biopsychosocial disease that affects Simon Dedalus in *Portrait* has infected the family dynamic. In this scene Simon's only interest is in using all the money he can to stand himself and others rounds of drinks at the bar. He is desperate not only to defend his right to drink, but to hide that drinking is his intention. Dublin pub culture sanctioned his behavior.

Roles are reversed. Dilly becomes the responsible parent. Her "job" is to obtain as much money as she possibly can from Simon because she and her sisters literally cannot afford to buy food. Earlier in the chapter, when Boodie had come home, she had picked up the lid of a simmering pot on the stove and had found in it—shirts (*U* 226). The one pot of food on the stove was pea soup, and that was given to the Dedalus family as a charity portion from Sister Mary Patrick (*U* 226).

Simon's violence and subterfuge in protecting his right to drink are evident. The "trick" he'll "show" her is, presumably, the back of his hand (*U* 238). Simon attacks Dilly's posture and insists that she is neither feminine nor attractive; his abuse derides her lacks rather than his drinking (*U* 237). As abhorrent as these behaviors are to feminist readers aware of the patriarchal privilege of male violence in the family, perhaps the most poignant is Dilly's single-mindedness. No matter what Simon does or says, she perseveres. Her very persistence suggests that Dilly has been through this series of maneuvers previously. The skewed gender relations in turn-of-the-century Ireland underline a connection to Elizabeth-Jane's role in *Mayor:* daughter Dilly, unlike son Stephen, has no rights to an artistic myth of the self, nor to any self not in service to another. To those familiar with the effects of alcoholism on families, it is not ahistorical after studying this scene to conclude that Simon Dedalus is an alcoholic whose drinking has degraded his once promising life and has forced his family into extreme poverty.

But at the end of *Portrait,* the first-time reader does not know that Stephen returns to Dublin from the continent, convinced he is an artistic failure, immobilized by guilt about his mother. At the end of *Portrait,* the first-time reader may share with Stephen the hopeful and exuberant embrace of life that is the courageous response of a young man determined to survive his childhood in a family where the father's drinking creates serious problems.

CHAPTER THREE

"THE HORRORS OF FAMILY LIFE"

A Feminist Interrogation of the Politics of Codependence in *To the Lighthouse*

BIOGRAPHICAL INTRODUCTION

CURRENTLY THERE IS LITTLE DISAGREEMENT among many North American scholars that Virginia Woolf's family of origin was dysfunctional.[1] The Anglo-Indian family system in which Julia Stephen, Virginia Woolf's mother, spent a chaotic childhood and adolescence adversely affected her self-care abilities, encouraging her to develop an exaggerated devotion to the needs of others at the expense of herself. Julia Stephen's response to her mother's chronic illness—an illness, I will suggest, which may have been exacerbated rather than relieved by a use of opium-derived drugs—predisposed Julia Stephen to a life of compliance in an extremely patriarchal household and society.

Although I agree with some of the feminist critiques of the medical concept of codependence, I reformulate that concept, using it as a political lens through which to examine the white middle-class Victorian ideal of the wife as a self-sacrificing figure, demonstrated in aspects of Julia Stephen's life, and fictionalized in the family system of *To the Lighthouse*.

The Stephen Family

Interpretations of the life of Virginia Woolf's father, Leslie Stephen, have clarified important points relevant to the family dynamic fictionalized in *To the Lighthouse*. Lord Noel Annan and John Bicknell were the first to interpret Leslie Stephen's familial and cultural context, an analysis recently repeated by Hermoine Lee. Because the information is now so well known, a brief summary will suffice.

Leslie Stephen's male forebears' lives were deeply bifurcated, their masculinity, while culturally normative, depended on the racial and gender subordination operative in England and in the British Empire. Both Leslie Stephen's grandfather and father used their Evangelical Christian beliefs to sustain the work ethic that underpinned their public achievements (Annan 8–14). However, Leslie Stephen's father could not consistently maintain the facade of the masculinity he had learned from his own father, and throughout the course of his productive public life, he paid the price for this by suffering several nervous breakdowns (Annan 14–15). The masculinity Leslie Stephen saw modeled was exaggerated even more in his older brother, Fitzjames Stephen. The "rind" as Thomas Hardy might have called it, of Leslie Stephen's public male self covered, as did his father's, a sensitive interior self that could not consistently navigate the cultural expectations of masculinity. The bifurcation between public and private self redounded on Leslie Stephen's wives and children in ways as difficult for them as for himself.

In both Leslie Stephen's grandfather and father may be observed similar behavioral patterns. At home, they came first. Devout Evangelicals, they were intolerant of religious laxity in others and refused to acknowledge sensual pleasure (Annan 16–17). Like his own and other Victorian fathers, James Stephen, Leslie's father, was distant and inaccessible; as a boy Leslie called his father "Sir" (Annan 43). Leslie Stephen's mother oversaw the upbringing of the children, and interceded between them and their father (Annan 16). James and

Elizabeth Stephen had four children, only three of whom survived into adulthood—Fitzjames, Leslie, and Caroline Stephen.

Some branches of contemporary American academic feminist theory connect the paternalism of Leslie Stephen's father James's home life to his beliefs about the British colonies (Marcus, "Britannia;" M. Ferguson 1–7, 65–89; McClintock). Lord Noel Annan explicitly ties patriarchy in the Stephen home to imperialism abroad, although he cautions against too extreme an interpretation of such connections (13–14). However, as Jane Marcus was among the first to point out, the recognition that the patriarchal family was inextricably connected to the British Empire structures the argument of *Three Guineas* (*Languages* 78–80, 84–85). There Woolf was rereading her own family as well as the life of certain middle- and upper-class Victorians and Edwardians.

Sibling rivalry, whereby one sibling was assumed to exemplify the gender ideal in which the other was decidedly lacking, seems to have structured the relation between Fitzjames and his younger brother Leslie Stephen.[2] Lord Annan calls Fitzjames their father's favorite (23) and points out that "[a]lways in Leslie's youth the figure of Fitzjames loomed above him; broad and strong, successful and competent" (23; 29 n). But Fitzjames, like his father and brother, suffered from emotional instability, revealed publicly late in his life by Fitzjames's handling of the Maybrick case (Hussey, *A to Z* 266). After his son Jem died mad, Fitzjames had a nervous breakdown and died two years later.

Growing up in an Evangelical home where physical pleasure was not countenanced (Annan 16–17), where self-sacrifice to the point of exhaustion at work was the definition of public duty, where there was only one way to believe in religious matters though claims were made of religious tolerance, Leslie Stephen received certain ideas about what constituted mature manhood. One was the absolute right of the father to rule the Victorian middle-class family (Annan 14).

Anthony Fletcher has recently argued that for centuries boys were gendered as British middle-class gentlemen through brutality at school and separation from their mothers (297–321). The pattern Fletcher has traced was followed by Leslie Stephen's family (Annan

16) in making him ready to assume his masculine role. Outwardly schooling toughened him. Although both Stephen boys found life difficult at Eton, they survived; Fitzjames excelled at sports and studies alike, and protected his younger brother Leslie from bullies (Annan 19).

During his undergraduate years at Cambridge University, Leslie Stephen mastered the rudiments of the male persona, although "he was ashamed of his nervous sensibility and boyish ill-health" (Annan 29). As a Don at Cambridge, Leslie Stephen successfully hid his poetic, intellectual side—even appearing to some at Cambridge to feel contempt for intellectuals (Annan 29, 32). For example, he buttressed his public male persona by coaching the rowing team (Annan 31–33).

Leslie Stephen left his teaching post at Cambridge in 1862, having renounced Holy Orders only after his father's death in 1859 (Bicknell, "Mr." 57–58; Annan 42–47). He lived with his mother in London, supported by his father's bequest (Annan 46). In London Stephen continued dealing with some of his emotional needs through sports, a culturally appropriate means for doing so (Houghton 243, 248n). He became an expert Alpine climber and the head of a loosely organized group of assiduous hikers who called themselves the "Sunday Tramps" (Annan 97–98).

Leslie Stephen was one of the most respected men of his generation; his friendships with male peers were among the most important aspects of his life (Annan 54, 79). The forms of conventional public manhood in Victorian England perhaps offered Leslie Stephen a safe arena in which to hide his more fragile interior being.

Hence, like many other men of his social class in Victorian England, Leslie Stephen had never been allowed to think of meeting his own emotional or physical needs for which there was a staff of female servants. He had been raised by a doting mother and sister to expect pampering and emotional sustenance. Far from allowing him to respect women, this seems to have encouraged his contempt of them. In his writing about his sister Caroline Emilia, who adored him, such contempt is obvious (MB 55–56; Annan 129–130). His responses to his sister-in-law Annie Thackeray, though expressed in a more mature manner, reflect contempt as well (MB 23–25; Annan

72–76; Stephen, *Letters* I 157–58; II 363, 426–27, 445–46). Interestingly, both his wives had been adversely affected by their mothers' illness before their marriages to him. His first wife's mother had been institutionalized for madness, a condition from which she never recovered, while Julia Stephen's mother's failing health shaped the circumstances of Julia's upbringing. Perhaps, partially as a consequence, both the Mrs. Leslie Stephens regarded their marital duty as meeting Leslie Stephen's every need (Annan 64, 104–105).

Like many other middle-class Victorian professional men, Leslie Stephen had never needed to integrate his public and private selves. When his colleague (and nephew by marriage) F. W. Maitland was writing the authorized biography of Sir Leslie Stephen, Maitland had difficulty believing what Leslie Stephen's daughters revealed of his family life (Annan 130). But how could it have been otherwise? Sanctioned by his culture and social class, his bifurcated masculinity was also modeled on that of his father and grandfather (Annan 136). Like them, Leslie Stephen married wives who supported his childishness. Crippled emotionally as had been his father, in public Leslie Stephen was a rational man of conventional morals. At home he was emotionally intemperate and tyrannical (Stemmerick 62–63; DeSalvo, *Impact* 30). Thus by the time of his marriage to her, Leslie Stephen had been fashioned as an appropriate mate for Julia Prinsep Jackson Duckworth, the mother of Virginia Woolf (Caramagno 121).

The Jackson Family

The Victorian British Empire and the patriarchal system that maintained it were central to Julia Stephen's upbringing. Describing Julia Stephen's Anglo-Indian forebears, Boyd narrates a fable of empire (Boyd 9–10,144–5; Q. Bell I, 14; Stephen, MB 26). Virginia Woolf's great-grandmother, Adeline de l'Etang, had married James Pattle in 1811. The Pattles lived in Calcutta among the highest echelons of the colonial ruling class, a position assured by James Pattle's descent from a wealthy and powerful Anglo-Indian family. He became a senior member of the Board of Revenue and the oldest active member of the Bengal Civil Service, although scholarship substantiates the family legend that he had a severe alcohol problem (Q. Bell, I, 14; Boyd 8–9, 14–15, 123–25; but see Lee 87). Quentin Bell character- izes James Pattle as "a quite extravagantly wicked man ... [who] drank himself to death" (I, 14). Of the Pattles' ten children, seven daughters survived. "Their early years were spent between India, France and England," (Christian 5) culminating in what were then termed "brilliant marriages" (Boyd 9).

Virginia Woolf's maternal grandmother, Maria Pattle, had mar- ried Dr. John Jackson in Calcutta in 1837. Dr. Jackson had been born in England in 1804, educated at Cambridge University, and had migrated to Calcutta to practice medicine in the 1820s (Stephen, MB 25). At the time of his marriage he served on the staff of the Bengal Presidency General Hospital, and in 1841 was ap- pointed a professor at the Medical College (Boyd 12). Dr. and Mrs. Jackson did not have the colonial rank of the families of several of the other sisters who had married men of greater wealth and power, although Leslie Stephen reported that "Dr. Jackson made a modest fortune in India" (MB 26).

Julia Jackson was the third daughter of Maria and John Jack- son, born in 1846 in Calcutta. Her sister Adeline was born in 1837 and married Henry Vaughn in 1856, when Julia was ten. Mary, born in 1841, married Herbert Fisher in 1862, when Julia was sixteen.

Leaving Dr. Jackson behind in 1848, Mrs. Jackson brought Julia to England, where the two elder girls were already settled with their aunt Sara Prinsep. In 1843 the Prinseps had left Calcutta on Thoby Prinsep's retirement from the civil service to settle in London (Christian 5), moving in 1850 into what came to be known as Lit- tle Holland House, the nucleus of the other Pattle sisters' families' lives in London when they, too, emigrated to England from India. It was in this extended family setting amid artists and writers, that Julia Jackson, Virginia Woolf's mother, was raised.

Until 1855 when Dr. Jackson retired and returned to his family in Britain (Boyd 32), Mrs. Jackson and her daughters lived in vari- ous lodgings, with the Prinseps at Little Holland House, or with Julia Margaret Cameron, another Pattle sister, at her estate, Dim- bola (Gillespie and Steele xvii-xviii). Leslie Stephen speculated that

Julia Jackson had not "acquired the filial sentiment" about Dr. Jackson "generated in early familiarity," because her uncle Thoby Prinsep had stood in for her father (MB 27).

Mrs. Cameron had wanted Dimbola to rival Sara Prinsep's Little Holland House (Boyd 18). Sara Prinsep's "vision—inspired perhaps partly by her French antecedents—was to establish a salon to which people eminent in every walk of life would be drawn" (Christian 6). She succeeded: the Prinseps' guests included some women and many men prominent in art, politics, literature, and science (Boyd 17–18; Christian 7).

As patrons of the Pre-Raphaelites, the Prinseps allied themselves with the revolutionary in art and the unconventional in behavior. "Indeed all the sisters revelled in breaking the rules" (Christian 7). Some Victorians thought Little Holland House was not quite respectable (Hill qtd. in Love 54). Jean Love refers to "Mrs. Prinsep's equivocal reputation . . ." (54). Virginia Woolf herself called the Pattle sisters (with the exception of Maria Jackson) "worldly" (MOB 88).

These resettled Anglo-Indian "tribes" (Boyd 16) differed from typical Victorian middle-class Anglican households, offering "a respite from the formality, the regularity and the stuffiness of mid-Victorian society" (Q. Bell I, 15). The Pattles had not been raised from infancy in a culture where the worldview became daily more rigid, where many people even of a certain rank publicly observed Victorian decorum. It would seem that Julia Jackson's mother and aunts, heretofore having only visited Victorian England, escaped "Victorianism" because they had lived in the closed circle of the empire from whence they drew money and status. Their ancestors were French, and it does not seem inaccurate to speculate, as John Christian does (6), that they were raised to behave as the wealthy French had behaved before the revolution, a point of view that can only have been exacerbated by their experience of wielding colonial power.

Julia Stephen's social position, understanding of the female role, and education were thus inextricable from her maternal family's successful participation in the systems of dominance, repression, and appropriation that maintained the British Empire.

Virginia Woolf analyzed her mother's socialization in the female role at Dimbola and Little Holland House: "She was taught . . . [to revere] distinguished men; to pour out tea, to hand them their strawberries and cream; to listen devoutly . . . to their wisdom" (*MOB* 88). Julia's letters, stories, and now-published essays attest to her wit and observational powers (Gillespie and Steele). She was educated enough to teach her own children Latin, history, and French (Q. Bell I, 26). But as a young girl in her Anglo-Indian extended family, Julia had been trained to be an ornament, an aide to her mother, and an artist's model.

Given her family's views, Julia's stunning beauty (Gersheim 89, 99, 149; Mulligan, *et al.*, plates III, IV, V) seemed to invite artistic use. Leslie Stephen defends the respectability of Maria Jackson's mothering, noting that Mrs. Jackson refused to allow Mary and Julia to sit as models for William Holman Hunt and Thomas Woolner "on the ground that their simplicity might be injured by the implied homage to their beauty" (MB 28). In fact, Julia served as an artist's model from puberty (Boyd 32; MB 31; Gillespie and Steele xvii–xviii). In the circles of Dimbola and Little Holland House, where art was almost a religion and where male artists were its high priests, such homage to a young girl's beauty was acceptable. However, it is probable that more conventional middle-class mid-Victorian mothers—even someone as liberal as Mrs. Gaskell—would not have permitted such use of an unmarried girl.

Some North American and British historians have argued that the reassertion of Puritanical harshness noted in some families, was mitigated by a softening of Victorian attitudes toward children (Stone 667–73; Pollack 96–202; Gorham 16–17). However, the rigid, gendered role dichotomies in these male-dominated families meant that mothers and children, particularly girls, were neither perceived nor treated as the equal of their brothers (Dyhouse, "Mothers" 34–36). Further, wives and children were heavily circumscribed in their movements, secondary to the patriarch (Davidoff, L'Esperance and Newby, "Figures" 53, 60). Although Julia Stephen's Anglo-Indian aunts were not subordinate to husbands (Love 55) in their homes, children obeyed parental dictates.

The difficult circumstances of resettlement in England might account in part for the unusual, even unprotected nature of Julia Jackson's childhood and adolescence. Maternal illness in addition inadvertently resulted in Julia Jackson's becoming an object for her mother's use from 1856 onward, when Maria Jackson became increasingly ill from rheumatism.

MORPHIA AND CHLORAL: GENDER AND DEPENDENCE

Two life-changing events occurred in Mrs. Jackson's life at the onset of her illness: her husband's return to England and the family and the marriage of her oldest daughter. By 1856, Mrs. Jackson's suffering from rheumatism compelled her to visit spas such as St. Moritz, Aigle, and Malvern (Stephen, MB 34). Bruce Haley points out that such visits were not unusual for the wealthier Victorians (16). Uprooted from an already unsettled life, Mary at fifteen and Julia at ten wandered dutifully with their mother as she sought better health, although they spent part of these years in London or with their aunts. Then in 1862 when Mary married, Julia at sixteen assumed the entire nursing care of her mother (Stephen, MB 34). British and American daughters were expected to nurse ailing parents, but the more usual arena was the family home, not fashionable British or Continental spas (Dyhouse, *Feminism* 25–26; Lerner 148–50).

Mrs. Jackson "treated" her rheumatic pain "with morphia and chloral" (Q. Bell I, 17), which at that time were frequently dispensed in dosages neither standardized nor controlled by the medical profession (Haley 13; Berridge and Edwards 21–72). Chloral and opium use was legal and socially acceptable. "Chloral was being prescribed increasingly in general practice from the 1860's for sleeplessness . . ." (Berridge and Edwards 70; see also Gilman, et al. 364).

Morphia is an opiate: "Opiates . . . are drugs of the morphine type, which have the common property of relieving pain and inducing euphoria" (Berridge and Edwards xvi). The body reacts physiologically to prolonged usage and/or to specific amounts of addictive substances, no matter whether the language to conceptualize addiction exists and no matter how drug use is socially constructed. Even though Berridge and Edwards problematize the medicalization of addiction, they do not deny that opiates are always addictive: "The opiates are drugs of addiction. There are variations in individual susceptibility, but anyone who takes an opiate for a long enough period and in sufficient dose will become addicted.... Opiates are drugs to which the individual's central nervous system will, on repeated exposure, develop a high degree of *tolerance* [which can lead the user to] ... escalate the dose.... Tolerance is then intimately linked to the onset of *withdrawal symptom* experience and *physical dependence*" (Berridge and Edwards 278–79; emphasis in original).

Both her medical history and letters within the University of Sussex collection point to a change in Maria Jackson's use of chloral and morphia. In 1855 and 1858, papers on the hypodermic administration of morphine (for many complaints, among them, neuralgia and rheumatism) were published (Berridge and Edwards 139–40). By the 1860s, such usage was popular, although Dr. Clifford Allbutt had published warnings "as early as 1864" that hypodermic injections of morphine led to addiction (Berridge and Edwards 142).

David Musto, considering the differing impact on rates of addiction that different methods of administering opiates might produce, notes that "the ingestion of crude opium before the nineteenth century would have had milder effects than hypodermic injections of purified opium derivatives" (87). After reviewing Maria Jackson's letters at the University of Sussex, Panthea Reid has recorded that Maria Jackson was receiving morphine injections in her later life ("Another" 6). The regularity of these, however, is unclear.

The morphine injections of women of Maria Jackson's class were almost always under the control of a doctor. There is little evidence of hypodermic self-administering of morphine of the sort associated with twentieth-century American drug use (Berridge and Edwards 147). However, as hypodermically injected morphine usage increased, so did medicalized gender concerns: "[w]omen were said to be peculiarly susceptible to morphinism . . . [c]onventional ideas about the weakness of the female sex were also soon linked with the spread of morphine use" (Berridge and Edwards 144–45). Although in America at the turn of the century, most known morphine addicts were women (Courtwright 55), in Britain, the number of women was equal to the number of men who were addicted (Berridge and Edwards 148). Although Leslie Stephen notes that Dr. Jackson did not practice medicine on his return to England, Jean Love has stated that he did so (MB 26; Love 56). Certainly the fact that her husband was a doctor might have increased Maria Jackson's belief in the efficacy of and her access to opiate drugs.

Because I cannot say with certainty what dosage of chloral and morphia Maria Jackson used, I cannot prove that Maria Jackson developed a physiological dependence on chloral or on morphia, nor can I prove that her behavior in her later life developed in part because of her use of morphia and chloral. My objective is to problematize Maria Jackson's drug use yet avoid anachronism: Berridge and Edwards have successfully documented that the problem of "drug addiction" as late twentieth-century middle-class North Americans might define it did not exist in mid-Victorian England, the time that Mrs. Jackson was increasingly incapacitated by chronic rheumatism.

Nevertheless, certain current medical models of addiction suggest that the focus (even the obsession) by the user on the lifestyle to sustain addiction is worth examining. Haley reports that many Victorians were obsessed by questions of health, for many ailments that today are treatable could cause death in the nineteenth century. Thus the Pattle sisters were not unusual in their shared family focus on issues of health and its treatment (Love 50–51). However, when Quentin Bell says of Mrs. Jackson that "her grand topic was health," (I, 17) I wonder whether more was involved than might have been thought at the time?

Did Maria Jackson focus on her chronic pains solely because of their severity? Without denying the reality of the chronic pain of rheumatism, which can be incapacitating, is it possible that such a focus may also have resulted from the fact that such pain would have enabled Mrs. Jackson's continued reliance on substances such as morphia and chloral? Was the use over a long period or the overuse of such medications as morphia and chloral implicated in what Jean Love reports as Mrs. Jackson's difficulty with her "nerves" (117)? Was Maria Jackson's later life, curtailed certainly by increasing rheumatism (Stephen, MB 72–73; Rothenstein qtd. in Boyd 36–37), further limited by her use of these substances? Did her drug use, even though legal and under a doctor's care, impinge on and perhaps increase the retreat from daily life that her increasing incapacity from rheumatism brought about? Did it increase what Reid has implied was her self-absorption (*Art* 459)?

Here I am asking the kinds of questions that doctors of the late Victorian era raised about the widespread legal use of opiates and morphine derivatives (Berridge and Edwards 113–23, 150–205). Such British debates were inseparable from discourse about British foreign policy in India (site of poppy cultivation) and China (site of sales from India), and were influenced by racial and class prejudice in context of opium use in the empire and indigenous drug use in England. By mid-century, "many Britons were critical of the policies behind the so-called opium wars with China and began to fear retribution for what they saw as immorally forcing a detrimental product onto an unwilling customer" (Milligan, "Opium" 93–94). Medical specialists who opposed unrestricted cultivation of opiates in India and the Indian sale of opiates to China "like most [British] medical specialists, saw moderate opiate use as impossible. Dosage was ever-increasing and addiction inevitable . . ." (Berridge and Edwards 192). Additionally, medical proof that people could use the drug moderately would "undermine both the case for ending the cultivation of the poppy and the medical argument that all regular users of the drug were the proper concern of the [medical] profession" (Berridge and Edwards 192).[3]

The trajectory of Maria Jackson's medical use of chloral and morphine coincided with the history of and debate about drug use in Britain in the mid- and late-nineteenth century. The view that morphia and chloral were not problematic could be seen as conclusively refuted when in 1908 the Poisons Act brought these drugs under medical control. Although Mrs. Jackson's increased disability due to arthritis is documented, her medically supervised reliance of hypodermically administered morphine as its corollary should not go unremarked.

Even had her mother not used, or perhaps even overused, chloral and morphia it is likely that Julia's character would have been shaped as it was because her mother's illness and dependence on her led the daughter to become an overly responsible adult who regularly sacrificed herself to take care of the ailing. Throughout her life, Julia Jackson's primary allegiance was to her mother, not to her second husband or her children.

In a conventional mid-Victorian family of this rank, Julia, Adeline, and Mary Jackson probably would have been raised by governesses and have lived in a separate world from that of their parents (Davidoff and Hall 339; Dyhouse, "Mothers" 29; Gorham 17, 162). Although prescriptive literature may have only a tangential relation to the actualities of nineteenth-century British women's lives (Lewis, "Introduction" 6), Victorian prescriptive literature depicted the daughterly ideal. Genderization was determined by social class (Abbott 31; Gorham 27, 162; Davidoff and Hall 29). Middle- and upper-class Victorian daughters were expected to put family duties above personal needs and pleasures (Dyhouse, *Feminism* 14, 24). The Prinseps and Camerons, wealthy, Anglo-Indian, and nonphilistine though they were, exhibited much the same gender hierarchy as more traditional middle-class Victorian homes: daughters did their elders' bidding.

However, Julia Jackson did not grow up in a traditional Victorian family. Possibly because of the peripatetic nature of her youth and adolescence and perhaps because her mother's illness exacerbated Maria Jackson's reliance on her daughter, the mother-daughter relation was deeply enmeshed (Q. Bell, I, 17; Stephen, MB 34, 71–75; Love, 58–59, 81, 93, 120–23, 136; DeSalvo, *Impact* 41). Such intensity characterized some conventional upper-class mother-daughter relations in mid-Victorian England (J. S. Lewis, *Family* 65, 69–70) Middle-class Victorian daughters could develop complicated feelings about their mothers that were not always positive (Dyhouse, *Feminism* 24–28; Davidoff and Hall 338).

In Julia's family, where Leslie Stephen speculated that the father played a subsidiary role (MB 26; Love 55), Julia's service to the mother, who served as head of her household, was the expected role for the middle-class Victorian daughter. The effects of such training influenced the course of Julia Stephen's adult life.

The analysis by which I read Julia Jackson Stephen's behavior as indicating an extreme lack of self-care with an almost indiscriminate insistence on care for others, was first made by her own daughter Virginia Woolf. Courageously facing her own experiences and feelings first and then by synthesizing this understanding with her wide reading in what might now be termed the documents of cultural studies, Woolf was able to question Victorian and Edwardian cultural expectations about women's role in the family. This work enabled her to analyze what had happened to her mother and to speculate about the specific ways in which this upbringing within that gendered cultural context had caused difficulties in the lives of Julia Stephen's children.

The Victorian Family System

Before I examine contemporary theories of codependence, it is necessary to state that the middle-class family as an institution was designed in Victorian England to foster codependence in the wife and daughter and to enforce this legally as a woman's role. Far from being considered unhealthy, a codependent middle-class female in Victorian England was performing her socially defined role.

The ideal Victorian middle-class woman was an obedient wife and loving mother, organizing household life to sustain the patriarch who had jurisdiction over the lives of women and children (Dyhouse "Mothers"; Roberts). She was expected to teach by precept and example the sharp demarcation between sons and daughters as to family resources, public and private manners and activities, and education, readying the son for economic life and the daughter for reproducing such households as those in which they were raised. This gendered "domestication" was inseparable from class and racial prejudice; hence it did not apply to working-class women or women of the color in the dominions who were delineated not as "women," but as "others" or as "animals" (Pratt 86–107; Spurr 76–80; McClintock 245–46). In her novels and two feminist tracts, Virginia Woolf documented and rejected this gendered inequality.

The economic situation of middle-class wife and mother diverged sharply from that depicted by prescriptive literature. In British Common Law before the reforms of the 1880s, the wife had no legal existence beyond her husband. A wife could not own property, incur debt, or retain any money she might earn without the husband's permission. She and her children were legally her husband's property. No legal category for marital rape existed (Hammerton 103–108, 119). Wife beating was legal. Dominated by social convention and legal restrictions, a woman was under as much pressure to perform her expected role to insure her economic stability and that of her children as her husband was to perform his (Holcombe; J. S. Lewis, *Family* 59–60).

To the Lighthouse assaults the Victorian ideology of gender division through an oblique narrative of the psychic costs to Victorian parents and children of living within such a family and imperial state. There were courageous Victorian intellectuals who advanced criticisms similar to Woolf's in *To The Lighthouse*. For example, John Stuart Mill described the typical result for women of the family and social system as severe character deformation. Mill suggested that the patriarchal ideology coupled with economic and social barriers precluded middle-class female rebellion against male power. Further, "[m]en do not want solely the obedience of women, they want their sentiments. All men . . . desire to have . . . not a forced slave but a willing one . . ." (141).[4] Further, Mill argued, middle-class wives need scope for their energies, but "[w]here liberty cannot be hoped for, and power can, power becomes the grand object of human desire" (238). Mill's is a gendered political analysis. He does not see women's behavior as natural, but as a deformation of personality that is the direct result of oppression. He is not analyzing women as schemers, but as survivors (Rossi 58–63).

John Stuart Mill could be describing both the gendered ideology that buttressed Julia Jackson's upbringing, and the power arrangements in the Ramsays' marriage in *To the Lighthouse*. Hence, Mill's reading of the family as a series of contested sites for power connects his insights to some current medical controversies about family systems theory and to the concept of codependence.

Feminist Definitions of Codependence

Behaviors labeled codependence appear in varied American discourses. The earliest term in alcoholism discourse was "co-alcoholism," implying that alcoholism affected the entire family (Dulfano 3–9). Even though the family dynamic was acknowledged, some clinicians blamed the wife for her choice of spouse (S. Brown, *Alcoholic* 249). Thus from its inception, the concept was problematic.

Diverse feminists dispute the concept of codependence. A series of critiques appeared in the popular American press within months of one another in 1990 (Kaminer; Tallen; Gordon and Marcus). These articles did not interrogate the diverse medical models of codependence, but focused on its mass media representation in such works as those by Sharon Wegscheider-Cruise, Robert Subby, and Anne Wilson Schaef. Each article presented negative views of "the Recovery movement," critiquing an often distorted representation of "12-Step programs" from a middle-class white feminist perspective.

Concurrently with feminist journalists, many feminist clinicians have interrogated codependence as depicted in medical models. In *Challenging Codependency* North American and Canadian social workers argue that the medical diagnosis is yet another method by which male psychiatric theory is given license to misread women's behavior as self-destructive rather than political, while male behaviors are rarely criticized (Kokin and Walker 85–87; Krestan and Bepko 106–109; Lodl 211–16; Asher and Brissitt 131). They suggest that many medical concepts of codependence pathologize behaviors that, when read as resistance, gain political credibility (Van Wormer 126–27; Walters 190–91). Those behaviors that may be labeled codependence are survival strategies within family and social systems wherein women are not in positions of strategic domination.

Their arguments are important but rely on problematic strategies. Almost none of the essayists state clearly which medical models of codependence they query. Most of the contributors essentialize women by claiming that many of the overlapping symptoms that are named codependent occur in "all" women in "all" circumstances of oppression in families in North America (McKay 223; Van Wormer 120–21; Krestan and Bepko 101–102; Hagen 199–203; Lodl 208–209). Arguing thus, many of the writers make the same universalizing claims that they object to in the discourses they interrogate. Overgeneralizations of this sort have been demonstrated to be based on a racialized tendency to obscure the experiences of women of different classes, races, and gender preference (Spelman). Such views are useful neither to political action nor to scholarly argument.

The feminist critiques I have summarized imply that women engage in behaviors that have been labeled as codependent. Their goal is to reframe and control the discourse. I agree that cultural constructions of family, gender, class, and race shape "codependent" behavior; codependence is not an individual pathology.[5]

Feminist social workers and psychologists, among others, formulate different definitions of codependence because the American Psychiatric Association, which authors the *Standard Diagnostic and Statistical Manual,* a work I have cited in the Hardy and Joyce chapters, does not recognize codependence as a psychiatric illness. Rather than a reflection of gender bias in psychiatric circles, Timmen Cermak, M.D., viewed the struggle as one between "grassroots" healing modes and the entrenched power of the medical establishment ("Co-Addiction" 266–69).[6]

The term codependence describes a series of reactive patterns of behavior within a family system. For that reason, my definition of the term requires that it be embedded in a feminist examination of family systems theory. Thus I turn now to interpretations by David Elkin, Murray Bowen, Stephanie Brown, and Timmen Cermak of individual behaviors within family systems. Their work illuminates some aspects of both Julia Jackson Stephen's life choices and also the narrative construction of Mrs. Ramsay in *To the Lighthouse.* I will define Mrs. Ramsay's codependence as a survival strategy apparent in her obsessional focus on and attempts to manage the dominant male—and others—in a rigidly hierarchical Victorian family and its wider social network.

As I noted earlier, discussions of codependence originated in analyses of "co-alcoholism" within alcoholic families.

Elkin's *Families Under the Influence* is iconoclastic, arguing (like David McClleland whom I cite when discussing pub behaviors in *A Portrait of the Artist as a Young Man*) that relationships between the non-alcoholic and the alcoholic are battlegrounds for power. His assertion that the alcoholic has the upper hand in manipulative skill leads him to suggest that co-alcoholism is a survival strategy. In coping with the difficulties of living with familial alcoholism, the non-alcoholic partner struggles to exert whatever control is possible over a random, often violent, and usually economically limited life, while retaining some sense of respect for the self and its talents.

Fancifully speculating about advertising "for a position as the wife of the alcoholic," Elkin compiled a skill-based resume of 18 items. These include a "[h]igh level or organizational ability" often resulting in "overachievement" and "working consistently at 120% of capacity." The applicant should be "[resilient] with a high tolerance to pain," and "out of touch with her own needs." She must possess "a [h]igh level of nursing and care taking skills," and the "ability to delay gratification indefinitely." And finally she should excel at "[s]kill at diplomacy and emotional manipulation." (57–58).

Clearly, Elkin's respect for the many-faceted skills required to survive alcoholic family dysfunction is what some literary critics might name a "strong reading." Feminists would question Elkin's gendered view. Concerned not to misinterpret loss of self in alcoholic families as resilience, Stephanie Brown and Timmen Cermak might question Elkin's suggestion that the manipulation of others might be a survival skill rather than a problematic expectation that one can force others to do one's will if only one works at it hard enough.

Like that of David Elkin, Murray Bowen's work analyzes the family as a power nexus. Murray Bowen's pioneering work in family systems theory posited the family as a site of struggle for dominance, in other words as a series of differential and gendered power arrangements.[7] Bowen's gender-neutral categories may be part of his repeated refusals to label or to single out family members for blame (422, 444, 472, 492). As a family systems theorist, he posits family interactions as the site of dysfunction, not one gender, one race, or one patient.

Bowen conceptualized a "scale" of "differentiation" measuring the amount of a family member's enmeshment in the family system. Some people remained mired; others achieved relative autonomy. Family members unable to extricate themselves from the family power system Bowen noted were persons with "low differentiation of self." For those in the family with "low differentiation of self," fusion is both the method and the objective of self in relationships (472). Bowen's sophisticated readings of the minutia of family interactions such as triangulation and intergenerational "transmission," have a direct bearing on my reading of how Virginia Woolf formulated a fiction of family interactions (204–206).

In the Bowenian system, a person with "low differentiation of self" has no core self that is inviolable by the perceived needs or demands of others. Such a self's survival skills consist in hiding its core and in manipulating or pleasing others by bending to their domination (Bowen 200–201), trading "core self" in order to facilitate peace or appease someone more powerful in that system (Bowen 472–80).

I would read this self as "codependent" because, as Bowen states, his or her whole life is "totally relationship oriented" (201). Murray Bowen refers to the process by which a "pseudo-self that is involved in fusion and the many ways of giving, receiving, lending, borrowing, trading and exchanging of self" (366) as becoming "de-selfed" (366).

Although to his critics, Murray Bowen is no feminist, his insistence on power as the means of interaction among family members allies him to such feminists as Jane Lewis, Ellen Ross, and Leonore Davidoff, who read the family as the site of power struggles determined by gender and position in the hierarchy.

Stephanie Brown locates codependence as a developmental coping strategy necessary to survive in an alcoholic family. Like Elkin and Bowen, Stephanie Brown suggests that behaviors that she terms codependence are learned responses to familial dynamics. Children raised in alcoholic families develop a "false self" that helps them to circumvent familial chaos, frequent emotional or physical violence, the constant inconsistencies, and the denial of an alcohol problem in such families (S. Brown, *Adult* 60).[8] These children develop codependence as a coping strategy because "people who spend their days reacting to another rather than to following their own inner voice, will lose, or never develop, a sense of independent self . . . [but] one tied to the needs or dictates of the [other] person" (*Adult* 60).

Stephanie Brown points out similarities in adaptive strategies in alcoholic families to families wherein there is chronic illness in one or both parents (*Adult* 68–69). "The onset of the illness and its progression require a response and major adjustments from all family members" (*Adult* 68). The "disabled" parent's needs become central and "dominate" the family system (*Adult* 68).

Brown's analysis seems relevant to Julia Jackson's experience of her mother's illness. As Mrs. Jackson's condition worsened, Julia as a Victorian daughter shaped her life around caring for her mother. Whatever the complicating factor of her use of addictive medication, the fact of Maria Jackson's progressive illness and her emotional responses—such as the self-absorption apparent in her letters to Julia Stephen (Reid, *Art* 459)—to these had a formative effect on Julia Jackson. Her mother's needs seemed to have taken precedence over those of her second husband and children and herself. She was "over-determined" to develop the personality structure of a child who had had to sacrifice her own needs for nurturance and autonomy to the need of her parent for care (Love 48; DeSalvo, *Impact* 41).

In the theoretical discourses I have cited, codependence presupposes a survival strategy, not a personal neurosis or moral failing. The term codependence designates a relationship with someone on whom the self is dependent, usually economically, sexually, and/or socially. Elkin, Bowen, and Brown emphasize that family systems of power, dominance, and manipulation produce hierarchical situations in which the "low differentiated self," or the "co-alcoholic" or the "codependent" must survive as best as she or he can. They neither use the word "victim," nor claim that such behaviors are a widespread "addiction." Bowen, Elkin, and Brown's interpretations have informed my political analyses of Mrs. Ramsay's behaviors as fictionalized in *To the Lighthouse,* and have shaped my understanding of aspects of Julia Jackson Stephen's life choices.

Interrogating Julia Stephen's Behavior as Codependent

I have partially summarized Elkin, Bowen, and Brown's analyses of self-sacrifice within a nexus of family power, providing a context and methodology for interpreting codependence.

What I will interrogate as Julia Stephen's codependence appeared in her first marriage. The source for such information is not unbiased: Sir Leslie Stephen's description in *The Mausoleum Book* (the therapeutic journal he wrote shortly after Julia's death) of Julia's marriage to Herbert Duckworth must be qualified by Stephen's depression when he wrote it and his conventional expectations about women and family. He envied the devotion Julia had pledged to Herbert Duckworth, and may have exaggerated the couples' unity in order to exacerbate his own sense of loss (MB 35).

Reading Julia's letters written during her engagement to her first husband, Sir Leslie Stephen reports that "[s]he made a complete surrender of herself . . . [t]he two lives were to become one . . ." (MB 37). John Stuart Mill deplores the fact that women were expected to lose themselves in marriage. Even Mrs. Sarah Stickney Ellis's widely-read Victorian conduct book, *The Wives of England* advises dissimulation and manipulation, not merger as a marital strategy. Neither Julia Stephen's mother nor her aunts appear to have espoused fusion as a marital idea. In fact, in emphasizing what she calls Julia's "maternal" heritage, Jean Love speculates that the Pattle sisters had married men whom they could "dominate" (48, 55). Possibly Julia Jackson had learned that love required fusion from her relation to her mother, not from observing the marriages in her family.

During their short marriage, the Duckworths "were very rarely separated; she accompanied him upon [his duties as a Judge of the Northern] circuit whenever she was able" (MB 38).[9]

Whenever Herbert Duckworth was late, Julia Duckworth exhibited intense anxiety, as her sister Mary later reported to Sir Leslie

(MB 39). Unfortunately, Julia Jackson's fears were realized. Herbert Duckworth died within 24 hours of a sudden illness on September 19, 1870. Julia Duckworth was expecting her third child, born October 29, 1870, six weeks after his father's death.

Julia Duckworth was honest about her response to Herbert's sudden death. She wrote a letter to Sir Leslie when he was courting her (cited in full in his *Mausoleum Book*) acknowledging that she was aware that in her widowhood she had accepted social convention. This letter demonstrates cultural prescriptions for middle-class Victorian women's behavior: to put self first would harm a woman's children; a woman's expression of direct grief would make her a burden to others. Incessant service effectively redirected unacceptable feelings, disguising them under the appearance of cheerfulness. Mourning truthfully contravened the female role, for "there was Baby to be thought of" (MB 40).

The syntax of the letter suggests that Julia Jackson was not conscious that she had had a choice: "[t]here was nothing to be done" (MB 40). Putting her own health before the needs of others had occurred to her only as a thought to be suppressed.

After Herbert's death, Julia "became a kind of sister of mercy. Whenever there was trouble, death or illness in her family, the first thing was to send for Julia, whether to comfort survivors or to nurse the patients. She became a thoroughly skilful [*sic*] nurse" (Stephen, MB 40).

In spite or because of this life of service Julia Stephen experienced almost continuous depression (DeSalvo, *Impact* 114; Caramagno 115–24). John Bicknell notes that Julia had written to her aunt Julia Margaret Cameron five years after her husband's death, "[i]f only I could just die" ("Ramsays" 5). She later confided to her second husband "that death would be the greatest boon that could be bestowed upon her" (MB 41; see also Love 65).

Leslie Stephen believed that Julia's nursing was noble in itself but was also one of the ways she coped with her sadness (MB 41, 60–61). Indeed, Julia had stated in her letter that keeping busy kept her from dwelling on herself. Love speculates that "[p]ossibly there was also something incipiently suicidal in the extent of her self-sacrifice" (69).

The causes of Julia Stephen's self-immolation are numerous, though these seem connected to a complex mixture of her over-responsible—though socially approved—accession to her mother's increasing dependence on her; her severe depression after her widowhood; and the difficulties of meeting Sir Leslie's needs and those of her many children and other dependents. She died an exhausted woman at forty-seven. Photographs of her shortly before her death show a woman looking to me as if she were sixty-five or seventy (DeSalvo, *Impact* 232 ff.).

Almost immediately after reluctantly agreeing to marry Leslie Stephen (MB 51; Love 81–101), Julia Duckworth spent the six weeks before their wedding nursing her uncle Thoby Prinsep through his final illness (Gillespie and Steele xx). At any time that her mother's health was threatened, Julia Stephen left her husband and children to attend to Mrs. Jackson who also stayed "frequently with the Stephens until her death" in 1892 (Gillespie and Steele xxi). Additionally, she nursed other family and friends through illness, then sustained the bereaved survivors (Gillespie and Steele xx-xxii). Beyond her family duties, Julia Stephen performed unpaid volunteer nursing for the impoverished in London and in the area where the Stephens' summer home was located, St. Ives, Cornwall (Gillespie and Steele xxi).

Julia Stephen's martial duties included sustaining her husband through his increasing depressions (Annan 111–12; Love 111–38; DeSalvo, *Impact* 19–22, 115–16, 135–36) and raising eight children. In addition to her three children by her first marriage, Leslie and Minnie Thackeray had had a child, Laura, whom Julia now helped raise.[10] Four more children were born from Leslie and Julia's marriage: Vanessa, 1879, Thoby, 1880, Virginia, 1882, and Adrian, 1883. The Stephens were financially comfortable enough to employ seven servants (Q. Bell I, 20). Following the typical upper-middle-class Victorian arrangement, the children lived separated from the adults in the nursery where they were attended by a staff of servants (DeSalvo, *Impact* 115–16, 162–63).

Woolf scholars dispute the efficacy of Julia Jackson's mothering. Leslie Stephen's conventional view of his wife as a "saint" contrasts sharply with Jean Love's conviction that "[s]he never deliberately neglected the children, but all too often they were low on her list of priorities" (110). Louise DeSalvo compassionately remarks that "it would be incorrect and unfair to underestimate the amount of stress and sheer physical labor that were required of Julia" (*Impact* 117). Nevertheless, DeSalvo's complex assessment of Julia Stephen's mothering reveals that her rigid enforcement of male prerogative left her daughters continuously exposed to male violence or its threat (*Impact* 48). Further, Virginia Woolf felt unmothered, acknowledging her continued need for maternal protection and attention (*D3* 52).

Woolf observed that her mother favored sons over daughters; she thought that Adrian had been her mother's favorite (*MOB* 83). Martine Stemmerick makes the point that Julia and Leslie Stephen had raised their sons and daughters in accordance with the rigid Victorian division of male and female roles (56–57, 60). However even Sir Leslie had questioned Julia's harshness to her oldest daughter, Stella Duckworth (MB 59). Did Julia Stephen's treatment of Stella reenact her own self-surrender to her mother?

Significantly, Julia had told Leslie that "she was hard on Stella because she felt Stella [to be] 'part of myself'" (*MOB* 96). Just as Julia had never left her own mother, the relationship that took precedence over all others after her first husband's death, so Stella was expected to serve Julia. Julia's view of Stella as "a part of herself" (Stephen, MB 59) who must sacrifice self for mother and men suggests a pattern that Murray Bowen refers to as "transmission" of family behaviors from one generation to the next (491). In her young adulthood, and after her mother's death, Stella's life of extensive service was modeled on her mother's.

Summarizing his wife's behavior before and during her second marriage, Sir Leslie noted "[w]hen she had saved a life from the deep waters, that is, she sought at once for another person to rescue, whereas I went off to take a glass with the escaped" (MB 41). He describes his wife's as a life of caretaking at the expense of self, a remarkable assessment as he expected self-sacrifice in women. However, his tone may arise from the fact that he resented Julia's caring for anyone beside himself (Love 117–26).

Woolf repeated her father's description in a 1907 memoir: her overextended mother "sank, like an exhausted swimmer, deeper and deeper in the water" (*MOB* 39). In 1939 Woolf admitted that she felt shortchanged by Julia's behavior: "She had not time, nor strength, to concentrate ... upon me. ... Can I remember ever being alone with her for more than a few minutes? Someone was always interrupting" (*MOB* 83).

According to her own description and that of her second husband and daughter Virginia Woolf, Julia Jackson seems to have fulfilled almost all if not the complete list of fanciful requirements Michael Elkin suggested that a spouse would need to flourish in a contemporary alcoholic family: brilliant management skills, over-responsible care of others, and neglect of self. Elkin also implies that an ability to manipulate others so that they do one's will, experienced as for their best interest, is characteristic of such a spouse (57–58).

Murray Bowen's suggestion that those with "low differentiation of self" seek fusion might apply to Julia Jackson's relation to mother and her daughter Stella Duckworth. I have already noted Bowen's analysis of intergenerational "transmission" in Stella Duckworth's reenacting her own mother's self-sacrificing family behavior.

Additionally, Timmen Cermak's diagnostic criteria ("Co-Addiction" 270) offer an illuminating reading of much of Julia Jackson's behavior. Cermak states that codependents make "[c]ontinued investment of self-esteem in the ability to influence/control feelings and behavior, both in oneself and others, in the face of serious adverse consequences" ("Co-Addiction" 270). Virginia Woolf attests to her mother's "imperious" will, expressed in controlling behavior that undermined her health and cut short her life span (*MOB* 39).

Codependents assume "responsibility for meeting others' needs, to the exclusion of acknowledging [their] own needs" (Cermak, "Co-Addiction" 270). Woolf and Leslie Stephen cite numerous examples of such behavior, including the number of people from whom Julia Stephen received letters begging for emotional sustenance (V. Woolf, *MOB* 38), and her continuous familial and community nursing care.

Codependents are enmeshed "in relationships with personality disordered, chemically dependent, and impulse-disordered individuals" (Cermak, "Co-Addiction" 270). Leslie Stephen's emotional fragility, outbursts of rage, and his constant demands for emotional sustenance suggest problems with impulse control. I have also speculated that Maria Jackson, with whom Julia Jackson had her first codependent relationship, might have been chemically dependent.

Codependents exhibit "at least three of the following: (5) Compulsions (6) Anxiety (9) Stress-related medical illnesses" (Cermak, "Co-Addiction" 270). Both Virginia Woolf and Leslie Stephen observed Julia's compulsion to control and care for others besides herself, her severe anxiety states, and her early death in partial reaction to severe stress.

Virginia Woolf's self-analysis was extensive, occurring in fictionalized narrative, letters, diaries, and conversations. As part of that self-analysis, she fully explored the Victorian family dynamic and its impact on women, children, and the British Empire. She thought a great deal about her mother's choices (for example, her antisuffrage activity; her infantalizing of Sir Leslie). Insofar as she could, Woolf rejected the life her parents had led. Although doing so was difficult, she refused to suppress her will or ideas that were not acceptable to the men of her class and acquaintance.

I will argue that, as part of her self-creation, Woolf speculated that some white privileged women's oppression in nineteenth- and twentieth-century British culture could result in behaviors similar to those that her mother chose. Woolf theorized that such behaviors were culturally reinforced rather than the result of personal weakness. Much of this behavior she read as a survival skill, one of resistance to annihilation. Hers is an inherently political analysis (Black). Woolf's narrative of the Ramsays' as a complex relationship in which threats of violence are a continuous presence ties that marriage to the sustaining of male violence by the imperial state (Lilienfeld, "Lion"; "Can She?").

Woolf also saw in some women like her mother and Mrs. Ramsay the potential for self-destruction. Woolf refused to interpret all women as always agents or always victims, but she did acknowledge that some white privileged women were sometimes victims, even though they struggled not to be, and were themselves implicated in the oppression of other women, for example, women of color or working-class women. These privileged women, she appears to suggest, were not sufficiently or consistently allied with other women to resist oppression or protest against their part in it. Virginia Woolf's feminist analyses meant that she had the privilege of leading a life very different from that of Julia Jackson Duckworth Stephen's.[11]

NARRATIVE STRATEGIES IN *TO THE LIGHTHOUSE*

I read *To the Lighthouse* as Virginia Woolf's feminist analysis of Victorian family, Victorian culture, and Victorian empire. Virginia Woolf herself created the reading strategies for such a feminist analysis, as the collective efforts of explication by American academic feminist critics have made clear. These feminist analyses of Woolf's essays, letters, polemics, diaries, holographs, and writing strategies over the last 25 years have established the theoretical framework that underpins my readings.[12]

This theoretical framework suggests connections between narrativity in *To the Lighthouse* and *A Portrait of the Artist as a Young Man*, for both novels deploy multiple narrative voices. The implied authorial voice of *To the Lighthouse* is "polyphonic" and "communal" (Du Plessis 62–67) or "collective" (J. H. Miller, "Rhythm" 174) because it is located in several coexistent, nonhierarchical consciousnesses. This multi-layered narrative obliquely interprets plot and character through "image plots" which interconnect images of violence, domination, empire, and male aggression. Ironically, Lily Briscoe's obsessional focus on Mrs. Ramsay enacts codependence at the level of both characterization and narrative, for it is primarily in Lily's *oratio obliqua* that such connections are voiced. Lily Briscoe's feminist interpretations of the Ramsays' marriage and its cultural meanings support my political analysis of Mrs. Ramsay's codependence. Further, codependence operates as a narrative strategy observable in characters' "hypervigilance" (Cermak, "Co-Addiction" 270), observations of others that might be termed "mind reading," and other codependent survival strategies of resistance to domination.

From 1917 through 1927, Virginia Woolf theorized and created a narrative praxis that uncoupled narrator from omniscient intervention in plot and characterization. From metaphor to grammars of solution, Woolf split the biographical from the implied author and narrator. That which was submerged as narratorial voice reemerged without embodiment as ruptured, subversive plot and image-clusters.

Woolf had determined that what she termed the "damned egotistical self" (*D2* 14) must be jettisoned, replaced by, "a wall [separating] the book from [the] self" (*D2* 14) and from any political agenda or what Woolf repeatedly termed "personal grievance" (*AROO* 76). However, as Jane Marcus, Herbert Marder and Naomi Black, have argued, Virginia Woolf wanted her novels to advance "feminist, socialist, pacifist" ideas (Marcus, "Soap Operas"; Marder 18–21, 156–169; Black 180–197). The narrative of *To the Lighthouse* balances these contradictory goals, avoiding the appearance of omniscience, while indirectly presenting a feminist interpretation.

Woolf has dispensed with any visible narrating presence in *To the Lighthouse* (Auerbach 469–70). Writing in her diary on September 5, 1926, Woolf states: "[*To the Lighthouse*] is all in *oratio obliqua*. Not quite all; for I have a few direct sentences" (*D3* 106).

According to *New Latin Grammar* published in New York in 1888 by Ginn and Co., the literal translation for this term is "indirect discourse."[13] Different readers experience different degrees of narratorial control in Woolf's use of what is now called "free indirect discourse," but most agree that, the technique disperses "[the power of the] unitary authorial voice, by attributing discourse to many different voices and undermining distinctions between them . . ." (Mezei 85; see also Lanser 113–19). Free indirect discourse is polyvocal, containing at least "two styles, two languages, two voices, two semantic and axiological systems" (Prince 34–35). This technique disguises the originating point of the narrative voice (Rimmon-Kenan 113; Chatman 201).

Additionally, other voices come from the points of view of subsidiary characters, while still other voices circulate as "gossip" (Poole, "'We'" 86–87). Usually this gossip is presented through Lily Briscoe's *oratio obliqua* as "people said." For example, Lily recalls what she had heard about Mr. Carmichael's grief at Andrew's death (*TTL* 289), and what she has observed and has heard about Mr.

Ramsay's notorious temper—"[people said] [s]he let him make those scenes" (*TTL* 291). Other kinds of gossip, however, float without attribution throughout Book One. Observing her, the narratorial voices speculate on Mrs. Ramsay's unhappiness: "Never did anybody look so sad" (*TTL* 46). Those voices repeat speculation: was there perhaps "some other, earlier lover, of whom rumors reached one" (*TTL* 46)? More voices are heard in *To the Lighthouse* than those of the characters and the implied author (DuPlessis 162–67; Poole, "'We'").

Critical disputes about Woolf's narrator(s) are inseparable from critical disputes about plot (Leaska; Espinola 646; Lanser 116; Minow-Pinkney 105–106; Lilienfeld, "Spear" 160–61). In 1919, Woolf had appeared to reject the tyranny of Victorian and Edwardian plot conventions in order to represent consciousness. Thought, inseparable from feeling, would provide a new kind of plot (V. Woolf, "Modern" 154). To that end, Woolf "decentered" "the heterosexual couple" to focus on "non romantic pairings"; Woolf reversed traditional hierarchies, demonstrating that the so-called "trivial" was crucial and the so-called important was "inessential" (Du Plessis 48, 56–57).

Woolf replaced omniscient narration by a flexible polyvocality. A narrative of imagery takes the place of what would be the storytelling function of an omniscient voice. Harvena Richter named these "symbol clusters" which accrue increasing meaning at each appearance (Richter 201).[14]

Feminist critics have proven that what Richter identified as "symbol clusters" may also be read as a series of allusions (Marcus, *Languages* 36–56). North American feminist Woolf critics have traced these allusions to their sources and have discovered them to reveal more than a character's personal psychology or the cultural unconscious. They are, in fact, sustained cultural and political commentaries. These indirect commentaries reject violation, re-present the interpenetration of social being by cultural ideologies, and convey an ongoing class and gender analysis. In its explication of simile, metaphor, and allusion, almost all North American feminist criticism of Woolf's fiction from the mid-1970s to the present will bear out this assertion.[15]

The combination of ruptured, subversive plots, which cause cognitive dissonance in the reader's mind by flouting readers' expectations, the undecidability of "who is speaking" word by word in *oratio obliqua,* and image-plots, orchestrates a text rich in varied voices.

Woolf's narrative strategies have created in *To the Lighthouse* a novel that is often impenetrable to first-time readers (Daugherty, et al., "Roundtable"). David Lodge has suggested that the reader is destabilized in time and space where she or he expects, by conventions of psychological realism, to be fully informed about both.

It is clear that *To the Lighthouse* refuses to root the reader in a stable universe. In any given sentence, the reader is located in an approximate physical space, usually an unclearly defined area of the Ramsays' summer house in the Hebrides or its spacious grounds. Without warning the reader is wafted miles away from this unclear though fixed point, as the mind of the character (or narratorial voices) focuses on a spot often many miles removed. Spatial shifts are matched by temporal displacement (J. H. Miller, "Rhythm" 173–77; Spencer 156–57)). Because of Woolf's superb manipulation of *oratio obliqua,* a definite assessment of consciousness is as difficult to establish as is clarity about time and space. This occurs partly because the characters, whose interior thoughts are unreliably reported by the narratorial voices, swing repeatedly from one extreme emotion to another. No feeling is unambivalent; all feelings revert to their opposites.[16]

Marcy Bauman has argued that such processes of modernist narrative as I have analyzed pertain to alcoholism, a reading she and I arrived at independently of each other. Interrogating the narrative strategies of William Faulkner's *The Sound and The Fury,* Bauman argued that these "force [the reader to adopt] the meaning-making strategies that children of alcoholics are forced to assume" (291). The narrative of *To the Lighthouse* arises from codependence obsession, as I will show. Both Lily's codependent focus on Mrs. Ramsay and Mrs. Ramsay's obsessional fixation on her husband are integral to the narrative strategy of *To the Lighthouse.*

Virginia Woolf embeds a consistent feminist interpretation of *To the Lighthouse* within the text, though not all readers accept it.

To do so, Woolf interrogates Mrs. Ramsay's obsessional fixation upon her husband through Lily Briscoe's obsessional focus on Mrs. Ramsay.

The reported thoughts of a surrogate daughter in *The Mayor of Casterbridge*—Elizabeth-Jane, and Lily Briscoe in *To the Lighthouse*—assume a narrator's role. Lily Briscoe's worldview is similar to that shared by some upper-middle-class and middle-class women in late Victorian and Edwardian England (L. Bland; P. Levine). Gender is the lens through which Lily Briscoe interprets people, events, and even her painting techniques. She is highly critical of the double standard and is hypersensitive to the sacrifice of the female to the male's need, if not to his lust. She is amused by Mr. Ramsay's view of her as a useless spinster, rather than ashamed of her status (*TTL* 228). She is fiercely determined to remain an artist (*TTL* 77–78). She willingly rejects marriage. Even though she is thought to be living with her father in reduced circumstances, she is not shown as giving up her independence to take care of him (*TTL* 31). She is empathic, restrained in speech, but aggressive in thought. She has been deliberately crafted as a specific kind of feminist whose political analysis is integral to the novel. Her lesbian obsession with Mrs. Ramsay (Lilienfeld, "Mother"; Risolo 241; P. J. Smith 64–70) provides the rationale for her use as a narrative eye. Further, her observations are reiterated by the image-plots, and both counteract Mrs. Ramsay's persistent denial of the negative consequences of her marriage for herself and her children.

To describe the narrative's covert critique of the socially prescribed behaviors of Mrs. Ramsay as codependence would appear to be an anachronism. On the contrary: Virginia Woolf described some of the behaviors now named in medical literature as codependence before Michael Elkin, Murray Bowen, Stephanie Brown, and Timmen Cermak became therapists. Virginia Woolf understood that individuals were shaped in families that were systems of power reflecting and reproducing the power of the imperial state (*TG* 39, 53, 74, 78, 142; "Mary Wollstonecraft").

To the Lighthouse is ostensibly set in the early twentieth century, but explores a late Victorian family whose parents, according to internal dating, were born in the 1850s and 60s (*TTL* 14, 213,

304). Woolf recognized that the prescribed Victorian role for women upheld the Victorian family structure by forcing the wife to sacrifice her well-being in the service of husband, sons, and maybe daughters, a system complexly interwoven in Woolf's analysis with the oppressions of empire. Woolf satirized these behaviors in defining "the Angel in the House" ("Professions" 278–89) whose job was to negotiate what Woolf later called in *Three Guineas* "the pettiness," "the tyrannies," "the hatreds," "the cruelties of the private house." As a member of a group of friends, many of whom recognized that they had been emotionally damaged by their upbringings in late Victorian family systems, Woolf well knew that the Victorian female role was, by definition, life and soul endangering codependence.

Mrs. Ramsay is economically, psychologically, and socially inscribed in a series of power relations over which she has less control than she would like to believe. The narrative method represents both Mrs. Ramsay's consciousness and the family and cultural systems that shape it. Minute shifts back and forth between the narrated internal consciousness of Mrs. Ramsay and those of other characters, are mediated by at least one, if not several, disembodied, unreliable, larger consciousness(es)—what J. Hillis Miller described as a "ubiquitous bugging apparatus" ("Rhythm" 177). I will refer to these as the narratorial voices. This narrative method keeps the reader aware, if the character is only so intermittently, that Mrs. Ramsay is embedded in a debilitating power system. Such narrativity, with its breathtaking refusal to use one omniscient, narrative voice to simplify the human mind, or to privilege one character's truths over another's, is well positioned to represent the conflicting points of view of consciousnesses in a family such as that of the Ramsays where women and children are silenced.

CODEPENDENCE AS OBSERVATIONAL AND NARRATIVE STRATEGY

In *Three Guineas* Woolf named a feminist strategy of observation necessary for survival in constricting if not dangerous circum-

stances, the use of "the private [and] the public psychometer" (81).
Woolf defines this instrument, which she feels is a part of her implied female reader, as "the psychometer that you carry on your
wrist, the little instrument upon which you depend in all personal
relationships" (*TG* 81). It might resemble "a thermometer," for "[i]t
has a vein of quicksilver in it which is affected by any body or soul,
house or society in whose presence it is exposed" (*TG* 81). Responding to the objections of an implied speaker that such an instrument is too "personal and fallible," Woolf asserts that this
instrument of truthful observation is "now easily within the reach
even of the poorest of the daughters of educated men," (*TG* 81) an
unstably positioned though still privileged group. Woolf asserts that
certain women endowed with this instrument can comprehend the
"effect of power and wealth upon the soul" (*TG* 81). Woolf substantiates her argument by citing Creon's fight with Antigone, which
resulted in Antigone's resistance and eventual death. Using this example, Woolf implies that certain women can comprehend the in-
terrelations between the female self, the family, the state, the empire,
and (at great cost) resist the implied tyranny of these institutions.

How did certain women of the elite classes develop this instrument? In *A Room of One's Own*, writing about how women became diarists, letter-writers and then novelists, Woolf speculated
that the need to survive familial oppression and cultural imprisonment in certain constricted roles had forced some privileged women
to develop acute observational skills and hence to become excellent
judges of power strategies in human behavior. "People's feelings
were impressed on her"; she wrote, "personal relations were always
before her eyes" (*AROO* 70).

Some theorists of codependence also posit an instrument by
which an oppressed child or spouse may develop a way to monitor
his or her environment to observe, if not to circumvent, the situation: "hypervigilance" (Cermak, "Co-Addiction" 270). Such a strategy of intense looking implies the ability to interpret body language,
to listen to tones of voice, to differentiate what is said from what is
done. In traumatic situations, such observation may reach almost
hallucinatory proportion, for such surveillance is a necessity for survival (Herman, *Trauma* 99).[17] "Hypervigilance" is a survival strategy,

but it may at times become maladaptive if the observer believes that such observation confers the power to control (Cermak, "Co-Addiction" 270). Such looking can become obsessional, implying to the observer that she or he knows what others are thinking and planning, or that she or he is able "to enter into projective identifications as the 'receiver' of someone else's projections" (Cermak, "Co-Addiction" 270). Although Elkin suggests that manipulative obsession is a strategy of self-care, I doubt that Cermak would find "projective identification," one of Mrs. Ramsay's survival skills and an essential narrative device in *To the Lighthouse,* to be healthy.

The Ramsays' Family System

I will use specific techniques developed to interpret behaviors in family systems theory to read characters' interactions and consciousnesses in *To the Lighthouse.* In doing so, I suggest that Mrs. Ramsay's codependence is not only a mechanism for her survival, but that certain narrative techniques as well can be interpreted as similar to strategies of codependence.

The Ramsays are not literal representations of Woolf's parents, but are instead generalized images of the Victorian paterfamilias and the Victorian mother onto whom the reader can project feelings about his or her parents. Mr. Ramsay's voice is repeatedly censored or parodied (Naremore, *World* 131), reinforcing a depersonalized characterization of "the" Victorian middle-class father. His philosophical inquiries, moral views, and concepts of literary criticism do bear some resemblance to those of Leslie Stephen, but these, too, are unflatteringly flattened and thus misrepresented (Annan 86, 112–113, 317, 346–348; Bicknell, "Mr." 53–56).

If there is little evidence of Leslie Stephen's mastery of journalism, literary criticism, and the history of eighteenth-century British philosophy, there is even less indication of Julia Stephen's achievements. Julia Stephen was smarter, stronger, and much more self-aware than Mrs. Ramsay. Unlike Mrs. Ramsay, who has little time to read or think and is never shown writing, Julia Stephen was a published author. Mrs. Ramsay is ashamed that her efforts to understand and to help the poor are ineffectual, "half a sop to her own indignation" (*TTL* 18), but Julia Stephen worked as a volunteer nurse outside the home. For Mrs. Ramsay, care of Mr. Ramsay is paramount. Julia Stephen refused to relinquish other family obligations to minister solely to Leslie Stephen. The fact that her daughter, husband, and some critics interpret her rescue work as excessive need not diminish her considerable achievements.

With the collusion of the narratorial voices in *To the Lighthouse,* Mrs. Ramsay's few public utterances and much of her reported *oratio obliqua* are guarded. Julia Stephen's letters to Sir Leslie reveal a tough-minded woman, unafraid to discover and tell the truth. Further evidence that Julia Stephen did not censor herself comes from Virginia Woolf's admiring memories of her mother's satiric wit (*MOB* 35–36).

Mrs. Ramsay has been deprived of Julia Stephen's achievements, self-knowledge, and voice for a reason. She represents a woman with fewer resources, much less self-esteem and ability for consistent self-assertion. Her characterization depicts the difficult negotiations required of some privileged women to navigate the Victorian patriarchal family system. Similarly, Mr. Ramsay's deflation from the complicated, often sympathetic Leslie Stephen enables the reader to see Mr. Ramsay more as a villain than as an equal sufferer in a marital arrangement unfair to both parties.

I will analyze image, narrative, and characterization in chapters 6 through 8 of the novel. I will demonstrate that Mrs. Ramsay's codependent behaviors, sustained by cultural prescription and necessitated by her situation, harm herself and her son, yet represent her courageous struggle to make them safe in an unsafe family setting. I will decode the imagery of violation, demonstrating that patriarchal domination is a strategy found in family as well as empire.

To the Lighthouse begins by representing Victorian patriarchal family dynamics. The first words uttered in the text are a mother's promise to her favorite child that he can go to the lighthouse the next day. The husband's immediate reaction is to interfere between mother and son and attack the child (*TTL* 9–12). Murray Bowen describes such absorption of a third into a twosome as "triangulation," that is, the use of a third person exchanged between two family members as an indirect means of communication and a deflection from problems between the two (306–307). Family systems theorists might interpret this scene not as evidence of the Oedipal struggle (Abel, *Fictions* 48–58), but rather as an example of the minutely shifting balance of power among family members (Bowen 199–200). The little boy James's reaction to his father's envy is the self-protective one of a child with uncertain allies within a complex family dynamic.

The hatred that James feels for his father makes sense for reasons in addition to his father's harshness and envy. Family theorists believe that certain members of families may experience or exhibit feelings that are repressed or denied by the other members (Bowen 198–99). In Book One, no other son or daughter of Mr. Ramsay is reported as acknowledging as much hatred and fear of the father as James. This fact may result partially from the narrative methods of characterization, which use condensation, laconic abbreviations, and multiple mirrorings of characters by one another rather than detailed representation of each consciousness (Richter). The result is that James has been selected in this novel and by this family to voice inside himself the animosity attributed by narrative voices to all the Ramsay progeny. Here a narrative technique doubles as a dynamic of family politics.

Besides the children, there is someone else who may feel as much rage as James toward Mr. Ramsay, but who may never be able to express it. Mrs. Ramsay's silences are almost legendary in *To the Lighthouse*. Mrs. Ramsay's reticence is understandable, given the Victorian middle-class insistence on female suppression of all except positive feelings (Gorham 38–39). However, social constraint need not prevent consciousness of one's feelings. But Mrs. Ramsay rarely voices her feelings to herself. For example, she thinks that "she had had experiences . . . (she did not name them to herself)" (*TTL* 92). Such suppression may add to the necessity of having James say to himself that which she cannot acknowledge.

Timmen Cermak notes that codependent behavior never occurs in a vacuum, but in relationships: "interaction[s] [are] symmetric and synergistic" ("Co-Addiction" 270). Mrs. Ramsay's silence is a reaction to a family system rather than a personal failing. Her refusal to utter that which might be painful to others and her husband's equal refusal to tolerate that which mi____ self forges a covert bond between them. The b____ not always work to his advantage, however, a____ tell him she loves him (*TTL* 184–86). In add____ fusal between the parents to verbalize feelin____ even more plausible that James has become t____ the unspeakable. Beyond harm to James, the result of Mrs. Ramsay's inability to name feelings to herself and her refusal to do so with her husband are quite serious. They may cause her early death and they almost certainly reinforce the use of the children by the parents as a means to carry on their own relations.

Mrs. Ramsay's silence suggests the need to repress secrets. While there is no alcohol in *To the Lighthouse*, there is a serious behavior problem that is denied. The problem is what a late-twentieth-century reader might find as the erratic, inconsistent, childish, and often abusive behavior of Mr. Ramsay. The narrative voices specify that his is a non-willed behavior, similar, perhaps, to that which some might now label a compulsion: "an enormous need urged him, without being conscious what it was, to approach any woman, to force them, he did not care how, his need was so great, to give him what he wanted: sympathy" (*TTL* 225).

Characters in the text never know what will set him off and so must be constantly on guard. When his infantilism is activated, usually by severe anxiety about his worth and achievements, he must have immediate assurance that he is an original thinker whose work will be immortal. Needs this incessant and grandiose cannot be met. When his needs are not met, Mr. Ramsay erupts into violent temper.

Mr. Ramsay's temper and grandiose needs cause anxiety in Mrs. Ramsay similar to the anxiety that may be produced in the spouse of an active alcoholic. Questions may haunt the spouse of an alcoholic. Will the alcoholic drink? How much? Will she or he be in a fight? Will she or he be killed on the road? Will she or he be seen staggering, slurring, vomiting, or exhibiting public drunkenness? The incessant anxiety about the uncontrollable nature of drinking and its effects may cause reactive deformations in the behavior of the alcoholic's family members (Dulfano 3–9; S. Brown, *Adult* 63). Often these reactive deformations result in an unknowingness about

aviors at a conscious level and a determination to keep up
arances, if the knowledge is conscious.

Thus it is that throughout the first part of *To the Lighthouse*,
while Lily Briscoe is obsessively focused on Mrs. Ramsay, Mrs.
Ramsay is obsessively focused on how to manage Mr. Ramsay
(*TTL* 14). If not, she is under constant threat that "something violent would explode" (*TTL* 144). She feels he must be watched, jol-
lied, cajoled, tricked if necessary. His needs must first be imagined
and then met. Furthermore, no one besides herself must know the
truth about Mr. Ramsay; his reputation must be protected and appearances must be maintained. Her interiority, however, is not the
secret the text claims it is, for 12 of the 19 sections of the first part
of the book appear to report aspects of her consciousness. Nevertheless, at the time that the reader meets her, Mrs. Ramsay's identity is almost eradicated, submerged in her need to keep Mr.
Ramsay intact in public. Mrs. Ramsay has reason to remain "silent
always" (*TTL* 46).

An intricate dynamic involving James as a vehicle for parental
transactions occurs in chapters 6 through 8. Chapter 6 takes place
immediately or almost immediately after chapter 1, even though it
is placed five chapters later than the opening of the book. Mrs.
Ramsay is sitting on the steps with James while Mr. Ramsay circles
the terrace. As the scene opens, Mr. Ramsay's vanity has been "shattered, destroyed" (*TTL* 49). Mrs. Ramsay has learned from her experience of trying to control his tantrums not to speak to him when
his ego has been threatened and therefore, "she stroked James's
head; she transferred to him what she felt for her husband" (*TTL*
49), making the use of triangulation clear.

Knowing that he will not indicate how his vanity has been "destroyed," Mrs. Ramsay selects a third party in order to communi-
cate with her husband. Listening, she realizes that the silence
indicates that her husband had acted out his aggression against his
graduate student: "That was of little account to her. If her husband
required sacrifices (and indeed he did) she cheerfully offered up to
him Charles Tansley, who had snubbed her little boy" (*TTL* 28).
Mrs. Ramsay's hypervigilant "antennae" (*TTL* 161) monitor her
husband, even when she is not in his presence.

This passage demonstrates the effective use of *oratio obliqua*. Would Mrs. Ramsay have voiced to herself the savagery of her feelings about Tansley's usefulness to Mr. Ramsay? Would she have stated that she was delighted to "sacrifice" a young, vulnerable male? This seems unlikely, for almost all of her behavior rather than reported speech up to this point in the text, indicates that the narrative voices reporting her daughters' insights were correct: her motive seems to have been to have "the whole of the other sex under her protection" (*TTL* 14).

Some other voice than the character's seems to ripple through this passage, questioning the basic assumptions of that series of feelings that it reports. In light of what the reader has been told up to this point, the only words that might seem to be Mrs. Ramsay's are those of protective rage in defense of James.

This is a remarkable passage for more than its flexibly polyvocal narration. It underlines that which Mrs. Ramsay acknowledged elsewhere, that her "psychometer" is always trained on her husband to monitor his needs, partly for self-protection so that he won't bear down on her unannounced, and partly because his needs are her paramount concern.

Mrs. Ramsay's relief that neither she nor her children are the victims of the father's aggression becomes punitive toward another person even more dependent on Mr. Ramsay's power than she is. Charles Tansley's role and lower-class status enable Mr. Ramsay to act out aggression against Tansley without losing status; similarly, Tansley's class status allows Mrs. Ramsay to support her husband's use of the young man. Tansley has little recourse but to humor the professor's behavior. Nor is he merely a victim. He is as aggressive as Mr. Ramsay and gladly absorbs much of the older man's concepts of the power that professorial status conferred on the British male of his generation. That this is the case is clear to Lily Briscoe who analyzes Tansley's mode of lecturing audiences during the war (*TTL* 292–93).

Thus, this seemingly simple example of narrative reveals "hyper-vigilance," triangulation, class domination, and a woman's participation in an upper-middle-class man's abusive use of a lower-class man. That the lower-class man becomes highly aggressive when he gains power demonstrates (to Lily, who witnesses it [*TTL* 292–93]) a line of transmission of male aggression from one generation to the next and as such is central to one of the image-plots in the narrative.

The narrative voices report that inside Mrs. Ramsay's consciousness is the sense that she "cheerfully" complies with what are termed "sacrifices," suggesting that Mrs. Ramsay is an integral part of this transmission line. According to this passage, Mrs. Ramsay appears to accept as her duty the providing of "sacrifices" upon whom Mr. Ramsay may vent his feelings. For example, when Mr. Ramsay begins to suffer over the future of his works at the dinner party, Mrs. Ramsay manipulates Minta into rescuing him, as I will discuss later. Putting others in his way so that they may deflect feelings he cannot face is similar to Mrs. Ramsay's use of others as topics or social objects of exchange in her conversations with her husband.

Some of her behavior can be explained as a necessity of the narrative method. Because there is almost no access to Mr. Ramsay's interior monologue that is not parodic, Mrs. Ramsay's observations of him seem to display his interiority. Further, her use as an ear to her husband's mind serves to convey aspects of their marriage relation. Both as narrative device and as a character with "low differentiation of self" or codependence, Mrs. Ramsay sees one of her functions as serving as Mr. Ramsay's interconnection between self and others. The Ramsays' interactions consistently follow this pattern.

Verbally demolishing Charles Tansley, however, has only offered Mr. Ramsay temporary relief. He turns on his son, "ironically, flicking" James with a "sprig" (*TTL* 50). No recognition of this "flicking" of James is recorded in Mrs. Ramsay's *oratio obliqua* (50). However, Mrs. Ramsay may be anxious to deflect attention from James by deliberately provoking Mr. Ramsay. In response to her remarks, Mr. Ramsay loses control and "snapped" at her "irascibly" (*TTL* 50).

Mrs. Ramsay challenges her husband's omniscience by reminding him that he does not control the shifting winds (*TTL* 50). However, what they actually say to each other is unclear, reported rather than quoted dialogue. Mr. Ramsay's unassuaged anxieties erupt into abusive rage. In his tantrum, Mr. Ramsay curses his wife. "He stamped his foot . . . 'Damn you,' he said. But what had she said? Simply that it might be fine tomorrow. So it might" (*TTL* 50).

Almost no direct, attributable dialogue occurs in *To the Lighthouse*. Yet this curse is placed in quotation marks. Attributed dialogue in a narrative almost wholly formed of *oratio obliqua* may be seen as a textual enactment of the actual curse. The quoted line stands out on the page, just as the curse does in the marital interaction.

For a middle-class Victorian reader, the aftermath of the scene might be less noteworthy than the ungentlemanly act itself. Yet Mrs. Ramsay seems unaware that her husband has verbally abused her. That which is absent, the idea that might be phrased as "my husband cursed me," is moved from being silenced in the mind of the character to echoing loudly in the mind of the reader sensitive to the nature of verbal violence in certain twentieth-century family transactions. Mrs. Ramsay's consciousness cannot acknowledge the remark because an oppressed person with no options other than remaining in place cannot challenge power without directly threatening his or her existence. Mrs. Ramsay's response reveals her subservient position. She thus does not name his behavior to herself and argues back only in the terms he has set—the debate on the weather conditions.

Although some readers might dismiss Mr. Ramsay's outburst as a childish tantrum, contained within emotional and verbal violence of this sort is the implicit threat of physical violence. Uncontrolled rage may suggest the physical force implicit behind the social control of women (Schecheter 216–34).

In response to her husband's behavior, Mrs. Ramsay experiences self-pity. Her husband's behavior "was to her so horrible an outrage of human decency that without replying, dazed and blinded, she bent her head as if to let the pelt of jagged hail, the drench of dirty water, bespatter her unrebuked. There was nothing to be said" (*TTL* 51).

Mrs. Ramsay cannot verbalize anger because she cannot put into words the violence of the tantrum she has seen. Her *oratio obliqua* is cast in the language of Victorian ideology, not the language of self-awareness. Where is the word "I" in this passage? Where is the recognition that "I" was beaten verbally? Where is the recognition that a child witnessed the father cursing and stamping his foot? As is clear to the reader, Mr. Ramsay is not pursuing truth. He is pursuing the advantage the powerful have over the powerless. Where is the "I's" recognition of this? Silenced.

Nevertheless, even though the absent "I" cannot name its own violation or that of the child, encoded in this passage is a recognition of "brutality" toward generalized "human decency." The unnamed thing is not called violence but is trivialized into a "lack of consideration" for generalized "people's feelings." But it is given an equivalent: "wanton," "brutal," "outrage." For the phrase, "the thin veils of civilization" encodes the implication that in "uncivilized" places like the empire, such behavior is acceptable. In the white Victorian middle-class home it is not supposed to happen. Yet it has, even though the witness cannot name it. But the "I's" body language speaks. Mrs. Ramsay bends her head because "there was nothing to be said," acknowledging subservience to the out-of-control patriarch (*TTL* 51).

Why is there "nothing to be said"? As I have noted, Mrs. Ramsay, now fifty (*TTL* 14), in a narrative set in 1909, was thus born around 1860 and raised as an upper-middle-class Victorian woman. It is neither cowardice nor lack of intelligence that partially blinds Mrs. Ramsay; her upbringing seems to have ensured that she will lack the tools to recognize verbal violence. To middle-class Victorians, anger was unacceptable in women and children. Mrs. Ramsay's behaviors in her marriage and in her mothering suggest to me that in the process of being raised in a traditional Victorian middle-class family she has been "de-selfed" (Bowen 366).

Instead of confrontation, Mrs. Ramsay manipulates her husband by what Patricia Lawrence has called "strategic silence," maintaining her ladylike composure. Shaming him thus produces results, but leaves her without direct means of self-care.

Mr. Ramsay indirectly apologizes, or tries to, for what he may have said "at length" (*TTL* 51) is summarized in ten words. Mrs. Ramsay's immediate response is: "There was nobody whom she reverenced as she reverenced him" (*TTL* 51). To make it unmistakable, her response is set off in a paragraph to itself, and is later repeated almost exactly. Her husband's attempt at an apology elicits worship from her rather than emotions such as anger, acknowledgment of his limits, or worry that her son is a vulnerable witness to their debate.

Idealizing her husband serves many purposes. It protects her from having to admit some of the problematic aspects of her marriage. Idealizing Mr. Ramsay protects him, too, and protecting him from negative emotions is one of her primary goals. Rather than raging, which is as unladylike as it is unimaginable to her, Mrs. Ramsay "veils" her anger under self-abnegation: "She was quite ready to take his word for it, she said. Only then they need not cut sandwiches—that was all. They came to her, naturally, since she was a woman . . . one wanting this, another that . . . she often felt she was nothing but a sponge sopped full of human emotions" (*TTL* 51).

The key word here is "natural." Because she seems to see the female role as that which mops up after people, it is not surprising that Mrs. Ramsay may experience herself as a material whose sole purpose is to absorb others' unacceptable feelings and behavior.

What is revealed at this point in this parodic passage is the voice of a woman whose conviction that she must give all and take nothing has reached the point of self-immolation. The paragraph continues with no indication of a break in thought from her definition of woman's "natural" role to "Then he said, Damn you. He said, It must rain. He said, It won't rain; and instantly a Heaven of security opened before her. There was nobody she reverenced more. She was not good enough to tie his shoe strings, she felt" (*TTL* 51).

At no point in this passage of *oratio obliqua* is Mrs. Ramsay shown to acknowledge experiences the reader has witnessed. Reproduced in language is that which Mrs. Ramsay seems to choose as action: denial of her husband's violent outburst. Anger is absent. Idealization takes the place of any acknowledgment of how she might feel as a result of this verbal violence.

It is no accident that Mrs. Ramsay's idealization of her husband ends in her vision of herself as unfit to tie his shoes. The image reverses her daughters' comparison of her courtesy to that of "a Queen's raising from the mud to wash a beggar's dirty foot" (*TTL* 14), an image inextricable from her daughters' view of her as a symbol of the British Empire with her "ringed fingers and lace" (*TTL*

14). Although it does not strip her entirely of elite class position to equate her with the kneeling beggar, the image of Mrs. Ramsay as unfit to tie his shoes allies her with the myriads of servants—male and female—who scrubbed thousands of their employers' Victorian boots.[18]

Throughout this interchange, little James has stood silent. So intent are the parents on their struggle that James seems to have been eradicated from their consciousnesses, though not perhaps from the reader's. While Mrs. Ramsay may seem to some readers to be frozen in response to her husband's need to spew forth his infantile temper, James feels himself to be the recipient of his father's rage. Current family theorists speculate that children who witness emotional and physical violence against a parent experience themselves as violated (Krugman 132–33). Certainly James is powerless to protect himself or his mother. Perhaps equally harmful is the meaning that he might inadvertently attribute to the scene. He and his sister later make a "compact to fight tyranny to the death" (*TTL* 245). But parental interaction models no direct fight against tyranny. Mrs. Ramsay's subtle attempts to talk back to her husband in fact spur him to act out further.

This is an unfortunate legacy. That his mother cannot protect herself or him may not be obvious to her son. Certainly the legal and ideological reasons for her behavior would not have been obvious to a little boy. His mother's apparent inability to fight back, coupled with his father's obvious belief that women are to be harassed until they accede to male desires, impresses little James, its witness. Significantly, when this memory surfaces later, James blames his mother and sides with his father (*TTL* 277–78). As he sails to the lighthouse, he has become a hostile and selfish adolescent whose contempt for mother and sister far exceeds that of his own father. Thus does the narrative present intergenerational "transmission" of gendered responses.

To maintain the recognition that Mr. Ramsay's verbal violence is serious in spite of the fact that his wife can neither acknowledge it nor defend herself or her son against it, Mr. Ramsay must not be a sympathetic figure in the chapter following the argument with his wife on the terrace. The narrative achieves this objective in a variety of ways. First, Mrs. Ramsay's effort to deny the implications of her husband's behavior has little obvious effect. Rather than satiating his need for dominance, her self-sacrifice has delayed, not prevented, her husband's attack of self-hatred and conviction of his failure as a philosopher (*TTL* 53–57).

Thus when chapter 8 opens, some readers may see that Mr. Ramsay is a desperate man. His need, unlike in chapter 6, is now so fully focused on himself that he no longer perceives the existence of his son at all. Because James was silenced in chapter 6 by being removed from his parents' consciousnesses, the fact that much of chapter 8 is reported from James's *oratio obliqua* gives the effect of almost exact repetition. Chapter 8 depicts the same assault of the father/husband against the mother/wife resulting in the woman's same self-abnegation.

In challenging the "medicalizing" of battering, the British social scientists and activists R. Emerson Dobash and Russell P. Dobash characterize the American therapeutic analyses of women in family systems as blaming the victim (213–35). Although they almost certainly would not support my reading of Mrs. Ramsay as codependent, they might point to the political effect of reading James's hatred of his father in traditional Freudian terms. If in this scene James is read as wishing to kill his father and marry his mother, then what he feels about what he witnesses may be discounted. But what if James is not mistaken? What if it is not an exaggeration to read Mr. Ramsay's need as a violent, phallic weapon?

James experiences the interaction between his parents in chapter 8 as a brutal attack on his mother. During the transaction his is the only consciousness in the scene able to verbalize that which, as is clear from chapter 6, Mrs. Ramsay is represented as unable to acknowledge. James witnesses the exercise of male power over a female whose self is so erased as to experience intrusion as a voluntary act of giving.

So rapacious is the father that James "felt all her strength flaring up to be drunk and quenched by" his father's "beak of brass," which James felt repeatedly "smote" his mother (*TTL* 59). The "beak of brass" is not just a symbolic pen or a penis, but "an arid scimitar," a weapon of hand-to-hand combat (*TTL* 59). Once ripped open by this curved blade, Mrs. Ramsay's strength, her very blood and being, are being drunk. The metaphor of the "flar[ing]" blood hints at vampirism, later made explicit by Lily Briscoe's recognition that Mr. Ramsay is waiting to sink his "fangs" into Minta Doyle (*TTL* 154).

Here Mr. Ramsay receives milk, not blood: His wife becomes a "nurse" reassuring "a fractious child," not a grown man (*TTL* 60). Her efforts are successful. "[L]ike a child who drops off satisfied," he returns to his philosophical speculations "restored" (*TTL* 60).

This parental transaction resembles the one in chapter 6. At first Mrs. Ramsay is exhausted, almost completely emptied of self, but she "throbbed [with] . . . the rapture of successful creation" (*TTL* 60–61).

The narrative voice emanating from and surrounding Mrs. Ramsay dramatizes her denial of any point of view other than that which focuses on her husband's needs. In the moments of impact, she experiences as love the intrusions of what James calls the battering beak. If he needs, she must give; with each move he makes, she makes the move he wants (Cermak, "Co-Addiction" 271–72). Even his insatiability is unremarked by her consciousness as a problem.

Having seen her unable to acknowledge that her husband has cursed and abused her, a reader is not surprised that she has no language for that which James has more realistically defined as an intrusion into the wife by instruments of war. Both transactions in chapters 6 and 8 between husband and wife include weaponry and images of male incursions into the inner being of Mrs. Ramsay.

But what Mrs. Ramsay experiences is orgasmic: "the rapture" of having totally given over her consciousness (*TTL* 60–61). She feels that the beings of husband and wife have merged (*TTL* 61). Murray Bowen's reading of similar transactions among family members clarifies this interaction: "[i]t is the pseudo-self that is involved in fusion and the many ways of giving, receiving, lending, borrowing, trading and exchanging of self. . . . an automatic emotional process that occurs as people manipulate each other in subtle life postures" (366). Similarly, when living with Henchard, Elizabeth-Jane acceded to the demands of her stepfather, as did Stephen Dedalus when in Cork with his father.

During the scene, James voices that which is unknowable to the wife during it. But afterwards, Mrs. Ramsay is strong and courageous enough to acknowledge—though powerless to stop it except through death—the costs of her behavior.

After she feels "rapture" (*TTL* 61), Mrs. Ramsay has a series of physical uneasinesses. These she courageously follows to their emotional source and discovers discomfort. She suspected that she felt superior to her husband, and feared that she was not at times fully honest with him (*TTL* 61). Why should his rapacious need of her make her feel superior to him? "[I]t was their relation, and his coming to her like that, openly, so that any one could see, that discomposed her" (*TTL* 62).

Hiding the truth under false appearances becomes the goal of some members of twentieth-century North American alcoholic families (S. Brown, *Adult* 40, 43). Similarly, the fact that others can see rather than that she herself knows that such behavior is harmful is what causes Mrs. Ramsay discomfort: "for then people said he depended on her [but] . . . what she gave the world, in comparison with what he gave, [was] negligible" (*TTL* 62). She repeats her pattern of self-denigration to "veil" anger or self-pity. She cannot allow herself at first to acknowledge what is really bothering her, which is his publicly seen dependence on her, undermining her sense of herself, her mission, and her marriage.

But for a brief moment of narrative time, she voices the truth to herself. Perhaps such recognition is possible here rather than in the scene of his cursing her because his needing nursing is more culturally acceptable than the facts of male violence against women and their children; hence the insight may not require as massive a repression (*TTL* 62).

She acknowledges some of her fears about money, his fall from prominence, and even that their relation harms the children (*TTL* 62). She is rightly aware that she cannot reveal her sadness, worry, and fear. Her reluctance to acknowledge that his work may be dwindling in intellectual power is indicated by the twisted syntax: "to be afraid what he might guess, what she a little suspected" (*TTL* 62). She also acknowledges that the children are "burden[ed]" by the skewed parental interactions (*TTL* 62). (That this is accurate becomes clear in Book Three when Lily recognizes that the Ramsay children are "coerced" and "subdued" [*TTL* 222].) Mrs. Ramsay's regret is neither anger nor a decision to take action. She is incapable of direct anger, perhaps wisely, as she may have few alternatives to her financial and emotional dependence on her husband.

Buried in Mrs. Ramsay's consciousness, but available to a reader, is a more complete interpretation of her behaviors than she can voice to herself. The narrative method has made family interaction and characters' interiority the central "plot" of chapters 6 through 8. Making clear what is neither said nor thought, the narrative has represented three consciousnesses as they interact within this Victorian family system. The narratorial voices juxtapose Mr. Ramsay's agonized consciousness of his needs to Mrs. Ramsay's intense desire to meet these needs. These two consciousnesses are juxtaposed to that of little James. Encircling these mingled voices is the image-plot that, when read through the lens of 25 years of American feminist readings of the implied author's systems of allusion, substantiates James's interpretations.

Thus every behavior Mrs. Ramsay has adopted in chapters 6 and 8 is both culturally constructed and exhibits aspects of what Elkin might call co-alcoholism, Cermak and Brown might term codependence, or what Bowen might name "low differentiation of self." Mrs. Ramsay "invests" her "self esteem in the ability to influence/control feelings and behavior, both in [her]self and in others, in the face of serious adverse consequences" (Cermak, "Co-Addiction" 270). She is intent on using herself to protect and control her husband. Later I will demonstrate that her controlling Minta and Lily has "serious adverse consequences" for them. In dealing with her husband, Mrs. Ramsay clearly assumes "responsibility for meeting others' needs, to the exclusion of acknowledging [her] own needs" (Cermak, "Co-Addiction" 270). Her reading of verbal violation as the fusion that produces orgasm indicates "[a]nxiety and boundary distortions around intimacy and separation" (Cermak, "Co-Addiction" 270). Loving the infantile, bullying Mr. Ramsay whose lack of self-control, among feminist readers, is as legendary as Mrs. Ramsay's silences, indicates her "[e]nmeshment in relationships with . . . impulse disordered individuals" (Cermak, "Co-Addiction" 270).

Chapters 6 through 8 reveal that Mrs. Ramsay "discounts" her feelings, has trouble "identify[ing] her own needs," and shows "an extremely high tolerance for inappropriate behavior," which is dangerous to herself and her son. She reacts to her husband as if she were "nothing more than the sum of others' expectations." Yet she is honest enough to know, though powerless to change, her sense that she has "violated" her values and belief system (Mendenhall 16–17). But if focused only on Mrs. Ramsay, these interpretations are insufficient. The narrative method has revealed that Mrs. Ramsay's are not an isolated series of "self-destructive" behaviors. They are inextricably part of a larger family and cultural system. Her behaviors are predicated upon economic, social, and sexual dependency on Mr. Ramsay and cultural prescription. His self-aggrandizing and self-centered behaviors are encouraged by his culture. All the levels of narrative—the child's voice, the parents' voices, the image-plots—reveal that this family system represents and reproduces the culture that sustains it.

However, the supple, polyvocal narrative method, which refuses to privilege one voice over another, does not allow a single interpretation. Hence, it is possible to believe both James's view of Mr. Ramsay's behavior as violent and Mrs. Ramsay's view that it is loving, for, as James later realizes, "nothing was simply one thing" (*TTL* 277).

THE OPIUM NARRATIVE IN
TO THE LIGHTHOUSE

I have shown that in chapters 6 through 8 the Ramsays' family system is maintained by covert physical threat, hidden from the wife's view, but clearly revealed to the reader by the central characters' *oratio obliqua*. Thus codependence is both a behavioral and narrative strategy. I will now connect these interpretations to opium and to empire.

Mrs. Ramsay's interaction with Mr. Carmichael in chapter 8 demonstrates that, like her husband, she cannot maintain consistent control over her need to impose her will on those whom she considers inferior. The narrative deploys Mr. Carmichael's alleged opium addiction as a frame through which to view behaviors of Mrs. Ramsay's over which she cannot always exercise conscious control. Further, Mrs. Ramsay's interaction with Mr. Carmichael may be read through biographical reference to Maria Jackson and to Julia, her daughter.

In the published text, Mr. Carmichael's use of opiates is alleged, but not proven, highlighting the chronological superimposition of one time period over another in the text. The nature of family life and social conventions in this text replicate those of the 1850s and 1860s when opiates were legal. However, according to internal dating, Part One of *To the Lighthouse* occurs in 1909, the year after opiates were included in the Poisons Act of 1908, and at a time when British medical debates about opiates were embedded in political discourse about the effect of unrestrained opium use on subjects of the British Empire—both Indo-Chinese and British citizens. Mr. Carmichael's indolence, his self-absorption, his sleepiness, his inability to earn a living, the qualities Mrs. Ramsay attributes to him (*TTL* 62–66), are part of the racialized debate in British foreign policy that was subsumed into medical discourse from 1870 to the start of World War I (Berridge and Edwards 195–205). Tying the figure of Mr. Carmichael in *To the Lighthouse* to the British Empire, Kathy Phillips suggests that Mr. Carmichael may have become addicted to opiates "during his stay in India" (98), a fact clear in the holograph of the novel (J. Ferguson 48).[19]

Mr. Carmichael is an emblem of what may be an unhealthy dependence on false sources of sustenance. Mr. Carmichael is never directly shown interacting with anyone in the text. Ascriptions to him of love are rumors (*TTL* 289). Everything "known" about him is hearsay; John Ferguson notes that he speaks only 29 words in the text (47). Mrs. Ramsay's necessary reliance on self-suppression may mirror his reliance on opium. Hence her "demon" (*TTL* 63) may be something like his own. But her dependence on manipulating or serving others and his supposed opium reveries serve much the same purpose: escape from self.

Both appear to be isolated. He is consistently shown "lounging" (*TTL* 254) or lying "all day long on the lawn brooding presumably over his poetry" (*TTL* 154) or "asleep" (*TTL* 254), "basking" (*TTL* 265) in his lawn chair. Like Mrs. Ramsay, he remains aloof from intimate human contact. She, however, acknowledges repeatedly that she is tired from fighting with her adversary, life (*TTL* 92). She knows that life is harsh, "quick to pounce on you if you gave it a chance" (*TTL* 92). But Mr. Carmichael, although Mrs. Ramsay wishes to pity him for his wife's supposed shaming of him, is never shown in emotional pain. He exhibits no need for others' solace or admiration. He appears imperturbable. It is this difference between them that gives credence to the rumor circulated by voices of "gossip" (Poole, "'We'" 86–87) in *To the Lighthouse* that he is an opiate user (*TTL* 19, 63).

Opiate addicts whom Woolf had read and written about, Thomas De Quincey and Samuel Taylor Coleridge, accused each other of (and also themselves revealed) a dependence on what the Victorians called the "stimulant" use of the drug (Berridge and Edwards xxv), its ability to "produce a lessening of emotional distress. The [user] is in a way emotionally distanced from what is happening, and floats as it were on the surface of his [sic] experience. The drug has a *euphoric* effect" (Berridge and Edwards xxi; emphasis in original).

The opium narrative in *To the Lighthouse* consistently ties Mr. Carmichael to what Edward Said has named "Orientalism." Such Orientalism is inextricable from the artist narrative about Mr. Carmichael whose inscrutability, opacity, extreme aloofness, and constant dozing suggest both opium use and artistic necessity. Mr. and Mrs. Ramsay and Lily perceive him as doing the work of a literary artist—not as overcome by opium—while lying about on a lawn chair seeking the exact word. Because of these postures, the main characters accept the seriousness of Mr. Carmichael's writing. To Mr. Ramsay, Augustus is "a true poet" (*TTL* 145), the only recorded compliment Mr. Ramsay ever willingly is said to have paid to a male colleague. Lily Briscoe, who has never read Mr. Carmichael's published poetry, imagines it as Oriental in content and form: "It was seasoned and mellow. It was about the desert and the camel. It was about the palm tree and the sunset. It was extremely impersonal; it said something about death; it said very little about love" (*TTL* 289–90). The qualities of this poetry suggest images of Egypt and India, repeating racialized stereotypes about those cultures that were current in British governmental and scholarly writings of the early nineteenth century (Said 31–41).

John Ferguson has proven that Virginia Woolf read and wrote about De Quincey when she was writing *To the Lighthouse*. "Two thirds of the way through the unbound folder (the third volume) are nineteen lines from an article Woolf was writing in the summer of 1926 for the *London Times Literary Supplement* . . . a critical appraisal of Thomas De Quincey . . . [which] appeared . . . on September 16, 1926 while Woolf was writing chapter twelve of *To the Lighthouse*" (47).

In an essay on De Quincey of 1906, Woolf had noted that opium was inseparable from De Quincey's writing of "The English Mail Coach": "But if his mind is thus painfully contracted by *the action of certain foreign substances upon it,* the conditions in which it dwells habitually allow it to expand to its naturally majestic circumference" (*CEI* 367; emphasis added). These include the opening out and deepening down of space, the hallucinatory expansion of sound, the sense of involuntary movements of sinking down, the removal from experience as if cut off from others and imprisoned in another dimension (J. Ferguson 54; Hayter 95, 97, 113, 240–41, 250–54; V. Woolf, *CEI* 365–68).

Both Woolf and Alethea Hayter cite De Quincey's intermingling of spatial and musical imagery, not only in this essay, but as an integral aspect of all his writing. Woolf's analysis of De Quincey's essay as structured like a musical composition is substantiated by Hayter's reading of the same piece. There Hayter argues that "*[t]he English Mail Coach* . . . has a symphonic four-part structure, and within its four movements exhibits the musical forms of first and second subject, development, return to the first subject, and coda, with changes of key. . . . His experience under opium of the coalescence of memories and musical forms gave him a technique which underlay much of his subsequent writing" (Hayter 241–42; emphasis in original). Woolf would agree: "Indeed, De

Quincey's writing at its best has the effect of rings of sound which break into each other and widen out and out till the brain can hardly expand far enough to realise the last remote vibrations which spend themselves on the verge of everything where speech melts into silence" (*CEI* 368).

Alethea Hayter's view of the influence of opium upon De Quincey's style is extended by John Ferguson's assessment: "[s]ince Woolf was reading and writing about De Quincey as she was working on *To the Lighthouse,* it is certainly possible that some of De Quincey's . . . imagery spilled over into the novel" (50). For me, the imagery accompanying Mrs. Ramsay shedding her social self has similarities to Hayter and Woolf's analyses of De Quincey's opium reveries as crystallized in "The English Mail Coach." Possibly, then, what the narrative renders pictorially as Mrs. Ramsay's feeling as she submerges her social self into "a wedge-shaped core of darkness" in chapter 11 might be similar to those unspoken bodily sensations that Mr. Carmichael may experience while he is under the influence of opium and / or awaiting le mot juste (*TTL* 95–96).

In *Imperial Eyes: Travel Writing and Transculturation,* M. L. Pratt analyzes such passages in *To the Lighthouse* as examples of "the Monarch-of-all-I-survey" "discovery rhetoric" of the empire (204–5). Such discourses "estheticize" the landscape that is "represented as extremely rich in material and semantic substance" (Pratt 204). The rhetoric depicts great expanses of territory suggesting riches waiting to be plumbed by imperial commerce (Pratt 205; Spurr 17–18). Further, Mrs. Ramsay's conviction that this "de-selfed" (Bowen 366) core "could go anywhere'"; that it might travel anywhere in the world without restriction—"[t]hey could not stop it"—suggests an expansionist rhetoric marking "the lusts and ambitions—of a greedy, imperialist nation" (Winston 49). The mention of the "Indian plains" removes Mrs. Ramsay's meditation to the scene of British imperialism and the setting of Mr. Carmichael's first use of opium in the holograph of the novel (J. Ferguson 48). Indeed, the second half of this passage is replete with opiate imagery. The oceanic feelings conveyed by "it is all dark, it is all spreading, it is unfathomably deep," suggest a meditative state of mystical being, as Woolf scholars often remark (Overcarsh; Gough), yet also recall De

Quincey's extensive use of water imagery to suggest peaceful drowning, an oxymoron Ferguson notes (55–56).

With the mention of "freedom and peace," the revery spirals upward, continuing for four more pages. In the part I have cited, the segment certainly conveys the effects of what the Victorians refer to as the "stimulant" use of the drug, its ability to lull suffering and distill peace. Life's pain fades. The nonsocial being escapes "the fret, the hurry, the stir," that is the myriad demands of others upon one, and one's social responsibilities (conveyed by Mrs. Ramsay's knitting, with its suggested burden of bringing disparate strands together). The core "rest[ed]" on an inviolable foundation, not at all like the "iron girders" of "masculine intelligence" (*TTL* 159), made so problematic by Mr. Ramsay's irrationality, but on "a platform" of security. There was "peace," "rest," "eternity." This series of images thus could as well convey what might be behind the dreaminess and imperturbable repose in which Mr. Carmichael is often seen. It suggests his analgesic avoidance of human annoyance.

Here, as the passage nears its conclusion, it conveys what might be called in today's parlance "the smack of smack." A twentieth-century American addict informed a psychiatrist that injecting heroin, an opium derivative, was for him a physiological experience with similarities to "a 3-hour continuous [sexual] orgasm" (Imhof 294). As the passage continues, it effectively represents "the stimulant use of the drug." Fighting intrusive thoughts (*TTL* 97–98), Mrs. Ramsay focuses on the rolling ocean waves and the pulsating strokes of the lighthouse beam, its "silver fingers" mounting, swirling upward "stroking . . . some sealed vessel in her brain whose bursting would fill her with delight . . ." The beam "curved and swelled" until suddenly "the ecstasy burst in her eyes and waves of pure delight raced over the floor of her mind and she felt, It is enough! It is enough!" (*TTL* 99–100).

Four aspects of the biographical and the fictional "stories" are similar: India; opium use; emotional unavailability; and excessive self-sacrifice. Both Maria and Julia Jackson had lived in India, and India was the site—in the holograph of the novel—of Mr. Carmichael's increasing use of the drug.

In each case the drug use is obscured. Maria Jackson's drug use was culturally acceptable and hence unremarkable. Mr. Carmichael's drug use in the novel is merely rumor and supposition. Nevertheless, traces of drug use seem to cloud Mr. Carmichael's emotional accessibility, making him withdraw from others (*TTL* 290). Maria Jackson's maternal position ensured that Julia would honor her need for attention. Mrs. Jackson's self-absorption is a striking facet of her letters, according to Panthea Reid who characterizes Jackson as "enjoy[ing]" her "dependence" (*Art* 458), asserting that Mrs. Jackson "had no compunctions about exploiting anyone, even her much beloved daughter [Julia]" (*Art* 459). The very relationship between Mrs. Ramsay—importunate, longing for approval, and Mr. Carmichael, aloof, avoiding—depicts what it is like to desire recognition from an addict engrossed in the relation to his or her substance. Whatever its origin, however, the fictionalized relationship between Mrs. Ramsay and Mr. Carmichael suggests a veiled investigation of the role opiates played in the relationship between Maria and Julia Jackson.

The impact of empire on Mrs. Ramsay and Mr. Carmichael is consistent yet ambiguous. His opium use may resemble what I have called Mrs. Ramsay's codependence because both drug use and codependence suppress consistent rebellion in each, in her case allowing others' needs to dominate her daily life, while in his case, incapacitating him from close connection to others.

Perceived by Mr. Tansley as aptly framed by a picture of Queen Victoria, recognized by her daughters as an upholder of the system of empire and social class, Mrs. Ramsay is nevertheless deeply marked as a white woman of privilege (Winston 41, 49–52), who is herself usually subject to and unable to resist tyrannical demands.

Recent feminist studies such as those by Jeanette McVicker, Kathy Phillips, and Janet Winston of *To the Lighthouse* have revealed the presence of an ironic discourse on empire embedded in the text. Mrs. Ramsay's position as "subaltern" to Mr. Ramsay is interwoven with her position as white woman enforcing colonial rule over othered-women and men of lower social standing. Hence Mrs. Ramsay, who is herself subject to patriarchal/imperial rule within her home, nevertheless ambivalently reinforces that rule over others (R. Lewis 3).

Mrs. Ramsay's divided position is consistently demonstrated throughout the text. The British system of empire, which she supports, intrudes into the governance of her own home in an extreme of male dominance that causes her to have to watch what she says to her husband, to have to guard even her body language from his observation, and renders her so pressed at times to ensure her own emotional survival that she cannot closely monitor her son James's emotional safety.

The opium narrative in *To the Lighthouse* as crystallized in Mrs. Ramsay's "waking revery" suggests a complex series of modes and discourses of "subject(s)" of domination. The narrative represents both acceding to and resisting domination, played out in the intermingling of the imagery of codependence, opium, and empire.

INTERGENERATIONAL "TRANSMISSION"

Mrs. Ramsay is in contact with several other women who know that such a "domestic" world as hers is inimical to female health. Mrs. Ramsay's manipulation of her own daughters to immolate themselves in service to men—which the youngest girls resist while she lives (*TTL* 13–14, 16–17, 36)—is echoed in several of Mrs. Ramsay's interchanges with Lily Briscoe and Minta Doyle. These interactions may hint at some of the methods through which Mrs. Ramsay participated in the imposition of a patriarchal/imperial rule that attempted to suppress subjects'/daughters' rebellion and reinforce their acceding to oppression.

Janet Winston has clarified the narrative superimposition whereby Mrs. Ramsay's position as "Queen" of the home sphere reenacts the monarchical and imperial roles of Queen Victoria (Winston 41, 49–61). So positioned, Mrs. Ramsay can direct the unmarried women under her roof because she serves as both colonial subject and colonizer.

Mrs. Ramsay is explicitly drawn to Minta Doyle partly because Minta's awe grants Mrs. Ramsay influence over her. Further, Mrs.

Ramsay views Minta's parents as a ludicrous pair without any means of helping Minta to a good marriage (*TTL* 88). Thus Minta appears to need her help.

Mrs. Ramsay is more ambivalent about Lily than about Minta. Lily is stronger than Minta and more rebellious, a position strengthened by the narrative method that relies on Lily's insight to augment the observations of James and Mrs. Ramsay. Lily's dishevelment elicits negative responses from Mr. Bankes (*TTL* 31) and Mr. Ramsay (*TTL* 225). But Lily's dress suggests political choice as much as genteel poverty (*TTL* 31). As a feminist painter she may choose not to use her probably limited means to dress for sexual display just as she chooses not to succor men.

A plain, poor, and unadorned spinster, Lily occupies what Spurr might name as the site of abjection (77–81). The suggestion of her being stripped of the markings of appropriate class designation may denote her lower-caste status. The text marks her, in fact, as Oriental: Lily has "little Chinese eyes" (*TTL* 234).[20] Thus Lily is positioned as the most subservient of the subjects of patriarchal-empire, a woman invisible to the male gaze. So marked, Lily Briscoe is further aligned with Mr. Carmichael, himself a speaker and translator of "Hindustani," a student of a culture that the British Empire has attempted to incorporate.

Mrs. Ramsay's response to these women is an almost exact replica of Mr. Ramsay's response to her. As he needs his wife/the subjects of empire to accept his power over the complete range of family/country's resources—he must be "needed . . . not here only, but all over the world" (*TTL* 59)—so Mrs. Ramsay at times needs to have Minta and Lily support her goals of marriage and family. Imposing her values on them, she suppresses acknowledging that her marriage is not ideal. As a Victorian matron, Mrs. Ramsay enacted cultural imperatives to help younger women of her social class marry for position and security (Dyhouse, "Mother" 38–40). Her cultural role was an ingenious trap that encouraged those behaviors that she least admired in herself. She is intermittently aware of this.

Thinking about how she had finally gotten Minta Doyle to spend the summer with them, Mrs. Ramsay hesitates, marked in the text with ellipses (88). Yet she examines her feelings, as she could not do when with Mr. Ramsay: "Wishing to dominate, wish-ing to interfere, making people do what she wished—that was the charge against her, and she thought it most unjust" (*TTL* 88). Mrs. Ramsay's conscience speaks not only to her own discomfort with the expected matchmaking role of the Victorian matriarch, but also acknowledges that such domination might be interpreted as interference.

Once in her home Minta seems to be hers to influence. Mrs. Ramsay's use of Minta Doyle to assuage Mr. Ramsay's suffering is explicit at the dinner party where Mrs. Ramsay assembles all her guests. During the dinner party, Mrs. Ramsay focuses on her hus-band's emotional state. As Murray Bowen suggests, those with "low differentiation of self" intensely monitor others by close observation of body language, tones of voice, and gesture to maintain a fused re-lationship (202), an idea Timmen Cermak incorporates into his analysis of "hypervigilance" ("Co-Addiction" 270–71). Hence Mrs. Ramsay's mind reading serves both as a narrational device and an indication of codependent absorption into a family system.

Mrs. Ramsay uses Minta at the dinner party to deflect Mr. Ramsay's "fidgets" when guests discuss Sir Walter Scott's achieve-ments. Her "antennae" intercept overheard snippets of conversation so that "[s]he scented danger for her husband" (*TTL* 161). Discus-sions of Scott's immortality "would lead, almost certainly, to some-thing being said which reminded him of his own failure" (*TTL* 161). Mrs. Ramsay's "psychometer" prods her to protect her husband from what she believes is his now-activated sense of anxiety.

As her husband becomes more agitated, "[e]verybody, she thought, felt a little uncomfortable, without knowing why" (*TTL* 162). The fact that she can also feel the presumed reactions of oth-ers to the one to whom she feels connected as if by mental telepathy is a marker of codependence. It suggests the conviction that one has an omniscience that is belied by human limitation (S. Brown, *Adult* 48–49).

Mrs. Ramsay's transgression against Minta combines within it a reenactment of Mr. Ramsay's transgressions against his wife and those forces of patriarchal-empire that subvert the right to self-rule of subject peoples. "Then Minta Doyle, whose instinct was fine, said bluffly, absurdly, that she did not believe that any one really enjoyed reading Shakespeare" (*TTL* 162). Mr. Ramsay agrees (*TTL* 162). The word "fine" in Mrs. Ramsay's *oratio obliqua* is ironic, containing Mrs. Ramsay's view and questioning it at the same time. Minta's smoothing social relations by disparaging a third party (the deceased writer) so that Mr. Ramsay's fears can be soothed is not "fine." Minta's reward is to be abused by the man she has helped.

Mrs. Ramsay is further self-alienated, even as she herself participates in dominating Minta, an "othered" woman, in ways in which Mrs. Ramsay herself is dominated. "Mrs. Ramsay saw that it would be all right . . . he would laugh at Minta [who would intuit] . . . his extreme anxiety about himself [and] . . . would . . . see that he was taken care of" (*TTL* 162).

Again, Mrs. Ramsay's *oratio obliqua* both reports and critiques her point of view, for it is questionable that it is "all right" that Mr. Ramsay laugh at Minta. Minta Doyle assents to a social transaction in which a woman doing a man a favor by mimicking something he believes is then mocked by the man for whom she had demeaned herself.

In miniature and without the apparent threat of physical violence as conveyed by patterns of imagery, this interaction recalls the way Mrs. Ramsay allows herself and her son to be used by Mr. Ramsay. The Ramsays are ensuring the perpetuation of such a marital means of communication by implicating a just-engaged young woman into it. For Mrs. Ramsay is convinced that Minta is conscious of and reacting deliberately to her sense of Mr. Ramsay's uncertainties and her need to make him feel better at her own expense.

When Mrs. Ramsay meets her husband's needs on the terrace in chapters 6 through 8, her *oratio obliqua* reveals that she is not conscious that she does not want to do so, except for one moment of self-pity. But when Mrs. Ramsay forces Lily Briscoe to assuage Mr. Tansley's need as Mrs. Ramsay had been forced to assuage that of her husband, the effect is violent.

Lily's momentary surrender of her own ethics to help Mrs. Ramsay is a conscious act of self-sacrifice. Unlike Mrs. Ramsay, she does not feel "rapture," but instead, despair and self-hate. Lily

Briscoe rescues Mr. Tansley, who had become more and more agitated at the conversation of which he understands little except that his social class has not prepared him to partake of it. He behaves aggressively in response: "Mr. Tansley raised a hammer: swung it high in the air" (*TTL* 138), recalling Mr. Ramsay's scimitar. Lily intervenes, calming the young man by her feigned interest, because wordlessly but relentlessly, Lily feels, Mrs. Ramsay had implored her to "say something nice to that young man there . . ." (*TTL* 138). Lily experiences Mrs. Ramsay's request as coercive and threatening, for unless Lily rescues her, Mrs. Ramsay implies, "life will run upon the rocks. . . . My nerves . . . will snap . . ." (*TTL* 138–39).

Lily Briscoe is here shown reading Mrs. Ramsay's mind as ably as Mrs. Ramsay can read that of her husband. Lily's obsession with Mrs. Ramsay is fully the equal of Mrs. Ramsay's obsession with her husband, so that the same kinds of hypervigilant gazing enable continuous attachment to the focus of the obsession. Such gazing permits a reading of physical response that seems to give access to the feelings of the observed. Lily's codependence is thus made similar to Mrs. Ramsay's, and as with Mrs. Ramsay, her codependence is used both as narrative device and to show that her behavior is implicated in a complex and gendered cultural system.

Lily Briscoe has at times as little power against sacrificing herself to Mrs. Ramsay as Mrs. Ramsay has against sacrificing herself to her husband. But Lily Briscoe is continuously conscious, as Mrs. Ramsay is only intermittently aware, of the costs to herself of flattering men. In addition, she knows that she matters to neither hostess nor young man at this moment except as a tool to assuage their needs. Unlike Mrs. Ramsay, Lily is not convinced that this is enough of a reward. With jaded horror she watches Mr. Tansley ejaculate his self-aggrandizement into the air as a stream of conversation (*TTL* 139).

Lily knows she has sacrificed her own integrity to enable Mrs. Ramsay to relax from the work of forging a "civilized" ensemble of interlocking amiabilities (*TTL* 139). Little understanding the politics of Lily Briscoe's determination to let men meet their own needs, Mrs. Ramsay does not seek sincerity and authenticity between human beings in public settings.

Lily Briscoe's consciousness of her own sacrifice marks many kinds of silencing. Lily speaks for the silenced subjects of patriarchal/imperial domination. She speaks, too, for rejected and hidden Victorian and Edwardian spinsters and lesbians (P. J. Smith 64–70). After all, Lily's sacrifice is motivated by her longing to merge with Mrs. Ramsay, a feeling "which [Mrs. Ramsay] completely failed to understand" (*TTL* 78). Her rescue of Mr. Tansley is the last time in *To the Lighthouse* that Lily Briscoe is coerced into a self-sacrifice motivated by her unrequited love for Mrs. Ramsay.

As Lily's resistance gathers force, her refusal to participate in empire becomes more visible. Her rejection of her complicity in allowing domination offers an important rereading of Mrs. Ramsay's marital entrapment. As numerous feminist readers, myself among them, have remarked over the years, Lily Briscoe's rebellion makes valiant and visible one aspect of the narrative's anti-heterosexist, anti-imperialist, anti-patriarchal critique.

THE MARRIAGE IN THE GARDEN

If Woolf had entitled her chapters, 12 might be named "the Marriage in the Garden." Husband and wife are alone for the first time in the narrative, without James to voice that which the wife cannot say. Because of this, a more balanced love is evident between the Ramsays, although the couple's interactions follow the same patterns as demonstrated in chapters 6 through 8. Mrs. Ramsay's covert resistance continues, as does the representation of her denial.

As the Ramsays stroll around their garden, Mr. Ramsay hesitates to tell his wife that "[h]e did not like to see her look so sad . . ." (*TTL* 104). Mrs. Ramsay had hoped that his hesitation meant he would apologize, but he did not. "Had she known that he was looking at her, she thought, she would not have let herself sit there, thinking" (*TTL* 104). Mrs. Ramsay chooses to suppress further interchange: "No, they could not share that; they could not say that" (*TTL* 104). The ambiguity of the pronoun "that" reinforces the reader's recognition of all that Mrs. Ramsay must silence.

Mr. Ramsay, too, feeling grief, exerts himself to stifle his self-pity, but cannot, sighing "[p]oor little place" (*TTL* 106). Seemingly insignificant in comparison to his previous tantrum, this pitiful sigh evokes Mrs. Ramsay's anger: "All this phrase-making was a game, she thought, for if she had said half what he had said, she would have blown her brains out by now" (*TTL* 106).

With a life of its own in the text, the rage of Mrs. Ramsay's self-suppression rarely emerges as directly as this. The things that she never can say are here marked as lethal. His sufferings are rendered smaller than her own—never fully disclosed—reasons for suicidal despair. Thus his posturing is shown to be of lesser import than her despair, which goes unmarked so that he can safely have the space to speak his sadness. No wonder she is angry that he can voice what she cannot. The quality in her to which the narrative returns—"Never did anybody look so sad" (*TTL* 46)—may thus be a depression so severe that if voiced, it might lead her to suicide. Against the powerful silence of a woman, his fears for the world reveal the shadow of male dominance over empire, over nature, over fecundity, over the female body, so often in Victorian ideology marked as a trope for nature.

But she denies her anger by teasing him, knowing he was regretting that his marriage had lessened his scholarly achievements (*TTL* 106). Once again a narrative technique is also an indication of codependence. Frequently the text ambiguously implies that Mrs. Ramsay can read her husband's mind. Thus the text seems to indicate that she has narrative access to his voice that the text deflates by parody. But it is also true that Mrs. Ramsay has been shown to have reason to need to read her husband's feelings accurately.

Is love possible in such a marriage as this is seen to be? That depends on one's definition of love, which, as Mrs. Ramsay notes, has many forms. The Ramsays' sexual intimacy is not separate from, but draws part of its power and quality from the implied violence of the struggles over domination integral to the marriage. This interpretation sheds some light on the interaction between the Ramsays, which closes "the marriage in the garden," and is sustained by the narrative's repeated image clusters that link sex, violence, lust, beauty, war, and empire.

In response, Mr. Ramsay denies his regrets, like his wife knowing that some things were best left unspoken. "And he seized her hand and raised it to his lips and kissed it with an intensity that brought the tears to her eyes . . ." (*TTL* 106–107). Mr. Ramsay's formal gentlemanliness evokes images of "Queens," "ringed fingers," "lace" (*TTL* 14), the strategies of domination inherent in the Victorian empire (*TTL* 14)—the social structure upon which this marriage is based.

Mrs. Ramsay responds to his intense homage exactly as she had in response to his wooing of her after he curses her in chapter 6: denied anger becomes exaggerated veneration. Here her admiration for him springs up anew and with it, sexual desire. The Ramsays join together, walking "up the little path where the silver-green spear-like plants grew, arm in arm. His arm was almost like a young man's arm, Mrs. Ramsay thought, thin and hard, and she thought with delight how strong he still was, though he was over sixty . . ." (*TTL* 107).

The landscape once again wittily indicates through flora the feelings of the human beings. Yet the union displaced onto the plants reminds the reader that violence is inextricably connected to the twosome, for the plants that grow are "spear-like," a reminder of Mr. Ramsay's "scimitar," his "beak," his rapacious need, his warlike propensities shown earlier on the encounter on the terrace in chapters 6 through 8.

Nor can sexuality be separated from the spear of love, for Mr. Ramsay's arm is "thin and hard." She feels his body next to hers "with delight," drawn to his prowess, noting how "strong" he is still (*TTL* 107). There can be little doubt that Mrs. Ramsay desires her husband as he desires her.

Continuing to admire him she thinks of him now as "untamed and optimistic" (*TTL* 107). In the throes of her idealized view, any previous criticism is overridden. Now his maundering on the fate of the world (*TTL* 105–6) becomes its very opposite, for she now calls him cheerful and no longer pessimistic as she experiences desire (*TTL* 107). However, only several paragraphs earlier his pessimistic sighing had led her to disgust with his claims of despair (*TTL* 104). Her ability to need to deny that which has angered her about him was rarely more apparent. It has ceased to exist. It has become that which in fact it most certainly was not.

Chapter 12 demonstrates that the Ramsays' marriage depends on mutual self-suppression. Mrs. Ramsay's hypervigilance is once again used as a narrative device and codependent survival skill. The implied violence of their relationship is inextricable from their sexual attraction. Hence the imagery depicting the Ramsays' marriage, an ironic garden of Eden, extends the couples' relation to the narrative of empire, often depicted as a potential Eden (Pratt 168, 209–10.)

THE MARRIAGE IN THE STUDY

The dynamics of the Ramsay family as depicted in chapters 6 through 8 and in chapter 12 are repeated and elaborated in chapter 19. The ambiguity and pain in the Ramsays' marriage is unresolved, and their communication, overshadowed by the threat of violence, is differently interpreted by each partner.

In chapter 19, as elsewhere, Mrs. Ramsay's codependent "hypervigilance" is not a personal failing, but a complex survival strategy, incorporating behaviors that look compliant but in fact are not. As the chapter ends, her *oratio obliqua* registers her conviction that she is behaving lovingly when in fact she refuses to occupy the victim position, a "triumph" she believes to be consistent with social expectations about the middle-class Victorian female role (Lilienfeld, "Spear").

After the dinner party Mrs. Ramsay joins her husband in the study. They sit, reading silently to themselves (*TTL* 179–82). This nonverbalized interchange makes clear that he experiences her autonomy as his to control. The arrangement is discordant. While he draws strength from her peacefulness, she is unable to retain it without his permission (*TTL* 181).

She feels a need for intimacy with her husband, so many aspects of which the text has shown to be dangerous to herself and her children. The hint of threat contained in his protective, needy love for her is clear in the imagery: "(Every word they said now would be true.) . . . For the shadow, the thing folding them in was beginning, she felt, to close round her again . . ." (*TTL* 183–84). The parenthesis ironizes the mystery of narration in *To the Lighthouse*. Someone else's consciousness is inside the character's, a fact usually unremarked by the convention of free indirect discourse. Hence, the parenthesis insists on the audibility of other voices beside the character's, and leads a reader to ask which narratorial voice places the parenthesis and whether it is reliable. For the novel has persistently if indirectly demonstrated that no point of view is wholly reliable.

What shadow is this? Why does it enfold "them," but only close around her? Is it their mutual desire? Is it the penumbra of her denial? Is it the flag of empire, waving over subjugated territory? That it is threatening while perceived as comforting seems clear from the conflation of threat with help in Mrs. Ramsay's *oratio obliqua*.

The Ramsays' complex marriage is crystallized in the love-shadowed image: "But through the crepuscular walls of their intimacy, for they were drawing together, involuntarily, coming side by side, quite close, she could feel his mind like a raised hand shadowing her mind . . ." (*TTL* 184). The walls separating them are "crepuscular," both beautiful and darkening. Their "involuntary" union is both habitual and not always willed. Is the hand raised to strike a blow or hovering to protect her? The deliberate ambiguity simultaneously captures Mrs. Ramsay's denial and denies it. Just as the image of the raised hand recalls the brutality of the imagery often associated with Mr. Ramsay that Mrs. Ramsay experiences as protective, so, too, Mrs. Ramsay experiences her husband's doubts about the Rayley engagement as positive (*TTL* 184). Mrs. Ramsay is delighted at her husband's negative response, which seems to make her feel comforted, secure, perhaps even loved: in her denial, she once again experiences his negativity as positive; that which is, is not.

In this chapter, as in chapters 6 through 8 and in 12, Mrs. Ramsay's *oratio obliqua* is polyvocal, simultaneously presenting and critiquing Mrs. Ramsay's experiences and perceptions. The methods of narrativity have throughout the text balanced Mrs. Ramsay's positive views of the marriage with views of outside observers who recognize the potential brutality that underlies the husband's control of the wife. For while the Ramsays may experience their marriage as a protected space, the narratorial voices inside Mrs. Ramsay's *oratio obliqua*—as well as the voices of son James and of feminist observer Lily Briscoe—verbalize threat rather than safety. The ambiguity of the shadowed-love image shifts clearly toward the negative as it shades into Mr. Ramsay's desire to control his wife's thoughts. She must not be sad, "pessimistic," perhaps because he needs the reassurance of her happiness.

As he seems to sense her thoughts, she feels she can read his, a method of hypervigilant communication comically conveyed at the dinner party (*TTL* 143–45), a conviction Cermak calls "projective identification" in his analysis of codependence ("Co-addiction" 270). Although it would appear that the narratorial voices are reporting Mrs. Ramsay's accurate reading of Mr. Ramsay's thoughts, that cannot be known with surety. Whereas throughout the text she had been silenced, now he is. Because hers is the reported consciousness, she seems to represent the speaking subject; he appears to be suppliant (*TTL* 185). That she refuses to tell him she loves him moves to restore some balance in the unequal power relations between the two (Lilienfeld, "Spear" 160–63).

She is unable to imagine another way of life than her marriage, unable to recognize consistently his aggression against her and the children; certainly to do so would undermine her sense of female duty and of marriage. Although Lily Briscoe's consciousness is political, Mrs. Ramsay's is not. With no political analysis of her situation, Mrs. Ramsay continues to admire her husband's genius while disparaging his weaknesses, dependent on his intense need for her, yet unable to limit his need except by hiding, silence, and subterfuge. Refusing to acknowledge that she loves him protects her hidden self. She rationalizes her behavior: "He could say things— she never could" (*TTL* 185).

The repression of her speech has been revealed as a systematic though unconscious control her husband exerts over what he thinks his wife is thinking. Throughout the text when she has tried to tell him of her worries, sadness, the range of her feelings, he reacts in ways that indicate it is not safe to reveal her thoughts. These incidents seem to be synecdoches, repeated hints that may signify the whole (Richter 166–72), and examples of daily repressions during the marriage. Considering his response when she is honest, she is sensible to silence herself rather than risk his rages.

Her refusal to capitulate to his perceived need for her verbal surrender seems to arouse his desire (*TTL* 185). As in chapter 12, their quarrels fuel their physical attraction, a point underlined by the consistent linking of the imagery of male anger, male aggression, and sexual love. Threats of his violence, trivialized, turned into Homeric similes (*TTL* 144, 250) and so distanced, nevertheless point to the connection of his insistence here with his roughness to her elsewhere in the text.

Her happiness grows as she remains silent, all the while assuring herself that her husband knows she loves him (*TTL* 185–87). However, she appears to submit to him by agreeing that they will be unable to go to the lighthouse (*TTL* 186–87). She is convinced that by allowing him to win their unresolved quarrel she has shown her love. But in fact what he knows has been silenced. Her body language, however, is rejecting. She moves away from him toward the window, turns her back, stares at the lighthouse, and then turns to face him with a radiant smile. She is self-possessed. She becomes fully free just a few pages later as she escapes through death a marriage she would not have left when alive (*TTL* 194).

CONCLUSION: INTERRUPTING INTERGENERATIONAL "TRANSMISSION"

The family system that I have examined in *To the Lighthouse* by using the ideas of Bowen, Brown, Elkin, and Cermak includes intergenerational "transmission." Mrs. Ramsay had hoped that in their marriage, Minta Doyle and Paul Rayley would "carry it on when she was dead" (*TTL* 171), but it is within her own family that the reproduction and interconnection of family system and the imperial state is visible.

Feminist critics have suggested that the tragic nature of the conclusion be acknowledged. Elizabeth Abel's problematized Freudian reading proves that James Ramsay does indeed become

like his father. Louise DeSalvo suggests that Cam Ramsay symbolizes an incest survivor figure unable successfully as yet to negotiate
the family's gendered and hierarchical system of conflicts between
siblings and parents (*Impact* 172–79).

When Lily Briscoe notices the remaining Ramsay daughters on
her return to the restored summer house, she observes that without
Mrs. Ramsay to absorb Mr. Ramsay's use of the female to meet his
needs, the Ramsay girls have had no bulwark against his rapacity
(*TTL* 218, 233).[21]

While she had lived, Mrs. Ramsay had been able to absorb
(*TTL* 51) much of her husband's acting out through self-denial and
lack of perceived alternatives. She had thought herself successful in
keeping the private violence from becoming public knowledge. No
more. With her death her husband's rage—which she had once
imagined as "his anger fly[ing] like a pack of hounds into his eyes"
(*TTL* 144)—has been set loose to attack her daughters.

Nancy cannot protect herself. Lily observes that Nancy appears
"half dazed, half desperate . . . as if she were forcing herself to do
what she despaired of ever being able to do" (*TTL* 218). As her
mother modeled, Nancy does not seem to know clearly that one can
successfully acknowledge and resist male aggression. The suggestion
of unrestrained passion is further underlined by Lily's language.
"But it was a house full of unrelated passions . . . chaos" (*TTL* 221),
the very words often used by clinicians like Stephanie Brown to describe the dangers to the survivors in households where there is familial alcoholism or trauma (*Adult* 49–51, 55, 57). Nancy's
confusion recalls the paralysis experienced by the Dedalus girls and
their mother as their father whistles and curses upstairs while they
scramble to do his bidding (*P* 174–75).

Although World War I had wrought a revolution in English
manners, the middle-class life of the Ramsay girls shows no such
change (L. Bland). Mr. Ramsay is seventy-one in Book Three (*TTL*
304); yet he expects his daughters to live by the standards by which
daughters lived in his boyhood in the 1860s. Even in 1919, it would
take a strong young woman to leave her father's house, although the
universities admitted women of means, and professions in teaching,
office work, and in rare cases, medicine as well as nursing, were

open to women. Had the Ramsay girls been sent to school? If not, their options were limited. Ironically, there seems as little possible escape out of the Ramsay home for the daughters in 1919 as for the mother in 1909.

With Rose absent in Book Three, Prue dead, and Nancy stunned, narrative attention focuses on Cam Ramsay. Cam Ramsay's disappearance into her mother's role is noted by the reoccurrence of the ominously raised hand that shadowed the wife's mind in the study: "And as sometimes happens when a cloud falls on a green hillside and gravity descends and there among all the surrounding hills is gloom and sorrow, and it seems as if the hills themselves must ponder the fate of the clouded, the darkened, either in pity, or maliciously rejoicing in her dismay: so Cam now felt herself overcast, as she sat there among calm, resolute people and wondered how to answer her father about the puppy; how to resist his entreaty" (*TTL* 250–51).

This Homeric simile extends the "raised hand" (*TTL* 184) beyond the study to hover over a hillside. As such, it recalls the empire imagery, suggesting the British extending the patriarchal "home" rule to larger landscapes than the private home (Winston 52–53, 62). Dually presented in Mrs. Ramsay's *oratio obliqua* as protective and menacing, it has become Zeus/Apollo, the father as the Sun God, hovering over Cam.

While on the journey to the lighthouse, as James Ramsay becomes freer, Cam is forced into service to both her father and brother. Their father praises James's steering of the boat, and after that praise, James gives way, forgiving his father by shifting blame to his mother (*TTL* 277–79). Although she holds out silent a long while, emulating her mother in the study, at last she gives in and speaks to Mr. Ramsay (*TTL* 251). Both children surrender to survive, as their mother had had to do. But while in the boat James receives praise; Cam receives nothing but the silent expectation that she has done the duty her mother's behavior had modeled, a reminder of how Mr. Tansley and Mrs. Ramsay had treated Lily's self-sacrifice at the dinner party. Journeying to the lighthouse, both children learn to repeat their parents' gender roles in intergenerational "transmission" (Bowen 204–206).[22]

The Ramsay girls, however, are not the only women in daughterly roles. As I have explained elsewhere, Lily Briscoe is an important surrogate daughter to Mrs. Ramsay. Her freedom, which
encapsulates that of Minta (for it is Lily's memory that Minta's escape from the life Mrs. Ramsay had planned for her is contained
[*TTL* 257–60]), comes to represent the hope for freedom for all the
Ramsay girls. Her successful refusal to inhabit the Ramsay family
female role is clear when Lily resists Mr. Ramsay's demands for her
sympathy, immune to his withholding of sexual admiration of her
[Lilienfeld, "Mother" 368–69; *TTL* 229–30).

One of the burdens of those carrying the family secret is the
conviction that no one else knows about it. But what Mrs. Ramsay
had thought was her secret to protect was, in fact, the subject of
common gossip. Certainly Lily had known about it when she visited
them before the war. Now returned, remembering gossip about the
Ramsays, Lily recalled that people said "[t]hen she was weak with
her husband. She let him make those scenes" (*TTL* 291). Lily had
closely observed the Ramsay's marriage which, she dryly recalled,
was "no monotony of bliss" (*TTL* 296). Lily remembered that she
and Paul Rayley had witnessed several episodes of Mr. Ramsay's
rages: doors slammed, Mr. Ramsay bounded from meals in one of
his tantrums. They had even seen him "whizz his plate through the
window . . ." (*TTL* 296). Lily believed she understood the effect of
these dramatic passions on Mrs. Ramsay who appeared "tired" and
at times "cowed a little" (*TTL* 296).

Lily Briscoe had been briefly jealous of the Rayley's engagement
at the dinner party. On the one hand, Lily felt, "[i]t is so beautiful,
so exciting, this love, that I tremble on the verge of it . . . also it
is . . . barbaric . . ." (*TTL* 154). But at the dinner party Lily makes
several important connections between images while a witness to
the Rayleys' passion. The heat of Paul's love, "its horror, its cruelty,
its unscrupulosity" "scorched" (*TTL* 154) Lily who turned from it
to watch Minta being fed by Mrs. Ramsay to Mr. Ramsay. Lily had
briefly imagined the older man as a carnivore: "Lily, looking at
Minta, being charming to Mr. Ramsay at the other end of the table,
flinched for her exposed to these fangs" (*TTL* 154). The imagery of
Mr. Ramsay as a beast combines images of British monarchy (the

lion) with the hunted prey in the jungles of empire and is later made overt when Lily recognizes that in his pain in Book Three Mr. Ramsay is "like a lion seeking whom he would devour" (*TTL* 233). With Lily's mind making the connections, Paul Rayley, a beautiful young man, becomes the older man who is seen as a consumer of female flesh.

On her return in Book Three, Lily remembers the Rayleys' first love as an all-consuming fire, "[which] repelled her with fear and disgust . . . [although] she saw its splendour and power . . ." (*TTL* 261). Lily Briscoe experiences this fire as celebratory, set by "savages on a distant beach" (*TTL* 261). A resonant image, this raises the question of who are the "savages" and on which beach did they set the fire (Spurr 76–91)? The image could refer to Crusoe and Friday (Brantlinger 1–3), as well as to the beach the guests had walked on after the dinner party (*TTL* 189), as well as those lands of Asia and Africa under the domination of Britain. However, Lily Briscoe's *oratio obliqua* at the dinner party had inscribed European men like Mr. Ramsay and Paul Rayley as "savages." Thus the fire imagery and the figure of Mars, seen in Mr. Ramsay's war chariot (*TTL* 144), link men to rapacious colonialism and male feeding on the citizens of empire as well as on European women.

This fire was reflected in Book One at the dinner party where it became the candles lit to bring the disparate guests together (*TTL* 145); it shone there in the reflected glow of Prue's face as she shyly watched the engaged couple (*TTL* 164). But it was also the flash of the sparks Mr. Ramsay's rage emits as he pulled up short of explosion at the dinner party (*TTL* 144). This barely averted explosion was a reminder of the flash of Jasper's shooting gun, which had burst into Lily's thoughts about Mr. Ramsay's mind (*TTL* 40–41). It later became the exploding shell that in one instant destroyed soldiers, including Andrew Ramsay, in World War I (*TTL* 201).

The imagery makes clear that the fires of male temper and male love that raged at times in the Ramsay home reappear as conflated images in Book Three. A fire emanates from Paul Rayley in Lily's memory, and it shines on the poker she imagines him to have clasped to rattle at his estranged wife (*TTL* 258). In Book Three this light becomes the sun hovering over Cam in the boat (*TTL*

250), estranging her from herself, leading her to believe that love means sacrifice of the daughter to the father.

Lily Briscoe's vision, struggle as she may for balance, is focused most fully on women and hence is partial to Mrs. Ramsay. In moments narrated or envisioned by others than Lily Briscoe, the Ramsays' marriage did contain love as well as domination. Certainly both Mr. and Mrs. Ramsay thought it did.

When Lily Briscoe declares that "she has had her vision" (*TTL* 310), she refers to more than her completed painting. Her perceptual clarity at the novel's conclusion, obscured neither by the haze of her obsessional gazing at Mrs. Ramsay as in Book One (*TTL* 110–11), nor by a waking reverie such as Mrs. Ramsay's (*TTL* 95–100), shows there is "a way out of it all" (*TTL* 13). Consciousness of feminist solutions enables Lily Briscoe's *oratio obliqua* to contain the knowledge that the opium of codependent trance is not the sole option for a woman. Lily Briscoe enacts resistance to Mrs. Ramsay's model of heterosexual enmeshment (P. J. Smith 63–71), while also relinquishing her own obsession with Mrs. Ramsay. Further, positioned as signifying empire, for her "little Chinese eyes" (*TTL* 234) recall one site of the sale of the Indian poppy, Lily Briscoe marks an ironic narrative commentary on the Victorian and Edwardian fear of "Oriental contagion" (Milligan, *Pleasures* 20–21).

The narrative has rendered many of the family members' and its observers' points of view, revealing that the oppression of women and children was the linchpin of the Victorian family. Mrs. Ramsay is seen repeatedly in the very process of denial. Courageous and determined as she is, there are things she cannot see. Mr. Ramsay is seen repeatedly ensuring that she must remain in denial, as he insists that all her thoughts must focus on him.

The narrative method has thus presented many conflicting and still unreconciled views to the reader. Both through the image-plots and through the visions of other characters who appear to be peripheral to the Ramsays' interactions, other points of view break through Lily's bias and Mrs. Ramsay's denial to language. As a little boy, James Ramsay's anger voices what Mrs. Ramsay would never be safe enough to say. Lily Briscoe's role as an "insignificant" spinster enables her to "[know] all that" (*TTL* 137). It is her feminist vision that sees that which the Ramsays assume to be natural love is, in fact, socially constructed. Lily's courageous consciousness connects male rage in the domestic setting to the brutality of war as well as of lust, to the fires set by "savages" on the beach, a blazing, racialized image suggesting British governmental claims justifying the empire.

In this novel both Mrs. Ramsay and Lily Briscoe have searched for a way to maintain the complexities of truth without dividing things into opposites. The narrative method balances and expands their points of view, simultaneously enacting denial, yet exposing that which at first seems unsaid and unseen.

EPILOGUE

ALCOHOLISM IS A MULTIFACETED physiological illness, with a probable genetic component, inflected by gender, social class, and milieu, and expressed both within and outside of cultural norms. Characterization in narrative—even in narratives that are written to problematize the very concept of character—can reflect the complexity and multifaceted nature of alcoholism and its effects on the alcoholic and those involved with him or her. Further, the story line of a novel can simultaneously reveal and resist revealing the impact of alcoholism on a character and on his or her family. The properties of narrativity—management of time, space, consciousness, inclusion and exclusion of events—can mimic the effect of alcoholism on the human mind. Narratives can appear to collude with characters' denial and can, as well, demonstrate an expectation of the worst of circumstance, as if the narrative itself suffered from the hopelessness of alcoholic despair.

Repeatedly in this book I have noted that specific issues and discussions are contested sites. The very act of writing a book about alcoholism by examining biographical referents, characterization, and narratives that can behave as if they had an alcoholic mind-set is itself an act of engaged debate.

This book began in my efforts to inform my students about the complexities of alcoholism, but writing it led me to engage in debates about still-unresolved discussions of narrative, cultural criticism, and language-focused approaches to texts. The power of reading novels for me and for many of my students arises because novels invite readers to enter lives and cultures other than their own. Such entrance in turn deepens an understanding of the reader and the reader's world while encouraging an expansion of the constrictions of the private life. Reading *The Mayor of Casterbridge, A Portrait of the Artist as a Young Man,* and *To the Lighthouse* with many students has provided an important alternative to my reading of these novels in context of the critical debates still on going in literary theory. Writers mingle aspects of themselves in character and narrative in ways that also increase readers' interest in novels and characters. To see my students recognize (and occasionally reject) alcoholic characters and narratives has reminded me that novels can offer an important means of expanding readers' ability to grow in compassion and comprehension.

Michael Henchard's tragic suffering and enormous appetite for power and mastery over economics and other people is more than a story about the downfall of a man afflicted with alcoholism, although it is certainly that as well. No one reading of a novel can present the full meaning of a novel because readers construct novels from their varied standpoints (Harding 275–84). My interpretation, however, offers a coherent way to conceptualize disparate strands of the life story of a man who, to many readers, seems to cause his own losses, while to others, he is victimized by an author who delighted in the sufferings of his creations. Further, my argument brings to the fore Thomas Hardy's intimate knowledge of alcoholism and its interconnection with what would now be called the cultural construction of masculinity. Gender and social class, major themes in Hardy's novels, are inextricably intertwined with alcoholism and a narrativity of alcoholic despair in *The Mayor of Casterbridge*.

In their recent publication, *The Voluminous Life and Genius of James Joyce's Father, John Stanislaus Joyce,* John Wyse Jackson and Peter Costello re / joyce in the life-force of James Joyce's father. Refiguring him within his time and place, the authors read his drinking as both culturally normative and excessive. They claim—rightly—that this epic individual was at the heart of all of his favorite son's fiction, urging that the emerging shadow of John Stanislaus Joyce be seen behind the novels. My interpretation of *A Portrait of the Artist as a Young Man* tries to restore the fictionalization of John Stanislaus Joyce's problematic drinking to a visibility both denied and insisted upon by the novel. I have argued that Simon Dedalus's economic and personal failures are inextricable from an alcoholism enacted within the norms of a particular patriarchal culture. My methods of argument and my assertions are based upon insights enunciated slowly over several decades within the conversations of Joyce critics. By no means is mine offered as the sole reading. Like my work on Hardy, it is one view that brings out heretofore occluded aspects of a much-studied novel.

If alcoholism is a contested yet taboo topic, codependence is doubly taboo. Dismissed as a sexist label, a return to the worst kind of blaming the victim, the concept is disputed even among clinicians. My interpretation of *To the Lighthouse,* based on more than two decades of my published work on that novel, historicizes the concept of codependence from a feminist perspective. Few readers now disagree with the idea that the Ramsay family in its rigidly hierarchical/patriarchal structure is both destructive to its female members and the children, and is emblematic of sites of imperial domination beyond the private home. Because Virginia Woolf acknowledged it as a therapeutic narrative that had the effect of freeing her from the ghosts of her parents, especially her mother (*MOB* 81), many readers now assume it displays, while problematizing, a family system that at least encouraged the sacrifice of sisters to brothers, if not establishing an arena for sexual abuse. Further, the emergence of the British Empire as a central concern for Woolf scholars expands the concept of patriarchal advantage in *To the Lighthouse.* Mrs. Ramsay resisted and engaged in practices similar to those of her husband, and the novel's image plot makes this clear. That opium addiction and codependence are twinned in *To the Lighthouse* suggests an oblique commentary on the relation of Julia Jackson with her mother. These new interpretations of *To the Lighthouse* are, like my other readings, meant to reveal hitherto unremarked aspects of the novel, not to displace other arguments.

Who is speaking in all these novels also has reference to alcoholism discourse. There is an omniscient author in *The Mayor of Casterbridge,* sardonic, empathic yet distanced, not always reliable. He hides Elizabeth-Jane's parentage, he controls and refuses to reveal consistently Michael Henchard's interior monologues, and he also silences and occasionally mocks Farfrae. His work is expanded, however, by Elizabeth-Jane whose debased position as the bypassed admirer of Farfrae, and the emotionally battered daughter of an alcoholic stepfather gives her views piquancy. Her hypervigilance is necessary for her survival in an alcohol-impacted family. Her point of view adds compassion to a narrative structured by the trajectory of tragedy—and of alcoholic decline.

The problematic voices of the indirect interior monologues sharing the narrative *A Portrait of the Artist as a Young Man* with an implied narrator is not my central focus. As previous Joyce scholars like Margot Norris and Richard Pearce have argued, the narrative is dialogic. Norris's brilliant methodology has established methods by which to read Joycean narrative's "stifled 'back answers.'" The denied alcoholism narrative, one voice of the narrative's echoing "back answer[s]" (Norris, *Web* 97–98), can be made audible when analyzed by certain methods suggested by alcoholism discourse. The denied alcoholism narrative is further revealed through repeated paralipses, a method first identified by Hans Walter Gabler 25 years ago. The denied alcoholism narrative is also demonstrated by studying the symbolic image-plot, an analytic tool established by William York Tindall and elaborated by John Paul Riquelme and Michael Gillespie.

That a narrative would reveal as well as deny denial suggests a fascinating parallel to the complicated denial manifested by an alcoholic and also by those involved with him or her. The narrative of *A Portrait of the Artist as a Young Man* is the context for the character's own denial of his father's alcoholism and its effects on himself, increasingly estranged from his father and his father's world. In the emerging discourse about children of alcoholics, this concept is being further refined; it remains a useful model of understanding those who grew up in families shaped by parental drinking. Stephen Dedalus is the son of an alcoholic, and his father's drinking and the familial denial of that drinking, played out in cultural context, shapes Stephen's life choices and much of his artistic literary activity.

Like Elizabeth-Jane in *The Mayor of Casterbridge,* Lily Briscoe in *To the Lighthouse* is a derided female onlooker in a narrative that demonstrates the patriarchal power of an irrational father and the culture that gives him prominence. Like Elizabeth-Jane, because she is often disregarded, and because she must survive in a world that does not value her, Lily Briscoe's hypervigilance reveals much that the family members cannot see in *To the Lighthouse*. Lily's mind connects the multifaceted image-plot of the novel, connecting patriarchal "Home Rule" (Change 58) to British imperialism. But Lily's obsessive gazing upon Mrs. Ramsay is paralleled by Mrs. Ramsay's obsessive focus on Mr. Ramsay. She reads his mind and considers it her duty to meet his needs. She does not acknowledge that her obsessive focus on him exacerbates his aggression while lessening her ability to protect herself and her children. Through the image-plot, the novel suggests the cultural imperative that forces women like Mrs. Ramsay to serve others at the expense of themselves. Through the obsessional focus on the supposed thoughts and needs of others, *To the Lighthouse* demonstrates the lived experience of codependence as a gendered aspect of patriarchal/imperial culture.

In my dual discourse of theory I have argued that alcoholism is a major component of these novels, and their methodologies of storytelling and character creation.

My definition of alcoholism, like my analysis of the narratives, draws on many disparate voices. In using the biopsychosocial model, I have expanded the way in which many analyses that discuss addiction and literature characterize alcoholism. Further, I have followed the approach of those compassionate clinicians who can enter into their clients' feeling states without sharing their clients' denial. Acknowledging alcoholism as a non-willed illness, which can yet be brought into consciousness and the province of human will, they do not regard alcoholics as hapless victims. But neither do they disregard the irrefutable medical facts of alcoholism. In the cacophony of alcoholism discourse, their methodological examples—mindful of the alcoholic's human suffering, yet demonstrating that alcoholism is an illness that affects all those closest to the alcoholic—charts the course that I have followed.

I have argued that a biopsychosocial model of alcoholism and related theories about children of alcoholics and those affected by the alcoholism of a family member are useful tools by which to interrogate these novels by Thomas Hardy, James Joyce, and Virginia Woolf. Thomas Hardy and James Joyce were directly affected by the alcoholism or addiction of a family member or mentor, and Virginia Woolf's mother, Julia Stephen, had been affected by her mother Maria Jackson's chronic illness and Maria Jackson's consequent medicinal use of opiates and opiate-derivatives.

Michael Henchard's struggle with alcohol shapes the novel's plot, in which emotional aspects of alcoholism appear as narrative strategies. Alcoholism with "a life of its own" (Vaillant, Revisited 366) in *The Mayor of Casterbridge* surfaces in Henchard's denied dependencies on the men and women closest to him, in the drinking lives of the work-folk who serve as his doubles, and in Henchard's conception of a manhood which he cannot successfully enact without drinking.

My analysis of *A Portrait of the Artist as a Young Man* makes visible a deliberately submerged alcoholism narrative. The hidden presence of alcoholism reveals itself, not just in Simon Dedalus's financial and emotional decline, but in the adverse effects the father's drinking has on his son's psychological development. Alcoholism reveals itself in the narrative behaviors that simultaneously exhibit and deny the alcoholism that structures the characters' familial lives.

Reformulating the concept of codependence, I have used it as a political lens through which to examine the ambiguous critique of Mrs. Ramsay, an integral aspect of her characterization in *To the Lighthouse*. Codependence and opium addiction are embedded in this novel's narrative of empire, obliquely referring to the chloral and morphia use of Maria Jackson, Virginia Woolf's maternal grandmother. Presenting the multidimensional nature of alcoholism and the "transmission" of its effects across generations, *Reading Alcoholisms* foregrounds that which had been hidden or denied yet represented by narrative strategy: the unmistakable presence of alcohol, alcoholism, and their impact on the families affected by them.

NOTES

INTRODUCTION

1. Lloyd Sederer finds that the lack of hierarchical organization in the biopsychosocial model is problematic in some treatment modalities (192–93). Its egalitarian organization is appropriate to my objectives as a literary scholar.

2. The current *Diagnostic and Statistical Manual of Mental Disorders, IV* states that the contexts within which substance abuse and dependence occur are essential in diagnostic considerations (201).

3. Although the medical and biopsychosocial models assume that alcoholism is not within rational control, neither these nor AA absolves the alcoholic of accountability for behaviors when drinking or sober (Miller and Chappel, 197, 203–204; Bell and Khantzian, 280). "Although the alcoholic is not at fault for having the disease of alcoholism, personal responsibility is the cornerstone in the process of recovery" (Miller and Chappel 203).

   In responding to Fingarette's critique of the disease theory which is basic to the medical model, George Vaillant says, "Fingarette himself offers the best reason of all for labelling alcoholism a disease rather than a moral failing, namely self efficacy: 'Alcoholics are not helpless; they can take control of their lives. . . . The assumption of personal responsibility . . . is a sign of health. . . . ' A fervent advocate of Alcoholics Anonymous could not have made the point more forcefully" (*Revisited* 378).

4. Sandra Harding argues that "political and social interests are not 'add-ons' to an otherwise transcendental science that is inherently indifferent to human society; scientific . . . practices . . . are constituted in and through contemporary political and social projects, and always have been" (145).

5. The claim that narratives themselves can exhibit aspects of alcoholic behavior such as denial is one I used to analyze several narratives of addiction in 1993 at the MMLA in my essay, "'But I'm an English Teacher, Not a Therapist.'" John Crowley explores the use of denial as a kind of narrative emphasis of one of the themes of *Tender is the Night* in *The White Logic* (73–75). Earlier than the publication of *The White Logic,* James Joyce scholars such as Hans Walter Gabler and Susan S. Friedman had thoroughly interrogated Joyce's narrative constructions of disclosures of denial, as I discuss below in chapter 2. Margot Norris in *Joyce's Web* repeatedly demonstrates that Joycean texts brilliantly deploy and disclose narratives of denied denial.

CHAPTER 1—THOMAS HARDY

1. John Doheny argues that George Hand's alcoholism was family mythology with no factual basis (55–56).
2. Doheny argues that Betsy Hand was on relief for only a limited period of her life, contesting Gittings and Millgate's arguments (54–55).
3. For more than a century, British and American critics have disagreed on how to analyze Hardy's manipulations of causality and the underlying attitudes these may represent. Frequently critics patronize Hardy about his views, ascribing his "meliorism" and alleged "pessimism" to his autodidact's studies of German and British philosophers (Zabel 35–38) or to the traditional fatality of "folk wisdom" (Van Ghent 205). J. O. Bailey's summary of critical shifts in explanation for Hardy's characteristic attitudes is excellent ("Fashions"), as is John Holloway's exploration of Hardy's philosophy *(Sage)*. Recently Gillian Beer's return to Darwinian ideas as a context in which to understand Hardy's representations of causality has received critical assent, joining Roy Morrell's *Thomas Hardy: The Will and The Way* as a definitive critical formulation. Although he does not dwell on Hardy, Brian Richardson's *Unlikely Stories,* an analysis of causality, plot, and tragic inexorability, is a sophisticated theorizing of plot structures such as those of Thomas Hardy (69).

Hardy's philosophical theories of causality are not my central focus, although I do attribute part of his view of the futility of working-class efforts in the face of inexorable circumstance to his mother's complacent expectations of disaster, a view I believe may have been partly encouraged by her response to her father's alcoholism. My concern is Michael Henchard's reactions to the circumstances that face him as a result of Hardy's plotting. I seek to demonstrate that Henchard's tragedy is inextricably connected to his alcoholic perception of and reaction to challenging circumstances.

4. Opium was legal, although its addictive effects and the possibility of overdose were public knowledge (Berridge and Edwards 142). For a further discussion of Victorian attitudes toward drug use, see chapter 3.

5. The British temperance movement was influenced by the Scottish and Irish movements (B. Harrison 103–4). Thus it is not surprising that Henchard's oath is similar to the total abstinence pledge of Irish abstainers (J. Bland 24–25). For "[t]here were a variety of different pledges, rather than a standard one for the whole movement. In the 1830s and 1840s there were many battles about what was to be excluded and what allowed in the pledge" (Shiman 258 n. 160). The British temperance movement was factionalized between moderate drinkers and total abstainers, segregated by social class, and further divided geographically, with hostilities separating northern and southern British temperance groups (Shiman 18–42).

6. Steinglass and his coauthors do not call this denial; rather these researchers have established that the drinker's behavior becomes subsumed into a cyclical familial pattern of behavior whereby the drinking is essential to crucial familial interactions.

7. Commentary on the narrativity of spying in this and other Hardy novels by J. Hillis Miller remains an indispensable guide. (See Miller, *Distance* 7.)

8. For example, if Michael Henchard is analyzed according to the categories proposed in the *DSM-IV* (fourth edition of the *Diagnostic and Statistical Manual*) for "Substance Dependence," he might be said to demonstrate tolerance, as I have discussed earlier when noting his physiological reactions to the rum he drank. He appeared to have little or no hangover. Further, he tries to stop drinking by taking an abstinence pledge, an indication of his "desire . . . to cut down or control substance use" (*DSM-IV* 181). Tolerance in the *DSM-IV* is related to the loss of control of how frequently and how much one drinks (181) a symptom the medical model considers indispensable to a diagnosis of alcoholism (Miller and Chappel 202).

If Michael Henchard is analyzed according to criteria for "Substance Abuse," a diagnosis that does not depend on physiological dependence, Henchard demonstrates at least one of the criteria: his alcohol use impairs his social relationships. His wife had clearly worried—if not confronted him about—his drinking (*DSM-IV* 182–83).

If Michael Henchard is analyzed according to the Cahalan scale quoted in Vaillant in Table 1.2 and note a (1), he demonstrates belligerence, binge drinking, marital problems, financial problems, and admits his problem with control (qtd. in Vaillant, *Revisited* 27). Further, the narrator reports that his wife worried about his drinking, an indication of probable marital problems. E. M. Jellinek would diagnose Michael Henchard as a binge drinker, that is as having *"Episolon alcoholism,"* a form of alcoholism that Jellinek considered did fit the disease model (39; emphasis in original). According to all of these definitions, Michael Henchard clearly has a problem with alcohol.

9. Clinical portraits of a certain subset of male alcoholics overlap to some extent with the results of batteries of psychological and psychometric tests—such as the MMPI (Minnesota Multiphasic Personality Inventory) and the TAT (Thematic Apperception Test), among others—which continue to be administered to inpatient alcoholics as well as to those in outpatient treatment (Cox 149–51, 153). Reviewing the literature on such tests in 1976, Charles Neuringer and James R. Clopton critiqued these tests, criticisms that Gordon Barnes corroborated in his 1979 review of the literature. Discrepancies in test results due to the divergent severity of subjects' alcoholism, differences in subjects' race, social class, and differences in kinds of population tested (inpatient or outpatient) have undermined claims that such tests are "objective" and accurate assessment measures.

Nevertheless, some researchers and clinicians find that the results of the MMPI appear to substantiate two aspects of the clinical picture of a certain subset of male alcoholics (Cox 150; Levin, *Introduction* 125). Neuringer and Clopton found in reviewing MMPI results that alcoholics consistently scored high on Depression scale 2 (D) and Psychopathic Deviate scale 4 (Pd), or what might be termed antisocial interpersonal interactions (Cox 155–56; Neuringer and Clopton 21). Levin also cites these two MMPI scores as consistent and thus as significant (*Introduction* 125–26).

Further, perceptual styles of certain subsets of male alcoholics resulted in controversial but interesting findings. Early research into the psychological/physiological ways alcoholics experienced themselves in the physical world suggested that alcoholics perceived differently than nonalcoholics (Cox 158–60; Barnes 609–11, 617–18). Obviously, chronic alcoholism causes brain damage (Levin, *Introduction* 46–49) and might be expected to affect perception. However, current research in the area of neurobiological preconditions to alcoholism suggests the possibility that such early findings about alcoholics' perceptual differences from those of nonalcoholics may one day be substantiated (Jacobson 188; Windle 130–36; Noble 216). For purposes of my discussion, however, I regard the early test results as worth citing if not entirely verifiable, and will use such evidence as suggestive rather than as definitive.

10. It appears likely that genetically transmitted predisposing central nervous system disorders might be a factor in the development of alcoholism (Vaillant, *Natural* 64–70, but see *Revisited* 72–73; Wallace 24–26; Miller & C'De Baca 364, #42 and #48; Noble 216; Windle 130–35, 152–56). "The fact that alcoholism runs in families has been known for centuries" (Goodwin, "Genetic" 427). But while there is general agreement about the probable importance of genetic influences in alcoholism, the mode of transmission has not been clearly established (Goodwin 432; Noble 228; see also Cloninger, Bohman, Sigvardsson, "Inheritance." This last study ["Inheritance"] has recently been replicated, (see "Replication"), a fact that I will refer to later).

Summarizing the decision of the *DSM-IV* study group not to recommend familial alcoholism as a diagnostic category, Mark Schuckit nevertheless points out that "using the most restrictive criteria, between 20% and 35% of alcoholic persons who enter treatment have an alcoholic father and/or mother . . ." ("Familial" 163).

11. More recent psychodynamic theories develop Blane's hypothesis further "by pointing out that the alcoholic is often enraged at those on whom he or she depends" (Levin, *Introduction* 169), a finding pertinent to Henchard's feelings about Farfrae.

12. Hardy cannot say this relationship with Lucetta is sexual because of the conventions of the Victorian novel, so he uses the word "intimate" to indicate that it was sexual. The relationship was "explicitly sexual in the original manuscript" (Langbaum 127).

13. Further, considerations of alcoholism as a trauma point to depression as a result of loss of control of alcohol and consequent loss of self-esteem and seriously disturbed interpersonal relations, as Margaret Bean has analyzed. Vaillant's longitudinal studies suggest that depression is a result of alcoholism (*Revisited* 82–85), a supposition Schuckit's analysis in the *DSM-IV Sourcebook* substantiates ("Relationship" 55). Depression is consistently revealed by Minnesota Multiphasic Personality Inventory (MMPI) results as I have noted. Many sources agree that depression lessens for most alcoholics as they stay sober (Vaillant, *Revisited* 85 and Schuckit, "Relationship" 55). In his discussion of depression as consequent to alcoholism, Vaillant reviewed Lemere's findings (*Revisited* 150–56).

14. The postmodern revolution in the discipline of history has problematized the social construction of the human being in culture (Laslett, et al., *History*). Additionally, scholars debate the history of the family in England from the Renaissance to the early twentieth century (Ross 5–9; O'Day 163–67; Pollock 1–69, 96–143). To place the fictional Henchard's life in historical context is therefore difficult.

Social class shaped family life, particularly the extent of parental reliance on their children's labor (O'Day 168; Ittman 148). Henchard "was brought up as a hay trusser" (M 37), and was thus slightly above unskilled laborers in social rank (Williams and Williams 34).

The narrative opens in the early years of the nineteenth century when Henchard was 21. He thus was born in the 1780s. At that time in rural laboring British families, men and women died in their forties; children went to work with their parents before puberty; and most such families lacked sufficient food, secure dwellings, and physical comforts.

In the last decade of the eighteenth century and the first 13 years of the nineteenth century many harvests were bad (G. Smith 524, 549). These economic uncertainties and the precipitous rise and fall of wages, availability of work, and high costs of food, would have added to the ordinary difficulties of a child growing up in a rural working-class family.

The agricultural working-class family of that era is assumed by social historians to have differed significantly from the late-twentieth-century middle-class family. Children were expected to behave as adults. Physical punishment was ordained by church teaching and custom. The sadistic streak in Michael Henchard, exacerbated by drink but still evident when he is sober, might have arisen in part, not just from the violence that alcohol often engenders (Vaillant, *Revisited* 103; U.S. Department of Health and Human Services, *Final Report* 20; S. Brown, *Adult* 15), but from the brutalizations to which a child of his class and time would almost certainly have been subject.

The "[s]ons of alcoholics are four times more likely to be alcoholic than the sons of non-alcoholics" (Noble 216). What follows is my scholarly speculation about the origins of Henchard's inconsistent acts of cruelty. Given his approximate birth date, Henchard's father could have been alive during what is termed in British history as "the gin epidemic," well known from Hogarth's prints (Sournia 20–22; Vaillant, *Natural* 98–99). The epidemic was still virulent during the 1750s, and if Henchard were born in 1784 when his father were 30, his father would have been a young boy—and children drank gin—during the 1750s. Thus it is possible that the congruence of parental alcoholism with social sanction for physical brutality toward children might have shadowed Henchard's childhood.

To speculate further, Sigvardsson, Bohman, and Cloninger have replicated their influential Stockholm study of male adoptees. They posit "two distinct forms of alcoholism" (681): clinically, Type 1 male alcoholics have "adult onset and rapid progression of dependence," whereas Type 2 male alcoholics have "teenage onset and recurrent social and legal problems from alcohol abuse" ("Replication" 681). Is Michael Henchard a Type 2 alcoholic? Perhaps a prequel might depict Henchard's first 21 years and answer my questions.

15. Elaine Showalter argues that most critics elide the inclusion of the child in the wife sale because the sale of a girl child "seems almost natural" ("Unmanning" 103). Nevertheless, "[p]aternity is a central subject of this book, far more important than conjugal love" (Showalter, "Unmanning" 103). For a discussion of the narrative implications of this false father-daughter relation, see O'Toole 22–23.

16. John Paterson relates the furmity-woman's reappearance to the need for Henchard to expiate his "crime against natural law" (361–62) as if the novel were a Greek tragedy like *Oedipus Rex*. To Frank R. Giordano, Henchard's response to her reappearance is another proof of Henchard's inherently self-destructive nature (88).

17. Closely examining hundreds of pages deleted from the manuscript draft of *The Early Life of Thomas Hardy,* the autobiography published under the name of Hardy's second wife (Florence H. Hardy), Lloyd Siemens has documented that Hardy wrote numerous angry and hurt—in fact, retaliatory—responses to criticisms of his novels (73–78).

18. Michael Millgate delineates the complexities of Hardy's handling of the omniscient point of view in *Mayor*, demonstrating the shifts of voice placed inside numerous anonymous observers, the physical location of the omniscient speaker that authorizes the admirable visual audacity of observation, and the subtlety with which the omniscient voice incorporates the nuanced viewpoint of Elizabeth-Jane (*Hardy, Novelist* 228–32).

19. Robert Langbaum agrees that Henchard's attachment to Farfrae is partially homoerotic (130–32), but asserts that it is not fully so (127, 129, 135). I do not agree with his view that the fight in the granary loft between Henchard and Farfrae is less homoerotic than the wrestling scene between Birkin and Gerald in chapter 20, "Gladitorial," of D. H. Lawrence's *Women in Love*, with its intertextual homage to Hardy (129–30).

Henchard insists to Farfrae in their first talk that he is "by nature something of a woman hater" (M 60). Dale Kramer comments on this confession, noting "[t]hroughout the novel Henchard has more affection for Farfrae than for any woman" (87), citing his sexual disinterest in Susan and Lucetta. However, Kramer then rejects the very notion she has argued so convincingly (87). Showalter, too, denies Henchard's homosexuality ("Unmanning" 107).

20. Tess O'Toole explores the fraudulence of this tie between Michael Henchard and an Elizabeth-Jane who is not his blood relation. Ironically, as O'Toole notes, Henchard's "eventual puzzled recognition that sanguinal claims and the claims of human affection need not coincide, that this Elizabeth-Jane can adequately fill the role of his daughter, attests to the supersession of biological relationships by imaginatively created ones" (20). However, O'Toole does not acknowledge that had Henchard not had a problem with alcoholism, he would not have sold his wife and daughter, an act which indirectly may have resulted in the death of the first Elizabeth-Jane, his biological daughter.

CHAPTER 2—JAMES JOYCE

1. Hereafter cited as *CDD*.

2. Michael Gillespie questions John Paul Riquelme's view that Stephen's is the final recursive consciousness of *Portrait* (Riquelme 52, 63, 66–67, 80, 232–33), arguing that the dialogic heteroglossia

of *Portrait* "repeatedly [asks] the reader to participate in the creation of meaning" (82). The reader does so by filling in narrative lacunae (92–93), "creating links" (94), and by interpreting repeated figurative language (97).

3. In Chapter 1 I explain that denial as alcohologists use the term differs from its usage in Freudian therapy, an argument beyond the scope of my text. For alcohologists (to use Jerome Levin's term) the term denial encompasses the fact that an alcoholic is often unaware of how much she or he drinks, disconnects his or her drinking from its consequences, and structures (albeit often unconsciously) his or her daily life around drinking. For further discussion, see Bean's, "Denial" and Bean-Bayog's "Psychopathology." See note 11 for a brief discussion of a cultural approach to alcoholism.

4. Written for the general reader rather than the Joyce scholar, *The Voluminous Life and Genius of James Joyce's Father, John Stanislaus Joyce,* as its title suggests, presents the elder Joyce as an improvident charmer more than a progressively ill alcoholic. Under "character" the index lists "charm," "ebullience," "sociability," "wit" (486), while the chronological list avoids the word "alcoholism," although it lists eight citations for "drunken rages" (485). Viewing his drinking as an unfortunate aspect of his character rather than as the cause of his behavior, the biography disconnects John Joyce's drinking from his constant financial difficulties, his self-pity, and his grown children's estrangement from him. What emerges is an affectionate chronicle that nevertheless makes clear that John Stanislaus Joyce was at the very least a problem drinker and recognizably of a piece with the portrait of his father Stanislaus Joyce created in *The Complete Dublin Diary.*

5. Bonnie Kime Scott acknowledges that the deleterious effects of John Joyce's drinking most strongly impacted his wife and daughters, noting cultural permission for his behavior (*Feminism* 58–60).

6. Goldman's is an astute reading of the complex family dynamic enacted by John, Stanislaus and James Joyce (61–68). Goldman repeatedly quotes Stanislaus' descriptions of the drunken John Joyce (62–68). Goldman also notes the numerous inadequate male authority figures in James Joyce's fiction (68–74), more than a few of whom, Goldman notes, drink problematically.

7. John Wyse Jackson and Peter Costello note the compositional history and the missing passages from Stanislaus's [*Complete Dublin*] *Diary,* acknowledging that it is "neither entirely accurate nor quite

complete" (258). Nevertheless, they claim it is "full of useful insights on the family," and that "what survives is enlightening" (258), incorporating into their biography summaries of its major passages about John Joyce's drinking, invective, and violence. They agree with Joseph Kelly and George H. Healey that Stanislaus is biased, but they repeatedly note the reasons for his continued resentment of his father, which did not abate (Jackson and Costello 347).

8. Hereafter cited as *JJII*.

9. Kevin Dettmar interprets this as the result of Ellman's overidentifying with James Joyce by assuming his subject position (133).

10. Charles Steward Parnell was the charismatic "leader of the Irish nationlist movement until he was named as an adulterer in 1889" (Anderson 485 n 7.25). Parnell's loss of political power from 1889–1891 did coincide, as John Joyce claimed, with the change in John Joyce's circumstances, although, as Colbert Kearney makes clear, John Joyce began mortgaging the Cork properties ten years before the fall of Parnell (65). See note 20.

11. Anthropological models of alcoholism avoid imposing alien cultural norms on all cultures, acknowledging instead that "[t]he drinking patterns of a given population vary as do the beliefs, attitudes and values that members of that population hold with respect to beverage alcohol and its interaction with the human organism" (Heath 357).

   The World Health Organization previously subscribed to an anthropological model of alcoholism that was sensitive to the norms of the culture (qtd. in Steinglass, et al. 31). (Stanislaus thought John Joyce's drinking was culturally normative for some groups of Dubliners [*My Brother's* 60, 63, 74, 98] as I noted above.) The current WHO definition makes no mention of cultural norms, but follows the *ICD-10 Classification of Mental and Behavioral Disorders* (which resembles the *DSM IV* description of alcohol dependence) (The current definition was cited in the WHO website: *F10.2 Alcohol Dependence Syndrome*. World Health Organization on 22 July 1998; see <http://www.mentalhealth.com/lcd/p22sb01.html.>). The balance between the external observer and the norms of the observed culture is currently the subject of protracted debate in anthropological and sociological studies of drinking (Gusfield 8–10, 32–34; Barrows and Room, "Introduction" 4–19).

12. Currently the category "child of alcoholic" and the extensive critical evidence for the harmful effects on children of parental alcoholism is

under extensive reinvestigation (Rydelius; Kelly and Myers). This theoretical discourse on causality seeks to explain exactly what causes the familial disruption and impaired development of children raised in alcoholic families. Is it the drinking per se, or the processes set in motion by drinking that disrupts child development (Moore qtd. in Windle and Searles 175)?

Researchers want to know why some children seem immune to parental alcoholism ("resilient") while others—often in the same family—suffer severe developmental damage (Stout and Mintz 466). Are there divergent effects due to gender formation in alcoholic homes (Stout and Mintz 467)? Are the claims made about the impact on children of parental alcoholism scientifically verifiable (Stout and Mintz 466, 468–71)?

Some qualitative researchers are studying the connection of parental drinking to life problems that are often congruent with alcoholism, such as communication difficulties, money and employment problems, parental depression and rages, and emotional and sexual abuse of dependents. But "the results are often non specific to parental alcoholism [i.e., they seem to be related to parental deviance in general rather than to alcoholism per se] and do not necessarily persist [when parents stop abusing alcohol]" (Gotham and Sher 34). This conclusion would seem to prove that the difficulties are related to parental alcoholism if they cease with parental sobriety.

The final effect of this contentious debate is yet unclear. It demonstrates the wide divergence between kinds, methods of finding, and means of interpreting data. It reveals the chasm between scientifically verifiable laboratory research results and the lived experience arising from assessments made by clinicians about their therapeutic work with children of alcoholics.

13. For further discussion of the disputed theory of alcoholic progression, see Chapter 1, "Henchard's Return to Drinking," pp. 64, 74–76.

14. Perhaps as a way of gaining sympathy for his point of view, Stanislaus Joyce also gave portions of the materials in his diary to Josephine Murray, his mother's sister-in-law, to read (*CDD* 66). Interestingly, Josephine's husband, William, seems also to have had a problem with alcohol (Ellman, *JJII* 20). Josephine Murray was James Joyce's favorite aunt, a fact that appears to have complicated Stanislaus's relation to her and to her daughter, Katsy, on whom he had a crush. Although a cultural studies interpretation would most likely not

pathologize such an action, there is little doubt that Murray Bowen would have analyzed Stanislaus's sharing his diary with his aunt and his brother as evidence of unhealthy family enmeshment.

15. Richard Pearce's analytic techniques of narrative "'back answers'" are similar in some respects to those of Norris; see his *The Politics of Narration,* 43, 51–52.

16. "Others might assign the conventional narrative voice [of certain passages] to an amorphous figure like 'the arranger,' David Hayman's term denoting the ubiquitous, polyvocal presence disrupting conceptions that a dominant narrative voices guides the discourse of *Ulysses*" (Gillespie 88). Perhaps this "arranger" elides connections, but the implications of such connection are part of the novel's "stifled back" alcoholism narrative.

17. Charles Rossman analyses Stephen Dedalus in very similar terms in both of his essays.

18. This idea is a staple of Freudian theory (Kershner, *Bakhtin* 184).

19. Scholes and Kain note that Symons, Boyd, the early Yeats, Dowson, Swinburne, and Thompson are the poets on whose work Stephen modeled his poetry (258–65).

20. His Cork properties, which brought him a yearly annuity of L 315.14, were a part of John Joyce's considerable inheritance (Ellman, *JJII* 15). From 1881–1884, at the births of eleven of his thirteen children, he mortgaged these properties, so that by 1894 the properties "were gone" (Ellman, *JJII* 21). Their sale realized more than L1875, but Ellman does not indicate that John Joyce received this money which most likely went to the holder of the mortgage (*JJII* 748 n 49), a fact confirmed by Jackson and Costello (182–84). By 1902 John Joyce was reduced to living on a monthly income drawn from half his pension of L5/10/ 1 1/2 (*JJII* 105).

21. My interpretation differs from that of Restuccia and Brivic, for example. Brivic's Freudian and then Lacanian argument posits that Stephen's behaviors symbolically reenact the trauma of the loss of the mother; in his reading the plot arises from Stephen's attempts via writing and sexuality to return to the point of origin, the maternal body (*Veil* 42–48). Restuccia's elegant argument locates Stephen's masochism in his assuming the female subject position, ventriloquizing the female voice and point of view. Neither critic finds familial alcoholism as a possible cause of Stephen's behavior or emotional difficulties, although Brivic does discuss Simon's "fall" and identification with Parnell ("Disjunctive" 254–55).

22. Dominic Manganiello reminds readers that "the first work Joyce ever wrote was political . . . the poem (now lost), 'Et Tu, Healy,' which he composed at the age of nine shortly after Parnell's death on 6 October 1891" (3). Tim Healy led "the clericalist forces" ranged against Parnell, and Joyce's poem "was inspired by [his father's] invective" against Parnell's enemies. "John Joyce admired his son's poem and had it printed and distributed among his . . . friends" (3).

  My suggestion that Parnell is inscribed in problematic parental drinking and thus tied to Stephen's literary activity in *Portrait* does not examine the political implications of such connection. However, Thomas Hofheinz's essay, "'Group drinkards,'" explores some of Joyce's political views in an analysis of Irish drinking practices and their narrative ramifications in *Finnegans Wake* (650, 653, 655, 658).

23. Margot Norris interprets Stephen as writing on an eviction notice (*Web* 19). In his edited version of *A Portrait of the Artist as a Young Man,* Kershner defines the words as "legal notices involving bankruptcy" (71).

24. Robert F. Bales contextualizes the fact that in poor, rural Irish nineteenth-century households meals were irregular, reflecting Irish cultural attitudes toward food and drink (160–61). Margot Norris connects John Joyce's poverty to *Portrait's* diminishing meals: "This scene [*P* 163] is not fantasy, according to Stanislaus' [*Dublin*] diary, which argues that the specter of famine, which cast its apocalyptic shadow over modern Irish history, haunted in its depoliticized form the everyday lives of the Joyce children" (*Web* 199).

25. For a convincing argument that Stephen's love for Cranly is homoerotic, see Joseph Valente (184–86). Margot Norris interprets Cranly as representing the social responsibility of the artist, hence his stance to Stephen is both sustaining and oppositional (*Web* 74–82).

CHAPTER 3—VIRGINIA WOOLF

1. For example, Roger Poole and Stephen Trombley argue the family system rather than Virginia Woolf was irrational, a viewpoint further elucidated by Louise DeSalvo's *Conceived with Malice* (50, 52–53, 62–63, 67). Thomas Carramagno and Nancy T. Bazin argue that a biochemical imbalance and severe depression characterized Woolf's paternal and maternal forebears. Leonard Woolf believed

that Virginia Woolf's genius was allied to her "madness" (*Beginning* 75–79, 92–94). For a discussion of the extreme divergence between British and American academic interpretations of Woolf's life and work, see Jane Marcus, "Quentin's Bogey."

As part of this debate about Woolf's family or origin, many scholars dispute Louise DeSalvo's work, which emphasizes the impact of incest on Woolf's emotional life and writings (Anne O. Bell, "Letter" 2; DeSalvo, "Letter" 3; Olafson and Corwin 1–2). Research by Judith Lewis Herman and Bessel van der Kolk, which was concurrent with that of Louise DeSalvo, would suggest that part of the scholarly response to DeSalvo's argument reflects a larger pattern of cultural denial about the meaning of incest in family and society (Herman, *Trauma* 2–4, 7–9; van der Kolk, *Psychological*). The inability to acknowledge and to understand the implications of such violation are thought to enable the witness not to be contaminated by it (Herman, *Trauma* 8–9). One reason for such a taboo is that such discussion focuses on the perpetrator, the family, and the cultural systems that enable the abuse, showing that the incest survivor is not to blame, but that she or he was sacrificed to a systemic use of women and children by men in the patriarchal family and society (Armstrong). Hence, for example, Hermoine Lee doubts the facts about Woolf's incest, which Quentin Bell, not Louise De Salvo, first documented, calling Woolf's incest experience "sexual intereference" (Lee 151). Lee suggests that the coy tone in which Woolf told her male colleagues about her incest experiences (153) at the memoir club undermines the truth of the experience, ignoring how difficult it is and was to disclose such information, and the fact that Vanessa Bell told Dr. Savage at the time and Dr. Savage—hardly one to believe girls' testimony—intervened (Q. Bell, I 95–96). Lee also questions Woolf's reports to Janet Case (123; Q. Bell, I 43n). For further discussion of Lee's point of view, see Eberly.

2. A similar, exaggerated division of gendered roles may be observed in the family's comparison of the younger Virginia Woolf with her older sister Vanessa Bell (McNaron 95–101; DeSalvo, *Malice* 52–53).

3. Mrs. Jackson was not alone in her use of such medications. Use of the kind about which I am speculating can be studied by looking at Elizabeth Barrett Browning, whose reliance on opium was well known in certain circles. Interestingly, the Brownings had visited Little Holland House, but did not return as Mrs. Browning "disapproved of the 'class' represented by Mrs. Prinsep" (Love 54).

In 1995 Julia Markus's *Dared and Done* contradicted the established view that opium use had not impaired Mrs. Browning's life or art. Markus repeatedly interrogates Browning's insistence that morphine was necessary to her existence (40, 278, 304) by showing the poet's over-reliance on it during times of stress (2, 14–15, 277, 310). Further, her husband and her close friend Anna Jameson were convinced that her health would improve if she could give up the use of morphine (Markus 40, 51). Markus demonstrates that Browning gave up the drug during her pregnancy only with great difficulty, and returned almost immediately to its use after the birth of her son (130, 161, 171) suggesting that the poet herself had concerns about its use. Although some readers might find such an approach anachronistic, in fact, the Victorians themselves raised the very questions Markus asks.

4. Mill's use of slavery as an unproblematized equivalent for middle-class white women's oppression was a common strategy of late-eighteenth-century and Victorian feminists (M. Ferguson 8–33).

5. Current feminist critiques of codependence recall earlier arguments. As Phyllis Chesler (56–132) and Elaine Showalter (*Malady* 23–166) noted, for example, pathologizing women's behavior has long been a medical strategy to disempower women. The Dobashes (229–33) and Linda Gordon (*Heroes* 292) advance a similar line of argument when refusing to pathologize the effects on women of male violence. I will argue that Virginia Woolf's analysis of her mother's behavior is best read in political terms, an interpretation that is congruent with some definitions of codependence.

6. Definitions range from analyzing codependence as a strategy of communication, a series of relationship dysfunctions, a collection of psychological symptoms that could be better explained by other diagnostic categories, or as a set of psychological deficiencies that result from living as a child in an alcoholic family. The medical debates about codependence resemble those about children of alcoholics that Gotham and Sher analyze; see note 12 in Chapter 2. Nastasi, Serrins, et al., and C. Mitchell, for example, question the etiology, accuracy of clinical data, and precise definition of codependence. On the other hand, Ohannessian, Hinkin and Kahn, Schandler, et al., and Hardwick, et al., claim to have empirical research data to support a diagnosis of codependence. Crothers and Warren's article is a particularly convincing presentation of their research data and theoretical interpretation of the existing clinical literature in support of the concept of codependence.

7. Feminist clinician Deborah Luepnitz critiqued Murray Bowen's persistent mother blame, embattled and absent fathers, and one example of what she interpreted as Bowen's racial prejudice (38–39; 42–43; 46–47), believing that Bowen's deliberate refusal of gender and racial markers masks his prejudice. Bowen's arguments, developed in the 1950s, appear to reject North American psychiatric silence about race and massive woman-blaming. McGoldrick, Anderson, and Walsh, for example, demonstrate that Bowenian family systems theory can successfully be applied for feminist cultural analysis and therapeutic practice (33–36).

8. Stephanie Brown's concept of a "false self" is not dissimilar to that of Bowen's "pseudo-self" (S. Brown, *Adult* 60–62; Bowen 364–35).

9. It was socially acceptable for wives to accompany their husbands on circuit court duties (John Bicknell, Telephone Interview, July 13, 1995).

10. Scholars disagree about Laura's mental illness. After a thorough examination of her medical and asylum records, John Bicknell convincingly argues that Laura was mentally retarded (Stephen, *Letters* 2, viii-xi). Jean Love speculates that Laura was schizophrenic (162).

11. That Virginia Woolf could live as she did because of her family's money—dependent in part on Empire—and because she had heterosexual privilege must be acknowledged.

12. See, for example, Neverow, "Composition"; Richter 132–33, 136; Minow-Pinkney 153–58; Lanser 111–13.

13. Hugh Kenner uses this term to describe the narrative technique that underpins "the Uncle Charles principle." See Chapter 2 pp. 109–110. I thank Michael Beard for locating the *New Latin Grammar* definition.

14. In such comparisons I do not imply the cliched, gendered analysis whereby Joyce is the ur-modernist and Woolf's work but a trivial imitation of his. As I report in Chapter 2, Joyce critics have only recently begun to balance postmodern theoretical analyses of Joyce's narrativity with aggressive political interpretation; feminist scholars have explicated Woolf's artful politics for decades. On the other hand, both *Portrait* and *To the Lighthouse* are polyvocal texts that may usefully be interpreted as bildungsromans. The sources of their narrative voices are not disclosed, and both texts rupture narrative sequence and insistently foreground paralipses, creating a texture of denied disclosure. Although feminist Woolf scholars have over the decades forged a nuanced, multilayered mode of analyzing Woolf's

textual voices, it is not inaccurate to compare their scholarly methods of reading to those Margot Norris synthesized in order to read James Joyce's "'stifled back answers.'" See also, Henke, "Modern" 642–65.

15. See, for example Schlack; Marcus, "Years," "Soap Operas," "Rules Britania"; Neverow, "Composition," "Defying," Haller.

16. Caramagno argues that this is a narrative marker of manic-depression [247, 264–67], while Herman notes that such "oscillations" are characteristic of trauma survivors [*Trauma* 59].

17. Jane Flax problematizes feminist acceptance of many of Foucault's strategies, including his ideas about surveillance (*Thinking* 198–212, 216–17).

18. McClintock has interrogated the persistent Victorian iconography, notable in Hannah Culwick, Munby's wife/servant's careful count of the thousands of shoes she cleaned yearly (166), for "maids were especially tasked with keeping their employers' shoes scrupulously clean" (171). Mrs. Ramsay's role appears to be that of her husband's servant, a factual observation about married Victorian women's legal status, according to Fraser Harrison (6).

Although Michael Tratner dissolves the binary oppositions between Mrs. Ramsay and Mrs. McNab and Mrs. Bast (55–57), he delineates Woolf's ambivalence about working-class women whom she saw as "an emblem of artistic innovation and fairly obtuse figures" (58). He views Lily Briscoe as working class (74–75) (perhaps a reason she is associated with Mr. Ramsay's boots [TTL 229–30; Lilienfeld, "Mother" 368–69]), and believes that Woolf appropriated the voices of working women in *To the Lighthouse* (75).

19. His source for opium in 1909 would have been Turkey, part of the Ottoman Empire, which supplied 60 percent of British opium. Even in peak years, India's shipments never exceeded 13 percent, although France sometimes supplied 20 to 30 percent of England's opium (Berridge and Edwards 272–73).

20. See Janet Winston's discussion of this metaphor (57–59). For helpful discussions of Woolf's negotiation of the complex, nuanced positionality of privileged/oppressed white women, see Cliff; see also Abel's "Matrilineage."

21. Blaming the mother for not protecting daughters from incest is a contested aspect of clinical discourse. Biographically, Woolf preferred her father to her mother (Q. Bell, I 26). *To the Lighthouse* foregrounds Mr. Ramsay's aggression, but suggests that the mother's

position is such that she cannot consistently protect her children against a male violence that attracts and repels her. Accusations of Mrs. Ramsay's collusion with male violence are hinted within Lily Brisoce's indirect interior monologues, as I argue. Janet Liebman Jacobs's multiethnic studies of incest survivors reveal that "psychological survival [can become] linked to separation from the perceived failure of maternal power. . . . It is a painful consequence of mothering in Patriarchal society that daughters in abusive families are forced to devalue their mothers and women in general in order to achieve a sense of self" (30).

22. For a different interpretation of Cam Ramsay, see Abel, *Fictions* 58–67 and DeSalvo, *Impact* 174–79 and 222–27.

WORKS CITED

Abbott, Mary. *Family Ties: English Families, 1540–1920*. New York: Routledge, 1993.

Abel, Elizabeth. "Matrilineage and the Racial 'Other': Woolf and Her Literary Daughters of the Second Wave." Featured Presentation. The Third Annual Conference on Virginia Woolf. Jefferson City, MO. 13 June 1993.

———. *Virginia Woolf and the Fictions of Psychoanalysis*. Chicago: U of Chicago P, 1989.

Anderson, Chester G., ed. *A Portrait of the Artist as a Young Man*. By *James Joyce*. Texts, Criticism, and Notes ed. by Chester G. Anderson. New York: Viking, 1964; New York: Penguin, 1980. (Abbreviated in Text as *P*.)

Annan, Noel. *Leslie Stephen: The Godless Victorian*. New York: Random House, 1984.

Antell, John. "The Old Malthouse and the Antell Family." *The Thomas Hardy Journal* IV.2 (1995): 26–29.

Armstrong, Louise. "The Personal is Apolitical." *Women's Review of Books* 7.6 (1990): 1+.

Asher, Ramona and Dennis Brissett. "Codependency: A View from Women Married to Alcoholics." Babcock and McKay 129–49.

Auerbach, Eric. *Mimesis: The Representation of Reality in Western Literature*. Trans. Willard Trask. New York: Doubleday, 1957.

Babcock, Marguerite and Christine McKay, eds. *Challenging Codependency: Feminist Critiques*. Toronto: U of Toronto P, 1995.

Bailey, J. O. "Changing Fashions in Hardy Scholarship." *Thomas Hardy and the Modern World: A Symposium*. Ed. F. B. Pinion. Dorchester: The Thomas Hardy Society, Ltd., 1974. 140–54.

———. "Hardy's Mephistophelian Visitants." *PMLA* LXI (1946): 1146–1184.

Bales, Robert F. "Attitudes toward Drinking in the Irish Culture." *Society, Culture, and Drinking Patterns*. Eds. David J. Pittman and Charles R. Snyder. Carbondale: S. Illinois UP, 1962. 157–87.

Barnes, Gordon. "The Alcoholic Personality: A Reanalysis of the Literature." *Journal of Studies on Alcohol* 40.7 (1979): 571–633.

Barrows, Susanna, and Robin Room, eds. *Drinking: Behavior and Belief in Modern History.* Berkeley: U of California P, 1991.

———. "Introduction." Barrows and Room 1–27.

Barry, Herbert, III. "Psychoanalytic Theory of Alcoholism." Chaudron and Wilkinson 103–42.

Bauerle, Ruth. "Date Rape. Mate Rape. A Liturgical Interpretation of 'The Dead.'" Scott, *New Alliances* 113–25.

Bauman, Marcy L. "Faulkner's Fiction Makes Addicts of Us All." Vice et al. 291–98.

Bayog-Bean, Margaret. "Psychopathology Produced by Alcoholism." Meyer 334–45.

Bazin, Nancy T. *Virginia Woolf and the Androgynous Vision.* New Brunswick: Rutgers UP, 1973.

Bean, Margaret, and Norman Zinberg, eds. *Dynamic Approaches to the Understanding and Treatment of Alcoholism.* New York: The Free Press, 1981.

Bean, Margaret. "Denial and the Psychological Complications of Alcoholism." Bean and Zinberg 55–97.

Beard, Michael. Letter to the author. 31 May 1995.

Beer, Gillian. *Darwin's Plots: Evolutionary Narrative in Darwin, George Eliot and Nineteenth-Century Fiction.* London: RKP, 1983.

Bell, Anne Olivier. "Letter." *Virginia Woolf Miscellany* 38 (1992): 1–2.

Bell, Carolyn M., and Edward J. Khantzian. "Contemporary Psychodynamic Perspectives and the Disease Concept of Addiction: Complementary or Competing Models?" *Psychiatric Annals* 21.5 (1991): 273–81.

Bell, Quentin. *Virginia Woolf: A Biography.* 2 vols. New York: Harcourt, Brace, and Jovanovich, 1972.

Benstock, Bernard. "The Temptation of St. Stephen: A View of the Villanelle." *James Joyce Quarterly* 14.1 (1976): 31–38.

Berridge, Virginia, and Griffith Edwards. *Opium and the People: Opiate Use in Nineteenth-Century England.* New Haven: Yale UP, 1987.

Bicknell, John. "Mr. Ramsay was Young Once." Marcus, *Celebration* 52–67.

———. "The Ramsays in Love." *Charleston Magazine* 9 (1994): 4–9.

———, ed. *Selected Letters of Leslie Stephen, 1864–1904.* 2 Vols. Columbus: Ohio State UP, 1996.

———. Telephone interview. 13 July 1995.

Black, Naomi. "Virginia Woolf and the Woman's Movement." Marcus, *Aslant* 180–97.

Bland, Lucy. "Marriage Laid Bare: Middle-class Women and Marital Sex, c. 1880–1914." Lewis, *Labour* 123–48.

Bland, Joan. *Hibernian Crusade: The Story of the Catholic Total Abstinence Union of America.* Washington: Catholic UP, 1951.

Blane, Howard T. *The Personality of the Alcoholic: Guises of Dependency.* New York: Harper & Row, 1968.

Blau, Melissa. "Recovery Fever." *New York* Sept. 1991: 31–37.

Booth, Wayne C. *The Rhetoric of Fiction.* Chicago: U of Chicago P, 1961.

Bowen, Murray. *Family Therapy in Clinical Practice.* Northvale: Jason Aaronson, 1985.

Boyd, Elizabeth French. *Bloomsbury Heritage: Their Mothers and Their Aunts.* London: Hamish Hamilton, 1976.

Brantlinger, Patrick. *Crusoe's Footprints: Cultural Studies in Britain and America.* New York: Routledge, 1990.

Brivic, Sheldon. "The Disjunctive Structure of Joyce's *Portrait.*" Kershner 251–67.

———. *The Veil of Signs: Joyce, Lacan, and Perception.* Urbana: U of Illinois P, 1991.

Bromley, Roger. "The Boundaries of Hegemony: Thomas Hardy and *The Mayor of Casterbridge.*" *Proceedings of the Literature and Society and the Sociology of Literature Conference.* 1976. University of Essex. 30–40.

Brooks, Edward. "Moule and a Whisper of Hardy." *The Thomas Hardy Journal* II.2 (1986): 56–57.

Brown, Douglas. "The Harsher Aspects of Agricultural Life." Robinson, *Mayor* 321–26.

Brown, Stephanie. *Treating Adult Children of Alcoholics: A Developmental Perspective.* New York: Wiley & Sons, Inc., 1988.

———. *Treating the Alcoholic: A Developmental Model of Recovery.* New York: Wiley & Sons, Inc. 1985.

Bulfinch, Thomas. *Bulfinch's Mythology: The Age of Fable, The Age of Chivalry, Legends of Charlemagne.* Rev. ed. New York: Thomas Y. Crowell, Co., 1958.

Cameron, Julia Margaret. *For My Beloved Sister Mia: An Album of Photographs by Julia Margaret Cameron.* Ed. Staff of the University of New Mexico Art Museum. Albuquerque: U of New Mexico Art Museum, 1994.

Caramagno, Thomas C. *The Flight of the Mind: Virginia Woolf's Art and Manic-Depressive Illness.* Berkeley: U of California P, 1992.

Carpenter, Dennis R. "Adult Children of Alcoholics: CAQ Profiles." *Alcoholism Treatment Quarterly* 13.2 (1995): 63–70.

Carpenter, William. "Joyce and Byron: Yet Another Source for the Villanelle." *James Joyce Quarterly* 28.3 (1991): 682–85.

Centola, Steven R. "'The White Peace of the Altar': White Imagery in James Joyce's *A Portrait of the Artist as a Young Man*." *South Atlantic Review* 50.4 (1985): 93–106.

Cermak, Timmen L. "Co-Addiction as a Disease." *Psychiatric Annals* 21.5 (1991): 266–72.

———. "Diagnostic Criteria for Codependency." *Journal of Psychoactive Drugs* 18.1 (1986): 15–20.

Chatman, Seymour. *Story and Discourse*. Ithaca: Cornell U P, 1978.

Chaudron, C. D., and D. A. Wilkinson. *Theories on Alcoholism*. Toronto: Addiction Research Foundation, 1988.

Cheng, Vincent. *Joyce, Race, and Empire*. Cambridge: Cambridge UP, 1995.

Chesler, Phyllis. *Women and Madness*. New York: Doubleday, 1972.

Chodorow, Nancy. *The Reproduction of Mothering: Psychoanalysis and the Sociology of Gender*. Berkeley: U of California P, 1978.

Christian, John, ed. *The Little Holland House Album by Edward Burne Jones*. North Berwirck: The Dalrymple P, 1981.

Cixous, Helene. *The Exile of James Joyce*. Trans. Sally A. J. Purcell. New York: David Lewis, 1972.

Cliff, Michelle. "Virginia Woolf and the Imperial Gaze: A Glance Askance." Featured Presentation. The Third Annual Conference on Virginia Woolf. Jefferson City, MO. 11 June 1993.

Cloninger, C. Robert, Michael Bohman, Soren Sigvardsson. "Inheritance of Alcohol Abuse: Cross-Fostering Analysis of Adopted Men." *Archives of General Psychiatry* 38 (1981): 861–68.

Courtwright, David T. *Dark Paradise: Opiate Addiction in America before 1940*. Cambridge: Harvard UP, 1982.

Cox, W. Miles. "Personality Theory." Chaudron and Wilkinson 143–72.

Crothers, Marciana, and Lynda W. Warren. "Parental Antecedents of Adult Codependency." *Journal of Clinical Psychology* 52.2 (1996): 231–39.

Crowley, John. *The White Logic: Alcoholism and Gender in American Modernist Fiction*. Amherst: U of Massachusetts P, 1994.

Dardis, Tom. *The Thirsty Muse: Alcohol and the American Writer*. New York: Ticknor & Fields, 1989.

Daugherty, Beth, and Mary Beth Pringle, Co-Moderators. "A Roundtable Discussion on Teaching *To the Lighthouse*." First Annual Conference on Virginia Woolf. New York. 8 June 1991.

Davidoff, Leonore, and Catherine Hall. *Family Fortunes: Men and Women of the English Middle-Class, 1780–1850*. Chicago: U of Chicago Press, 1987.

Davidoff, Leonore, Jeanne L'Esperance, and Howard Newby. "Landscape with Figures: Home and Community in English Society." Ed. Leonore Davidoff. *Worlds Between: Historical Perspectives on Gender and Class*. New York: Routledge, 1995. 41–72.

Davis, Donald I. "The Family in Alcoholism." *Phenomenology and Treatment of Alcoholism*. Ed. W. Fann, et al. New York: Spectrum, 1980. 111–26.

DeSalvo, Louise. *Conceived with Malice*. New York: Dutton, 1994.

———. "Letter." *Virginia Woolf Miscellany* 38 (1992): 3.

———. *Virginia Woolf: The Impact of Childhood Sexual Abuse on Her Life and Work*. Boston: Beacon P, 1989.

Dettmar, Kevin J. H. *The Illicit Joyce of Postmodernism: Reading against the Grain*. Madison: U of Wisconsin P, 1996.

Diagnostic and Statistical Manual of Mental Disorders. 4th ed. Washington: American Psychiatric Association, 1994.

DiCiccio, Lena. "Children of Alcoholic Parents: Issues in Identification." U. S. Department of Health and Human Services. *Research Monograph No. 4*. 44–59.

Dinwiddie, Stephen H., and C. Robert Cloninger. "Family and Adoption Studies in Alcoholism and Drug Addiction." *Psychiatric Annals* 21.4 (1991): 206–14.

Dobash, R. Emerson, and Russell P. Dobash, *Women, Violence and Social Change*. New York: Routledge, 1992.

Doheny, John. "Biography and Thomas Hardy's Maternal Ancestors: The Swetmans." *The Thomas Hardy Journal* XI.2 (1995): 46–60.

Dowling, Scott, ed. *The Psychology and Treatment of Addictive Behavior*. Madison: International UP, 1995.

Dulfano, Celia. *Families, Alcoholism, and Recovery: Ten Stories*. Center City: Hazelden, 1982.

DuPlessis, Rachel Blau. *Writing beyond the Ending: Narrative Strategies of Twentieth-Century Women Writers*. Bloomington: Indiana UP, 1985.

Dyhouse, Carol. *Feminism and the Family in England, 1880–1939*. Oxford: Blackwell, 1989.

———. *Girls Growing Up in Late Victorian and Edwardian England*. London: Routlege & Kegan Paul, 1981.

———. "Mothers and Daughters in the Middle-Class Home c. 1870–1914." Lewis, *Labour* 27–48.

Easingwood, Peter. "*The Mayor of Casterbridge* and the Irony of Literary Production." *The Thomas Hardy Journal* IX.3 (1993): 64–75.

Eberly, David. "On Reading Ill: Medical Narratives in Virginia Woolf." Virginia Woolf and the Medicalization of Influence. Seventh Annual Virginia Woolf Conference. Plymouth State College, Plymouth, New Hampshire. 14 June 1997.

Elkin, Michael. *Families under the Influence.* New York: Norton, 1984.

Ellis, Sarah Stickney. *The Wives of England: Their Relative Duties, Domestic Influence and Social Obligations.* New York: Appleton, 1843.

Ellman, Richard. *James Joyce.* Rev ed. New York: Oxford UP, 1982. Abbreviated as *JJII.*

Epstein, Edward. "James Joyce and *The Way of All Flesh.*" *James Joyce Quarterly* 7.1 (1969): 22–29.

———. *The Ordeal of Stephen Dedalus: The Conflict of Generations in James Joyce's* A Portrait of the Artist as a Young Man. Carbondale: S. Illinois UP, 1971.

Espinola, Judith. "Narrative Discourse in Virginia Woolf's *To The Lighthouse.*" *Virginia Woolf: Critical Assessments.* Ed. Eleanor McNees. Vol. 3. Mountfield: Helm Information, 1994. 638–49.

Ferguson, John. "A Sea Change: Thomas De Quincey and Mr. Carmichael in *To The Lighthouse.*" *Journal of Modern Literature* XIV:1 (1987): 45–63.

Ferguson, Moira. *Colonialism and Gender Relations from Mary Wollstonecraft to Jamaica Kincaid.* New York: Columbia UP, 1993.

Flax, Jane. *Disputed Subjects: Essays on Psychoanalysis, Politics and Philosophy.* New York: RKP, 1993.

———. *Thinking Fragments: Psychoanalysis, Feminism, & Postmodernism in the Contemporary West.* Berkeley: U California P, 1990.

Fletcher, Anthony. *Gender, Sex and Subordination in England, 1500–1800.* New Haven: Yale UP, 1995.

Flexner, Eleanor. *Century of Struggle: The Woman's Rights Movement in the United States.* Rev. ed. Cambridge: Harvard UP, 1976.

Forseth, Roger. "Alcohol and the Writer: Some Biographical and Critical Issues (Hemingway)." *Contemporary Drug Problems* (1986): 361–86.

———. "'Alcoholite at the Altar': Sinclair Lewis, Drink, and the Literary Imagination." *Modern Fiction Studies* 31.3 (1985): 581–607.

Friedman, Susan Stanford, ed. *Joyce and the Return of the Repressed.* Ithaca: Cornell UP, 1993.

———. "(Self) Censorship and the Making of Joyce's Modernism." Friedman 21–57.

Frosch, William A. "An Analytic Overview of Addictions." Milkman and Shaffer 29–38.

Gabler, Hans Walter. "The Christmas Dinner Scene, Parnell's Death, and the Genesis of *A Portrait of the Artist as a Young Man*." *James Joyce Quarterly* 13.1 (1975): 27–38.

———. "The Seven Lost Years of *A Portrait of the Artist as a Young Man*." Staley and Benstock 25–60.

Garis, Robert. *The Dickens Theatre*. Oxford: Clarendon P, 1965.

Genette, Gerard. *Narrative Discourse: An Essay in Method*. Trans. Jane E. Lewin. Ithaca: Cornell UP, 1990.

Gernsheim, Helmut. *Julia Margaret Cameron: Her Life and Photographic Work*. New York: Aperture, 1975.

Gillespie, Diane, and Elizabeth Steele. *Julia Duckworth Stephen: Stories for Children, Essays for Adults*. New York: Syracuse UP, 1987.

Gillespie, Michael. *Reading the Book of Himself: Narrative Strategies in the Works of James Joyce*. Columbus: Ohio State UP, 1989.

Gilman, Alfred, Louis Goodman, Theodore Roll, Alan Nies, and Palmer Taylor, eds. *Goodman and Gilman's The Pharmacological Basis of Therapeutics*. 8th ed. New York: McGraw Hill, 1990.

Gilmore, Thomas B. *Equivocal Spirits: Alcoholism and Drinking in Twentieth-Century Literature*. Chapel Hill: U of North Carolina P, 1987.

Ginsburg, Elaine, and Laura Gottleib, eds. *Virginia Woolf: Centennial Essays*. Troy, New York: Whitston, 1983.

Giordano, Frank R. *"I'd Have My Life Unbe": Thomas Hardy's Self-Destructive Characters*. University, Al: U of Alabama P, 1984.

Gittings, Robert. *Thomas Hardy's Later Years*. Boston: Little, Brown, 1978.

———. *Young Thomas Hardy*. Boston: Little, Brown, 1975.

Goldman, Arnold. "Stanislaus Joyce and the Politics of Family." *Atti del Third International James Joyce Symposium*. Trieste: Universita Degli Studi, 1974. 60–75.

Goodwin, Donald W. *Alcohol and the Writer*. New York: Penguin, 1988.

———. "Genetic Factors in the Development of Alcoholism." *Psychiatric Clinics of North America* 9.3 (1986): 427–33.

Gordon, Linda. *Heroes of Their Own Lives: The Politics and History of Family Violence*. New York: Penguin, 1988.

———. "More than Victims: Battered Women, the Syndrome Society, and the Law." *The Nation*. 24 March 1997: 25–26.

Gordon, Suzanne, and Isabel Marcus. "We Need to Recover from Self-Fulfillment." *Boston Globe*. 24 June 1990. A3.

Gorham, Deborah. *The Victorian Girl and the Feminine Ideal.* Blooming-ton: Indiana UP, 1982.

Gorski, Terence T., and Merlene Miller. *Staying Sober: A Guide for Relapse Prevention.* Independence: Herald House/Independence P, 1986.

Gotham, Heather J., and Kenneth J. Sher. "Do Codependent Traits Involve More than Basic Dimensions of Personality and Psychopathology?" *Journal of Studies on Alcohol* 57.1 (1996): 34–39.

Gough, Val. "The Mystical Copula: Rewriting the Phallus in *To the Light-house.*" Hussey and Neverow, *Third* 216–23.

Guerard, Albert J. *Thomas Hardy.* New York: New Directions, 1964.

Gusfield, Joseph R. *Contested Meanings: The Construction of Alcohol Problems.* Madison: U Wisconsin P, 1996.

Hagen, Kay. "Codependency and the Myth of Recovery: A Feminist Scrutiny." Babcock and McKay 198–206.

Haley, Bruce. *The Healthy Body and Victorian Culture.* Cambridge: Har-vard UP, 1978.

Haller, Evelyn. "The Anti-Madonna in the Work and Thought of Virginia Woolf." Ginsburg and Gottlieb 93–109.

Halliday, F. E. "Thomas Hardy, The Man in His Work." *Thomas Hardy After Fifty Years.* Ed. Lance St. John Butler. London: Macmillan, 1977. 126–34.

Hamill, Peter. *A Drinking Life: A Memoir.* Boston: Little, Brown & Co., 1994.

Hamm, John E., et al. "The Qualitative Measurement of Depression and Anxiety in Male Alcoholics." *American Journal of Psychiatry* 136:4 (1979): 580–82.

Hammerton, A. James. *Cruelty and Companionship: Conflict in Nine-teenth-Century Married Life.* New York: Routledge, 1992.

Harding, Sandra. *Whose Science? Whose Knowledge? Thinking from Women's Lives.* Ithaca: Cornell UP, 1991.

Hardwick, C. J., et al. "Are Adult Children of Alcoholics Unique? A Study of Object Relations and Reality Testing." *International Journal of Ad-diction* 305 (1995): 525–39.

Hardy, Florence Emily. *The Early Life of Thomas Hardy: 1840–1891.* New York: Macmillan, 1928.

Hardy, Thomas. *The Life and Death of The Mayor of Casterbridge: A Story of a Man of Character. An Authoritative Text, Backgrounds, Criticism.* Ed. James K. Robinson. New York: Norton, 1977. (Abbreviated as M in text.)

WORKS CITED
265

———. *The Personal Notebooks of Thomas Hardy.* Ed. Richard Taylor. New York: Columbia UP, 1979.

———. *Thomas Hardy's Personal Writings.* Ed. Harold Orel. London: MacMillan, 1967.

Harper, Jeane, and Connie Capdevila. "Codependency: A Critique." *Journal of Psychoactive Drugs* 22.3 (1990): 285–92.

Harrison, Brian. *Drink and the Victorians: The Temperance Question in England, 1815–1872.* Pittsburgh: U of Pittsburgh P, 1971.

Harrison, Fraser. *The Dark Angel: Aspects of Victorian Sexuality.* New York: Universe Books, 1978.

Hayter, Alethea. *Opium and the Romantic Imagination: Addiction and Creativity in De Quincey, Coleridge, Baudelaire and Others.* Rev. ed. Wellingborough: Crucible, 1988.

Healey, George H., ed. *The Complete Dublin Diary of Stanislaus Joyce.* Ithaca: Cornell UP, 1971. (Abbreviated in the text as *CDD*.)

Heath, Dwight B. "Emerging Anthropological Theory and Models of Alcohol Use and Alcoholism." Chaudron and Wilkinson 353–410.

Henke, Suzette, and Elaine Unkeless, eds. *Women in Joyce.* Urbana: U of Illinois P, 1982.

Henke, Suzette. "Modern Novels (Joyce)." *The Gender of Modernism.* Ed. Bonnie Kime Scott. Bloomington: Indiana UP, 1990. 626+.

———. "Stephen Dedalus and Women: A Portrait of the Artist as a Young Narcissist." *James Joyce and the Politics of Desire.* New York: RKP, 1990.

———. "Stephen Dedalus and Women—A Portrait of the Artist as a Young Misogynist." Henke and Unkeless 82–107.

Herman, Judith Lewis. *Trauma and Recovery.* New York: Basic Books, 1992.

Hinkin, C. H., and M. W. Kahn. "Psychological Symptomatology in Spouses and Adult Children of Alcoholics: An Examination of the Hypothesized Personality Characteristics of Codependency." *International Journal of Addiction* 30.7 (1995): 843–61.

Hirshey, Gerri. "Happy [] [sic] Day to You." *The New York Times Magazine.* 2 July 1995: 20+.

Hofheinz, Thomas. "'Group drinkards maaks grope thinkards': Narrative in the 'Norwegian Captain' Episode of *Finnegans Wake*." *James Joyce Quarterly* 29.3 (1992): 643–58.

Holcombe, Lee. "Victorian Wives and Property: Reform of the Married Woman's Property Law, 1857–1882." Ed. Martha Vicinus. *A Widening*

Sphere: Changing Roles of Victorian Women. Bloomington: Indiana UP, 1977. 3–28.

Holloway, John. "Hardy's Major Fiction." Robinson, *Mayor* 342–46.

——.*The Victorian Sage.* New York: Norton, 1963.

Houghton, Walter. *The Victorian Frame of Mind: 1830–1870.* New Haven: Yale UP, 1957.

Howe, Irving. *Thomas Hardy.* New York: Colliers, 1966.

Hussey, Mark. *Virginia Woolf A to Z.* New York: Facts on File, 1995.

Hussey, Mark and Vara Neverow, eds. *Virginia Woolf: Emerging Perspectives: Selected Papers from the Third Annual Conference on Virginia Woolf.* New York: Pace UP, 1994.

Hussey, Mark and Vara Neverow-Turk, eds. *Virginia Woolf: Miscellanies: Selected Papers from the First Annual Conference on Virginia Woolf.* New York: Pace UP, 1992.

——, eds. *Virginia Woolf: Themes and Variations: Selected Papers from the Second Annual Conference on Virginia Woolf.* New York: Pace UP, 1993.

The ICD-10 [International Statistical Classification of Diseases and Related Health Problems: Tenth Revision.] "F10.2 Alcohol Dependence Syndrome." "Alcohol Dependence: European Definition." World Health Organization. 22 July 1998. <http://www.mentalhealth.com/lcd/p22sb01.html>. (www.mentalhealth.com).

Imhof, John E. "Countertransference Issues in Alcoholism and Drug Addiction." *Psychiatric Annals* 21.5 (1991): 292–306.

Institute for Health Policy. Heller Graduate School, Brandeis University. *Substance Abuse: The Nation's Number One Health Policy Problem, Key Indicators for Policy.* Princeton: The Robert Wood Johnson Foundation, 1993.

Irwin, Michael, Mark Schuckit, and Tom L. Smith. "Clinical Importance of Age at Onset in Type 1 and Type 2 Primary Alcoholics." *Archives of General Psychiatry* 47 (1990): 320–24.

Ittman, Karl. *Work, Gender and Family in Victorian England.* New York: New York UP, 1995.

Jackson, John Wyse, and Peter Costello. *The Voluminous Life and Genius of James Joyce's Father, John Stanislaus Joyce.* New York: St. Martin's, 1997.

Jacobs, Janet Liebman. *Victimized Daughters: Incest and the Development of the Female Self.* New York: RKP, 1994.

Jacobson, Jacob G. "The Advantages of Multiple Approaches to Understanding Addictive Behavior." Dowling 175–90.

Jameson, Fredric. *The Political Unconscious: Narrative as a Socially Symbolic Act.* Ithaca: Cornell UP, 1991.

Jellinek, E. M. *The Disease Concept of Alcoholism.* New Haven: College and UP, 1960.

Joyce, James. *A Portrait of the Artist as a Young Man.* Text, Criticism, and Notes ed. by Chester G. Anderson. New York: Viking, 1964; New York: Penguin, 1980. (Abbreviated in text as *P*.)

———. *Ulysses.* Rev. ed. New York: Random House, 1961. (Abbreviated in text as *U*.)

Joyce, Stanislaus. *The Complete Dublin Diary of Stanislaus Joyce.* Ed. George H. Healey. Ithaca: Cornell UP, 1971. (Abbreviated in the text as *CDD*.)

———. *My Brother's Keeper.* Ed. Richard Ellman. London: Faber & Faber, 1958.

Kaminer, Wendy. "Chances Are You're Codependent Too." *New York Times Book Review* 11 Feb. 1990: 1+.

Karlen, Neal. "Greetings From Minnesober!" *The New York Times Magazine* 28 May 1995: 32–35.

Kearney, Colbert. "The Joycead." *Coping with Joyce: Essays from the Copenhagen Symposium.* Ed. M. Beja and S. Benstock. Columbus: Ohio State UP, 1989.

Kelly, Joseph. *Our Joyce: From Outcast to Icon.* Austin: U of Texas P, 1998.

Kelly, Virginia, and Jane Myers. "Parental Alcoholism and Coping: A Comparison of Female Children of Alcoholics with Female Children of Nonalcoholics." *Journal of Counseling and Development* 74.5 (1996): 501–504.

Keltner, N. L., C. W. McIntyre, and R. Gee. "Birth Order Effects in Second Generation Alcoholics." *Journal of Studies on Alcohol* 47 (1986): 495–97.

Kenner, Hugh. *Joyce's Voices.* Berkeley: U of California P, 1978.

———. "The Portrait in Perspective." *James Joyce: Two Decades of Criticism.* Ed. Seon Givens. New York: Vanguard, 1948. 132–74.

Kershner, R. B. "History as Nightmare: Joyce's *Portrait* to Christy Brown." *Joyce and the Subject of History.* Ed. Mark A. Wollaeger, et al. Ann Arbor: U of Michigan P, 1996. 27–45.

———. *Joyce, Bakhtin, and Popular Literature: Chronicles of Disorder.* Chapel Hill: U of North Carolina P, 1989.

———ed. *A Portrait of the Artist as a Young Man.* By James Joyce. New York: Bedford, 1993.

Khantzian, Edward, J. "Self Regulation Vulnerabilities in Substance Abusers: Treatment Implications." Dowling 17–42.

Kinney, Jean, and Gwen Leaton. *Loosening the Grip: A Handbook of Alcohol Information.* St. Louis: Mosby-Year Book, 1991.

Klein, James. "Out of Mere Words: Self-Composition and *A Portrait of the Artist.*" *James Joyce Quarterly* 13.3 (1976): 293–305.

Kokin, Morris, and Ian Walker. "Codependency is a Misleading Concept." Babcock and McKay 81–87.

Kramer, Dale. *Thomas Hardy: The Forms of Tragedy.* Detroit: Wayne State UP, 1975.

Krestan, Jo-Ann, and Claudia Bepko. "Codependency: The Social Reconstruction of Female Experience." *Smith College Studies in Social Work* 60.3 (1990): 216–32. Reprinted in Babcock and McKay 93–110.

Krugman, Steven. "Trauma in the Family: Perspectives on the Intergenerational Transmission of Violence." van der Kolk 127–51.

Langbaum, Robert. *Thomas Hardy in Our Time.* London: Macmillan, 1995.

Lanser, Susan Sniader. *Fictions of Authority: Women Writers and Narrative Voice.* Ithaca: Cornell UP, 1992.

Lanza, Joseph. *The Cocktail: The Influence of Spirits on the American Psyche.* New York: St. Martin's, 1995.

Laslett, Barbara, et al., eds. *History and Theory: Feminist Research, Debates, Contestations.* Chicago: U of Chicago P, 1997.

Lawrence, Patricia O. *The Reading of Silence: Virginia Woolf in the English Tradition.* Stanford: Stanford UP, 1991.

Leaska, Mitchell. *Virginia Woolf's "Lighthouse": A Study in Critical Method.* New York: Columbia UP, 1970.

Lee, Hermione. *Virginia Woolf.* New York: Knopf, 1997.

Lemere, Frederick. "What Happens to Alcoholics?" *American Journal of Psychiatry* 136: 586–58.

Lerner, Gerda, ed. *The Female Experience: An American Documentary.* Indianapolis: Bobbs-Merrill, 1977.

Levin, Jerome David. *Introduction to Alcoholism Counseling: A Bio-Psycho-Social Approach.* 2nd ed. Washington, D.C.: Taylor & Francis, 1995.

———. *Treatment of Alcoholism and Other Addictions: A Self-Psychology Approach.* Northvale: Jason Aronson, Inc., 1987.

Levine, George. "Victorian Studies." *Redrawing the Boundaries: The Transformation of English and American Studies.* Eds. Stephen Greenblatt and Giles Gunn. New York: MLA, 1992. 130–53.

Levine, Philippa. *Feminist Lives in Victorian England: Private Roles and Public Commitment.* Oxford: Oxford UP, 1990.

Lewis, Jane, ed. "Introduction: Reconstructing Women's Experience of Home and Family." *Labour and Love: Women's Experience of Home and Family, 1850–1940.* London: Blackwell, 1986. 1–26.

Lewis, Judith Schneid. *In the Family Way: Childbearing in the British Aristocracy, 1760–1860.* New Brunswick: Rutgers UP, 1986.

Lewis, Reina. *Gendering Orientalism: Race, Femininity and Representation.* New York: Routledge, 1996.

Lilienfeld, Jane. "'But I'm an English Teacher, Not a Therapist': Designing a Course on Alcoholism for the Traditional College Classroom." MMLA Convention. Minneapolis, MN. November 1993.

———. "Flesh and Blood and Love and Words: Lily Briscoe, Stephen Dedalus, and the Aesthetics of Emotional Quest." Scott, *New Alliances* 165–78.

———. "'Like a Lion Seeking Whom He Could Devour': Domestic Violence in *To the Lighthouse.*" Hussey and Neverow-Turk, *First* 154–63.

———. "['The Critic'] Can't Say That, Can She? Naming Codependence and Family Dysfunction in *To the Lighthouse.*" Hussey and Neverow, *Third* 151–56.

———. "The Deceptiveness of Beauty: Mother Love and Mother Hate in *To the Lighthouse.*" *20th Century Literature* 23.3 (1977): 345–76.

———. "Where the Spear Plants Grew: The Ramsays' Marriage in *To the Lighthouse.* Marcus, *Feminist* 148–69.

Liskow, Barry, et al. "Anti-Social Alcoholics: Are There Clinically Significant Diagnostic Subtypes?" *Journal of Studies on Alcohol* 53.1 (1991): 62–69.

Lodge, David. "Where Was Mr. Tansley When They were Talking about Him?" *The Virginia Woolf Miscellany* 10 (1977): 4.

Lodl, Karen M. "A Feminist Critique of Codependency." Babcock and McKay 207–18.

Logan, Deborah Anna. *Fallenness in Victorian Women's Writing: Marry, Stich, Die or Do Worse.* Columbia: U Missouri P, 1998.

Love, Jean. *Virginia Woolf: Sources of Madness and Art.* Berkeley: U of California P, 1977.

Ludwig, Arnold. *Understanding the Alcoholic's Mind: The Nature of Craving and How to Control It.* New York: Oxford UP, 1988.

Luepnitz, Deborah Anna. *The Family Interpreted: Feminist Theory in Clinical Practice.* New York: Basic Books, 1988.

Maddox, Brenda. *Nora: A Biography of Nora Joyce.* New York: Fawcett Columbine, 1988.

Manganiello, Dominic. *Joyce's Politics*. London: RKP, 1980.

Mannion, Lawrence. "Co-dependency: A Case of Inflation." *Employee Assistance Quarterly* 7.2 (1991): 67–81.

Marcus, Jane. "Britannia Rules the Waves." *Virginia Woolf: A Collection of Critical Essays*. Ed. Margaret Homans. Englewood Cliffs: Prentice Hall, 1993. 227–48.

———, ed. *New Feminist Essays on Virginia Woolf*. Lincoln: U of Nebraska P, 1981.

———. "Quentin's Bogey." *Art and Anger: Reading Like a Woman*. Ed. Jane Marcus. Columbus: Ohio UP, 1988. 201–14.

———, ed. *Virginia Woolf: A Feminist Slant*. Lincoln: U of Nebraska P, 1983.

———. "The Virginia Woolf Soap Operas." The Second Annual Conference on Virginia Woolf. Featured Event. New Haven. 14 June 1992.

———. "The Years as Gotterdammerung: Greek Play and Domestic Novel." *Virginia Woolf and the Languages of Patriarchy*. Bloomington: Indiana UP, 1987. 36–56.

———, ed. *Virginia Woolf and Bloomsbury: A Centenary Celebration*. Bloomington: Indiana UP, 1987.

Marder, Herbert. *Feminism and Art: A Study of Virginia Woolf*. Chicago: U of Chicago P, 1967.

Marks, John. "Hardy and Kindness." *The Thomas Hardy Journal* XI.1 (1995): 52–59.

Markus, Julia. *Dared and Done: The Marriage of Elizabeth Barrett and Robert Browning*. New York: Knopf, 1995.

Martin, Biddy. "Feminism, Criticism and Foucault." *Feminism and Foucault: Reflections on Resistance*. Eds. Irene Diamond and Lee Quinby. Boston: Northeastern UP, 1988. 3–19.

McClelland, David C., et al. *The Drinking Man*. New York: The Free Press, 1972.

McClintock, Anne. *Imperial Leather: Race, Gender and Sexuality in the Colonial Contest*. New York: Routledge, 1995.

McGoldrick, Monica. "Irish Families." *Ethnicity and Family Therapy*. Eds. Monica McGoldrick, John Pearce, and Josephe Giordano. New York: Guilford, 1982. 310–39.

McGoldrick, Monica, Carol M. Anderson, and Froma Walsh, eds., *Women in Families: A Framework for Family Therapy*. New York: Norton, 1991.

McKay, Christine. "Codependency: The Pathologizing of Female Oppression." Babcock and McKay 219–40.

McNaron, Toni. *The Sister Bond: A Feminist View of a Timeless Connection*. New York: Pergamon P, 1985.

McVicker, Jeanette. "Vast Nests of Chinese Boxes, or Getting from Q to R: Critiquing Empire in 'Kew Gardens' and *To the Lighthouse*." Hussey and Neverow-Turk, *First* 40–42.

Mendenhall, Warner. "Co-dependency, Definitions and Dynamics." *Alcoholism Treatment Quarterly* 6.1 (1989): 3–17.

Meyer, Roger, ed. *Psychopathology and Addictive Disorders*. New York: Guilford P, 1986.

Mezei, Kathy. "Who is Speaking Here? Free Indirect Discourse, Gender and Authority in *Emma, Howard's End* and *Mrs. Dalloway*." *Ambiguous Discourse: Feminist Narratology and British Women Writers*. Ed. Kathy Mezei. Chapel Hill: U of North Carolina P, 1996. 66–92.

Milkman, Harvey B., and Howard J. Shaffer, eds. *The Addictions: Multidisciplinary Perspectives and Treatments*. Lexington: Lexington Books, 1985.

Miller, Alice. *For Your Own Good: Hidden Cruelty in Child-Rearing and the Roots of Violence*. Trans. Hildegarde and Hunter Hannum. New York: Farrar, Strauss, Giroux, 1984.

Miller, J. Hillis. "From Narrative Theory to Joyce; from Joyce to Narrative Theory." *The Seventh of Joyce*. Ed. Bernard Benstock. Bloomington: Indiana UP, 1982. 3–4.

———. "Mr. Carmichael and Lily Briscoe: The Rhythm of Creativity in *To the Lighthouse*." *Modernism Reconsidered*. Ed. Robert Kiely assisted by John Hildebidle. Cambridge: Harvard UP, 1983. 167–89.

———. *Thomas Hardy: Distance and Desire*. Cambridge: Harvard UP, 1970.

Miller, Norman S., and John N. Chappel. "History of the Disease Concept." *Psychiatric Annals* 21.4 (1991): 196–205.

Miller, Norman S., and Mark S. Gold. "Dependence Syndrome: A Critical Analysis of Essential Features." *Psychiatric Annals* 21.5 (1991): 282–90.

Miller, William R., and Janet C'De Baca. "Alcohol Education Inventory: What Every Health Professional Should Know about Alcoholism." *Journal of Substance Abuse Treatment* 12.5 (1995): 355–65.

Millgate, Michael. *Thomas Hardy, a Biography*. New York: Random House, 1982.

———. *Thomas Hardy: His Career as a Novelist*. New York: Random House, 1971.

Milligan, Barry. "Opium Smoking and the Oriental Infection of British Identity." Vice, et al. 93–100.

———. *Pleasures and Pains: Opium and Orient in Nineteenth-Century British Culture*. Charlottesville: U of Virginia P, 1995.

Minow-Pinkney, Makiko. *Virginia Woolf and the Problem of the Subject*. New Brunswick: Rutgers UP, 1987.

Mitchell, Christina. "A Plea for Compassion toward Adult Children of a Functional Family." *TADC Journal* 17.2 (1989): 121–24.

Moreiras, Alberto. "Pharmaconomy: Stephen and the Daedalids." Friedman 58–86.

Morrell, Roy. *Thomas Hardy: The Will and the Way*. Singapore: U of Malaya P, 1968.

Morse, Robert M., and Daniel K. Flavin. "Special Communication: The Definition of Alcoholism." *JAMA* 268.8 (1992): 1012–14.

Mulligan, Therese, Eugenia Janis Parry, and April Watson, eds. *For my best beloved Sister Mia: An Album of Photographs by Julia Margaret Cameron*. Albuquerque, New Mexico: University of New Mexico Art Museum, 1994.

Musto, David F. *The American Disease: Origins of Narcotic Control*. Rev. ed. New York: Oxford UP, 1987.

Nadel, Ira B. "The Incomplete Joyce." *Joyce Studies Annual* 2 (1991): 86–100.

Naremore, James. "Consciousness and Society in *A Portrait of the Artist*." Staley and Benstock 113–34.

———. *The World without a Self: Virginia Woolf and the Novel*. New Haven: Yale UP, 1973.

Nastasi, Bonnie K. "Is Early Identification of Children of Alcoholics Necessary for Preventive Intervention: A Reply to Harvey and Dodd." *Journal of School Psychology* 33.4 (1995): 327–45.

Nelson, John R. *Hardy's People: Structure and Character in the Major Fiction*. Darmstadt: Thesen Verlag, 1974.

Neuringer, Charles, and James R. Clopton. "The Use of Psychological Tests for the Study of the Identification, Prediction and Treatment of Alcoholism." *Empirical Studies of Alcoholism*. Eds. Gerald Goldstein and Charles Neuringer. Cambridge: Ballinger, 1976. 7–35.

Neverow, Vara. "*A Room of One's Own* as a Model of Composition Theory." Hussey and Neverow, *Third* 58–64.

———. "Defying the Dic(k)tator: Virginia Woolf's Penis Mockery from Freud to Fascism." MLA Convention. San Diego. 27 Dec. 1994.

Newlove, Donald. *Those Drinking Days, Myself and Other Writers*. New York: McGraw-Hill, 1981.

Noble, Ernest P. "Genetic Studies in Alcoholism CNS Functioning and Molecular Biology." *Psychiatric Annals* 21.4 (1991): 215–29.

Norris, Margot. *Joyce's Web: The Social Unraveling of Modernism.* Austin: U of Texas P, 1992.

———. "The Politics of Childhood in 'The Mime of Mick, Nick, and the Maggies.'" *Joyce Studies Annual* 1 (1990): 61–95.

———. "Stifled Back Answers: The Gender Politics of Art in Joyce's 'The Dead.'" *Modern Fiction Studies* 35.3 (1989): 479–503.

O'Day, Rosemary. *The Family and Family Relationships, 1500–1900.* New York: St Martin's 1994.

O'Gorman, Patricia. "Prevention Issues Involving Children of Alcoholics." U.S. Dept Health and Human Services. *Research Monograph No. 4.* 81–101.

Ohannessian, Christine-McCauley. "Temperament and Personality Typologies in Adult Offspring of Alcoholics." *Journal of Studies on Alcohol* 156.3 (1995): 318–27.

Olafson, Ema and David Corwin. "The Sexual Abuse of Children." *The Virginia Woolf Miscellany* 34 (1990): 2–3.

O'Toole, Tess. *Genealogy and Fiction in Hardy: Family Lineage and Narrative Lines.* New York: St. Martin's, 1997.

Overcarsh, F. L. "The Lighthouse: Face to Face." *Accent* X (1959): 107–23.

Page, Norman. *Thomas Hardy.* London: RKP, 1977.

Paterson, John. "*The Mayor of Casterbridge* as Tragedy." Robinson, *Mayor* 346–66.

Pearce, Richard. *The Politics of Narration: James Joyce, William Faulkner and Virginia Woolf.* New Brunswick: Rutgers UP, 1991.

———. "Simon's Irish Rose: Famine Songs, Blackfaced Minstrels, and Woman's Repression in *A Portrait.*" Friedman 128–46.

Peterson, M. Jeanne. *The Medical Profession in Mid-Victorian London.* Berkeley: U of California P, 1978.

Phillips, Kathy. *Virginia Woolf against Empire.* Knoxville: U of Tennessee P, 1994.

Platt, L. H. "The Buckeen and the Dogsbody: Aspects of History and Culture in 'Telemachus.'" *James Joyce Quarterly* 27 (1989): 77–86.

Pollock, Linda. *Forgotten Children: Parent-Child Relations from 1500–1900.* 2nd ed. Cambridge: Cambridge UP, 1983.

Poole, Roger. *The Unknown Virginia Woolf.* Rev. ed. Cambridge: Cambridge UP, 1978.

———. "'We All Put Up with you, Virginia.'" *Virginia Woolf and War: Fiction, Reality, and Myth.* Ed. Mark Hussey. New York: Syracuse UP, 1991. 79–100.

Pratt, Mary Louise. *Imperial Eyes: Travel Writing and Transculturation.* New York: Routledge, 1992.

Prince, Gerald. *A Dictionary of Narratology.* Lincoln: U of Nebraska P, 1987.

Reid, Panthea. *Art and Affection: A Life of Virginia Woolf.* New York: Oxford UP, 1996.

———. "On Writing Yet Another Biography of Virginia Woolf." *The Virginia Woolf Miscellany* 46 (1995): 6.

Restuccia, Frances L. *Joyce and the Law of the Father.* New Haven: Yale UP, 1989.

Richardson, Brian. *Unlikely Stories: Causality and the Nature of Modern Narrative.* Newark: U of Delaware P, 1997.

Richardson, Ruth. *Death, Dissection and the Destitute.* New York: RKP, 1987.

Richter, Harvena. *Virginia Woolf: The Inward Voyage.* Princeton: Princeton UP, 1970.

Rieker, Patricia P. and Elaine H. Carmen. "The Victim-to-Patient Process: The Disconfirmation and Transformation of Abuse." *American Journal of Orthopsychiatry* 56.3 (1986): 360–70.

Rimmon-Kenan, Shlomith. *Narrative Fiction.* London: RKP, 1983.

Riquelme, John Paul. *Teller and Tale in Joyce's Fiction: Oscillating Perspectives.* Baltimore: Hopkins, 1983.

Risolo, Donna. "Outing Mrs. Ramsay: Reading the Lesbian Subtext in Virginia Woolf's *To the Lighthouse.*" Hussey and Neverow-Turk, *Second* 238–48.

Roberts, David. "The Paterfamilias of the Victorian Governing Classes." Ed. Anthony S. Wohl. *The Victorian Family: Structure and Stresses.* New York: St. Martin's 1978. 59–81.

Robinson, Bryan E. *Working with Children of Alcoholics: The Practitioner's Handbook.* Lexington: D. C. Heath, 1989.

Robinson, James K., ed. *The Life and Death of The Mayor of Casterbridge. An Authoritative Text, Backgrounds, Criticism.* By Thomas Hardy. New York: Norton, 1977.

Rocco, John. "Drinking, Ulysses: Joyce, Bass Ale and the Typography of Cubism." *James Joyce Quarterly* 33.3 (1996): 399–409.

Rosenberg, Carroll Smith. "The Female World of Love and Ritual: Relations between Women in Nineteenth-Century America." *Signs* 1 (1975): 1–29.

Ross, Ellen. *Love and Toil: Motherhood in Outcast London: 1870–1918.* New York: Oxford UP, 1993.

Rossi, Alice, ed. "Introduction: Sentiment and Intellect, the Story of John Stuart Mill and Harriet Taylor Mill." *John Stuart Mill and Harriet Taylor Mill: Essays on Sex Equality.* Chicago: U of Chicago P, 1970. 1–63.

Rossman, Charles. "Stephen Dedalus and the Spiritual-Heroic Refrigerating Apparatus: Art and Life in Joyce's *Portrait.*" *Forms of Modern British Fiction.* Ed. Alan W. Friedman. Austin: U of Texas P, 1975. 101–31.

———. "Stephen Dedalus' Villanelle." *James Joyce Quarterly* 12 (1975): 281–93.

Rydelius, Per-Anders. "Annotation: Are Children of Alcoholics a Clinical Concern for Child and Adolescent Psychiatrists of Today?" *Journal of Child Psychology and Psychiatry and Allied Disciplines* 38.6 (1997): 615–24.

Said, Edward. *Orientalism.* New York: Random House, 1979.

Schaef, Anne Wilson. *Co-Dependence: Misunderstood—Mistreated.* New York: Harper & Row, 1986.

Schandler, S. L., et al. "Spatial Learning Deficits in Preschool Children of Alcoholics." *Alcoholism Clinical Experimental Research* 19.4 (1995): 1067–72.

Schechter, Susan. *Women and Male Violence: The Visions and Struggles of the Battered Women's Movement.* Boston: South End P, 1982.

Schlack, Beverly Ann. *Continuing Presences: Virginia Woolf's Use of Literary Allusion.* University Park: Penn State UP, 1979.

Scholes, Robert. "Stephen Dedalus, Poet or Esthete?" *PMLA* LXXXIX (1964): 484–89. Reprinted in Anderson 468–80.

Scholes, Robert, and Richard M. Kain, eds. *The Workshop of Daedalus: James Joyce and the Raw Materials for A Portrait of the Artist as a Young Man.* Evanston: Northwestern UP, 1965.

Schuckit, Mark. "Familial Alcoholism." Widiger, et al. 159–67.

———. "The Relationship between Alcohol Problems, Substance Abuse, and Psychiatric Disorders." Widiger, et al. 45–66.

Scott, Bonnie Kime. "Emma Clery in *Stephen Hero:* A Young Girl Walking Proudly through the Decayed City." Henke and Unkeless 57–81.

———. *Joyce and Feminism.* Bloomington: Indiana UP, 1984.

———, ed., *New Alliances in Joyce Studies.* Newark: Delaware UP, 1988.

Sederer, Lloyd I. "Diagnosis, Conceptual Models, and the Nature of this Book." Milkman and Shaffer 183–96.

Serrins, Debra S., et al. "Implications for the Alcohol/Drug Education Specialist Working with Children of Alcoholics: A Review of the Literature from 1988–1992." *Journal of Drug Education* 25.2 (1995): 171–90.

Shaffer, Howard J., and Harvey B. Milkman. "Introduction: Crisis and Conflict in the Addictions." Milkman and Shaffer ix-xviii.

Shiman, Lilian Lewis. *Crusade against Drink in Victorian England.* New York: St. Martin's, 1988.

Showalter, Elaine. *The Female Malady: Women, Madness, and English Culture, 1830–1980.* New York: Penguin, 1985.

———. "The Unmanning of the Mayor of Casterbridge." *Critical Approaches to the Fiction of Thomas Hardy.* Ed. Dale Kramer. London: Macmillan, 1979. 99–115.

Siemens, Lloyd. "What Hardy Really Said about the Critics: Canceled Passages in the Manuscript of the *Life.*" *The Thomas Hardy Journal* VI. 3 (1990): 73–80.

Sigvardsson, Soren, Michael Bohman, Robert C. Cloninger. "Replication of the Stockholm Adoption Study of Alcoholism: Confirmatory Cross-Fostering Analysis." *Archives of General Psychiatry* 53.8 (1996): 681–87.

Smith, Goldwin. *A History of England.* 2nd Rev. ed. New York: Scribner, 1957.

Smith, Patricia Juliana. *Lesbian Panic: Homoeroticism in Modern British Women's Fiction.* New York: Columbia UP, 1997.

Sournia, Jean-Charles. *A History of Alcoholism.* Trans. Nick Hindley and Gareth Stanton. London: Basil Blackwell, 1990.

Spelman, Elizabeth. *Inessential Woman: Problems of Exclusion in Feminist Thought.* Beacon: South End P, 1988.

Spencer, Sharon. *Space, Time and Structure in the Modern Novel.* Chicago: Swallow P, 1971.

Spoo, Robert. *James Joyce and the Language of History: Dedalus' Nightmare.* New York: Oxford UP, 1994.

Spurr, David. *The Rhetoric of Empire: Colonial Discourse in Journalism, Travel Writing, and Imperial Administration.* Durham: Duke UP, 1993.

Staley, Thomas F., and Bernard Benstock, eds. *Approaches to Joyce's Portrait Ten Essays.* Pittsburgh: U of Pittsburgh P, 1976.

Steinberg, Edwin R. "The Bird-Girl in *A Portrait* as Synthesis: The Sacred Assimilated to the Profane." *James Joyce Quarterly* 17 (1980): 149–63.

Steinglass, Peter, et al. *The Alcoholic Family.* New York: Basic Books, 1987.

Stemmerick, Martine. "Virginia Woolf and Julie Stephen: The Distaff Side of History." Ginsberg and Gottlieb 51–81.

Stephen, Leslie. *Selected Letters of Leslie Stephen, 1864–1904.* Ed. John W. Bicknell. 2 Vols. Columbus: Ohio State UP, 1996.

———. *Sir Leslie Stephen's Mausoleum Book.* Ed. Alan Bell. Oxford: Oxford UP, 1977. (Abbreviated as MB in text.)

Stivers, Richard. *A Hair of the Dog: Irish Drinking and American Stereotype.* University Park: Pennsylvania State UP, 1976.

Stone, Lawrence. *The Family, Sex and Marriage in England: 1500–1800.* New York: Harper & Row, 1977.

Stout, Lisa, and Laurie Mintz. "Differences among Nonclinical College Women with Alcoholic Mothers, Alcoholic Fathers, and Nonalcoholic Parents." *Journal of Counseling Psychology* 43.4 (1996): 466–72.

Subby, Robert. *Lost in the Shuffle: The Co-dependent Reality.* Pompano Beach: Health Communications, Inc., 1987.

Sumner, Rosemary. "Indeterminacy in Hardy's Novels and Poetry." *The Thomas Hardy Journal* V.3 (1989): 33–45.

Syme, Leonard. "Personality Characteristics of the Alcoholic: A Critique of Current Studies." *Quarterly Journal of Alcohol Studies* 18 (1956): 288–301.

Tallen, Bette S. "Co-dependency: A Feminist Critique." *Sojourner* 15.5 (1990): 20–21.

Tarter, Ralph E., et al. "Neurobehavioral Theory of Alcoholism Etiology." Chaudron and Wilkinson 73–102.

Thomas, Denis W. "Drunkenness in Thomas Hardy's Novels." *College Language Association Journal* 28 (1984): 190–209.

Thompson, David. *England in the Nineteenth Century, 1815–1914.* Baltimore: Penguin, 1961.

———. *England in the Twentieth Century, 1914–1963.* Baltimore: Penguin, 1963.

Tindall, William York. *A Reader's Guide to James Joyce.* 1959. Syracuse: Syracuse UP, 1995.

Toolan, Michael. "Analyzing Conversation in Fiction: The Christmas Dinner Scene in Joyce's *A Portrait of the Artist as a Young Man.*" *Poetics Today* 8.2 (1987): 393–416.

Tratner, Michael. *Modernism and Mass Politics: Joyce, Woolf, Eliot, Yeats.* Stanford: Stanford UP, 1995.

Trombley, Stephen. *All That Summer She Was Mad: Virginia Woolf: Female Victim of Male Medicine.* New York: Continuum, 1982.

U.S. Department of Health and Human Services. Division of Prevention. National Institute of Alcohol Abuse and Alcoholism. *Final Report: An*

Assessment of the Needs of and Resources for Children of Alcoholic Parents. Rockville, MD: NIAAA, 1975.

U.S. Department of Health and Human Services. Division of Prevention. National Institute of Alcohol Abuse and Alcoholism. *Research Monograph No. 4: Services for Children of Alcoholics, A Symposium, September 24–26, 1979. Silver Spring, MD.* Washington: GPO, 1981.

Vaillant, George. *The Natural History of Alcoholism: Causes, Patterns, and Paths to Recovery.* Cambridge: Harvard UP, 1983.

———. *The Natural History of Alcoholism Revisited.* Cambridge: Harvard UP, 1995.

Valente, Joseph. "Thrilled by His Touch: Homosexual Panic and the Will to Artistry in *A Portrait of the Artist as a Young Man.*" *James Joyce Quarterly* 31.3 (1994): 189–206.

van der Kolk, Bessel A. "The Psychological Consequences of Overwhelming Life Experiences." van der Kolk 1–30.

———, ed. *Psychological Trauma.* Washington D.C.: American Psychiatric Press, 1987.

van der Kolk, Bessel, and Mark S. Greenberg. "The Psychobiology of the Trauma Response: Hyperarousal, Constriction, and Addiction to Traumatic Reexposure." van der Kolk 63–87.

van der Kolk, Bessel and Judith L. Herman. "Traumatic Antecedents of Borderline Personality Disorder." van der Kolk 111–26.

Van Ghent, Dorothy. *The English Novel, Form and Function.* New York: Rinehart, 1953.

Van Wormer, Katherine. "Codependency: Implications for Women and Therapy." Babcock and McKay 117–28.

Voelker, Joseph. "Clown Meets Cops: Comedy and Paranoia in *Under the Volcano* and *Ulysses.*" *Joyce/Lowry: Critical Perspectives.* Eds. Patrick A. McCarthy and Paul Tiessen. Lexington: UP of Kentucky, 1997. 21–40.

———. "27 April." *James Joyce Quarterly* 22.3 (1985): 325.

Vice, Sue, Matthew Campbell, and Tim Armstrong, eds. *Beyond the Pleasure Dome: Writing and Addiction from the Romantics.* Sheffield, England: Sheffield Academic Press, 1994.

Walkowitz, Judith. *Prostitution and Victorian Society: Women, Class, and the State.* New York: Cambridge UP, 1982.

Wallace, John. "Working with the Preferred Defense Structure of the Recovering Alcoholic." *Practical Approaches to Alcoholism Psychotherapy.* Eds. Sheldon Zimberg, et al. 2nd ed. New York: Plenum P, 1987. 23–36.

Walters, Marianne. "The Codependent Cinderella Who Loves Too Much . . . [*sic*] Fights Back." Babcock and McKay 181–91.

Walzl, Florence L. "Dubliners: Women in Irish Society." Henke and Unkeless 31–56.

Weissman, Myrna, and Jerome K. Meyers. "Clinical Depression in Alcoholism." *American Journal of Psychiatry* 13.3 (1980): 372–73.

Whitfield, Charles L. "Children of Alcoholics: Treatment Issues." U.S. Department of Health and Human Services. *Research Monograph No. 4.* 66–79.

Widiger, Thomas, et al., Eds. *DSM-IV Sourcebook.* Vol. 1. Washington, DC: American Psychoanalytic Association, 1994.

Williams, Raymond and Merryn Williams. "Hardy and Social Class." *The Writer and His Background.* Ed. Norman Page. London: Bell and Hyman, 1980. 29–40.

Wilson, G. Terence. "Alcohol Use and Abuse: A Social Learning Analysis." Chaudron and Wilkinson 239–87.

Windle, Michael. "Temperament and Personality Attributes of Children of Alcoholics." Windle and Searles 129–67.

Windle, Michael, and John Searles, eds. *Children of Alcoholics: Critical Perspectives.* New York: The Guilford P, 1990.

Winston, Janet. "Something Out of Harmony: *To the Lighthouse* and the Subjects of Empire." *Woolf Studies Annual* 2 (1996): 39–70.

Wolfe, Susan, and Julia Penelope. *Sexual Practice, Textual Theory: Lesbian Cultural Criticism.* Cambridge: Blackwell, 1993.

Woolf, Leonard. *Beginning Again: An Autobiography of the Years 1911 to 1918.* London: Hogarth P, 1968.

Woolf, Virginia. *A Room of One's Own.* New York: Harcourt, Brace & World, 1957. (Abbreviated in text as *AROO*.)

———. *The Diary of Virginia Woolf. Vol. 2: 1920–1924.* Ed. Anne Olivier Bell, assisted by Andrew McNeillie. New York: Harcourt, Brace Jovanovich, 1980. (Abbreviated in text as *D 2*.)

———. *The Diary of Virginia Woolf. Vol. 3: 1925–1930.* Ed. Anne Olivier Bell, assisted by Andrew McNeillie. New York: Harcourt, Brace Jovanovich, 1980. (Abbreviated in text as *D 3*.)

———. "Impassioned Prose." *The Essays of Virginia Woolf.* Vol. IV. 1925–1928. Ed. Andrew McNeillie. London: Hogarth, 1994. 361–69. (Abbreviated in text as *CE 1*).

———. *The Letters of Virginia Woolf. Vol. 1: 1888–1912.* Ed. Nigel Nicolson and Joanne Trautman. New York: Harcourt, Brace Jovanovich, 1975.

———. "Mary Wollstonecraft." *The Second Common Reader.* New York: Harcourt, Brace & World, 1960. 141–48.

———. "Modern Fiction." *The Common Reader.* New York: Harcourt, Brace & World, 1953. 150–58.

———. *Moments of Being: Unpublished Autobiographical Writings of Virginia Woolf.* Ed. Jeanne Schulkind. Sussex: U of Sussex P, 1976. (Abbreviated in text as *MOB*.)

———. "Professions for Women." Ed. Mitchell Leaska. *The Virginia Woolf Reader.* New York: Harcourt, Brace, Jovanovich, 1984. 276–82.

———. *Three Guineas.* New York: Harcourt, Brace & World, 1963. (Abbreviated in text as *TG*).

———. *To the Lighthouse.* New York: Harcourt, Brace & World, 1955. (Abbreviated in text as *TTL*.)

Wright, Doris T. "Stephen's Villanelle: From Passive to Active Creation." *The Colby Library Quarterly* 22.4 (1986): 215–24.

Zabel, Morton. "Hardy in Defense of His Art." *Hardy: A Collection of Critical Essays, Twentieth Century Views.* Ed. Albert J. Guerard. Englewood Cliffs: Prentice Hall, 1963. 24–45.

Zinberg, Norman E. and Margaret H. Bean, "Introduction: Alcohol Use, Alcoholism, and the Problems of Treatment." Zinberg and Bean 1–35.

INDEX

Dublin pub culture, 89, 93, 125, 126, 127, 128, 129, 156, 176; *see* cultural studies interpretations of alcoholism, social customs

Duckworth, Stella, 182, 183

Dulfano, Stephanie, 153

The Early Life of Thomas Hardy, 14, 15

Edwardian social class, 14, 15

Elkin, David, 73, 175, 176, 178, 179, 189, 192, 206, 225

Ellman, Richard, 89, 90, 91, 92, 93, 250 n.20

emotional characteristics, of children of alcoholics: *see* adult children of alcoholics, anger, Helene Cixous, codependence, cognitive "splitting," enmeshment, "external locus of control," "hypervigilance"

enmeshment, 102, 171, 177, 183, 206–207, 230, 250 n.14; *see* Joseph Kelly, Murray Bowen, family systems theory, "low differentiation of self," triangulation

epistemology, 5

Epstein, Edward, 130, 142, 152

etiology, 10, 253 n.6

"external locus of control," 44, 45, 53, 73, 92, 100, 149; *see* Stephanie Brown, "dual pattern of blaming," George Vaillant

familial alcoholism, 7, 20, 26, 91, 94, 176, 183, 236, 241 n.9, 250 n.21; *see* adult children of alcoholics, Stephanie Brown, "chronic" and "acute" trauma, Helene Cixous, Richard Ellman, genetics, Arnold Goldman, George H. Healey, James Joyce as child of an alcoholic, Joseph Kelley, Ira Nadel

family meals and Irish famine, 104, 116, 117, 138, 251 n.24

family structure, 2, 106, 173, 176–180, 226; *see* adult children of alcoholics, Stanislaus Joyce, *To the Lighthouse,* Victorian mores

family systems theory, 4, 26, 96, 107, 156, 173, 174, 176–180, 192, 194, 203, 205; *see* Murray Bowen, Stephanie Brown, Timmen Cermak, child rearing practices, gender, Thomas Hardy, James Joyce, secrets, Victorian mores, Virginia Woolf

family theorists, 10; *see* Murray Bowen, Stephanie Brown, Timmen Cermak, Louise DeSalvo, Russell P. and R. Emerson Dobash, Linda Gordon, Judith Lewis Herman, Deborah Luepnitz, Monica McGoldrick

fantasy, 9, 80, 82, 83, 109, 114, 123, 132, 136, 145

Farfrae, Donald, 13, 49–50, 52, 66, 71, 72, 75, 82, 155, 235, 243 n.11

female alcoholic (the), 6–7, 54; *see* the furmity-woman

feminism (in the Temperance Movement), 25

feminist criticism, 4–6, 10, 88, 111, 157, 174, 175, 185, 187, 206, 213, 219, 225; *see* Elizabeth Abel, codependence, Louise DeSalvo, Jane Flax, Sandra Harding, Jane Marcus, Harvena Richter, Martine Stemmerick

feminist theory, 9, 43, 161

Ferguson, John, 210, 211

fetus narrative, 113, 114, 117, 118, 120, 121–22, 123, 124, 125, 129, 130, 131, 136, 142, 143, 145, 146, 149; *see* annihilation panic

fictionalization process, 11, 14, 19, 23, 24, 85, 94, 173, 179, 234